Public Interest Design
Practice Guidebook

Public Interest Design Practice Guidebook: SEED Methodology, Case Studies, and Critical Issues is the first book to demonstrate that public interest design has emerged as a distinct profession. It provides clear professional standards of practice following SEED (Social Economic Environmental Design) methodology, the first step-by-step process supporting public interest designers. The book features an Issues Index composed of ninety critical social, economic, and environmental issues, illustrated with thirty case study projects representing eighteen countries and four continents, all cross-referenced, to show you how every human issue is a design issue.

Contributions from Thomas Fisher, Heather Fleming and David Kaisel, Michael Cohen, Michael P. Murphy Jr., Alan Ricks and Annie Moulton, and over twenty others cover topics such as professional responsibility, public interest design business development, design evaluation, and capacity building through scaling, along with many more. Themes including public participation, issue-based design, and assessment are referenced throughout the book and provide benchmarks toward an informed practice. This comprehensive manual also contains a glossary, an appendix of engagement methods, a case study locator atlas, and a reading list. Whether you are working in the field of architecture, urban planning, industrial design, landscape architecture, or communication design, this book empowers you to create community-centered environments, products, and systems.

'Public Interest Design pulses with community, equity, place and democracy. Its legacy of knowledge and practices, seamlessly interweaving design *with* community, is its DNA. Now, at this morphogenic moment, when PID is more than ready to prosper and grow, comes the *Public Interest Design Practice Guidebook.* With its many cases, process tools and SEED methodology, this book will fuel and energize PID culture and practice. It will fortify PID's role and value and without question, help shape and transform 21st century design.' – ***Paula Horrigan, Associate Professor, Cornell University, USA***

'This book is written for those that seek a new kind of design practice. The kind of practice that values on-the-ground engagement and thinking about the systematic impact of design labor. A practice that does not dictate form but rather seeks a radically contextualized understanding of "Public". Those new practitioners will find the critical essays and case studies found in this book to be invaluable tools.' – ***Quilian Riano, Founder and Principal, DSGN AGNC, USA***

'Bryan Bell and Lisa Abendroth have dedicated their respective careers to igniting the spirit of public interest design that exists within all of us who are charged with creating the *constructed* legacy of our time. If you have ever had the inclination to work on behalf of others whose needs are far greater than our own, then you will find the instruction, wisdom and inspiration contained within this book invaluable.' – ***R. Steven Lewis, SEED Network founding member, USA***

Public Interest Design Practice Guidebook

SEED Methodology, Case Studies, and Critical Issues

Edited by Lisa M. Abendroth, Bryan Bell

Routledge
Taylor & Francis Group

NEW YORK AND LONDON

First published 2016
by Routledge
711 Third Avenue, New York, NY 10017

and by Routledge
2 Park Square, Milton Park, Abingdon, Oxon OX14 4RN

Routledge is an imprint of the Taylor & Francis Group, an informa business

Library of Congress Cataloging-in-Publication Data
Abendroth, Lisa M.
Public interest design practice guidebook : SEED methodology, case studies, and critical
issues / Lisa M. Abendroth and Bryan Bell.
pages cm
Includes bibliographical references and index.
1. Architecture and society. 2. Architects and community. I. Bell, Bryan, 1959- II. Title.
NA2543.S6A24 2015
720.1'03–dc23
2014038114

ISBN: 978-1-138-81034-1 (hbk)
ISBN: 978-1-138-81035-8 (pbk)
ISBN: 978-1-315-74957-0 (ebk)

Acquisition Editor: Wendy Fuller
Editorial Assistant: Grace Harrison
Production Editor: Hannah Champney

Generous support for this publication was provided by the Surdna Foundation, the National
Endowment for the Arts, the Fetzer Institute, the Edward W. Rose III Family Fund, and the
Driehaus Foundation.

ART WORKS.

National
Endowment
for the Arts
arts.gov

Typeset in Univers by
Servis Filmsetting Ltd, Stockport, Cheshire
Printed by Bell & Bain Ltd, Glasgow

Contents

Acknowledgements

Thank you to all the SEED Network members, communities and partners, who have helped build the vigorous collaboration we have today. Thank you to the visionary SEED Founders, who saw what was needed to do as far back as 2005: M. Scott Ball, Barbara Brown Wilson, Brandy Brooks, Brent A. Brown, John Cary, Maurice Cox, Kathy Dorgan, Kimberly Dowdell, Roberta Feldman, Sarah Gamble, Frank Giblin, Steven Goldsmith, Lance Hosey, Steven Lewis, Steven A. Moore, Sergio Palleroni, David Perkes, Casius Pealer, Patrick Rhodes, James Stockard, Katie Swenson, JoEllen Wang, and Sally Young.

Above all, thank you to the primary editor, leader of this book and all things SEED, Lisa M. Abendroth, who always demonstrates the best of collaboration. Also my thanks to Eric Field, whose genius has made the SEED Evaluator highly functional on-line.

In the twenty-fifth year of Design Corps, I owe great thanks to our wonderful past and present board members: Evan Harrel, Beth Chute, Marcus Hurley, Drew Kepley, Melissa Tello, Cara Mae Cirignano, Melissa Hill Threatt, Andrew Sturm, James Wheeler, Jeremy Jepson, Barbara Brown Wilson, Scott Ball, Casius Pealer, Evan Supcoff, Jim Hamrick, Scott Scholz, Sharon Matthews, and Steve Weinstein. Thank you to the Design Corps Fellows, particularly Marie Schacht, Brooke Jones, Mary Haywood, Emily Axtman, Heather Ferrell, and Rasha Dumarieh, who have brought the energy, talent, and passion that makes Design Corps have a positive impact.

Design Corps could not have made it without the support of our funding partners: the Surdna Foundation, the National Endowment for the Arts, the Edward W. Rose III Family Fund, the Driehaus Foundation, and the Fetzer Institute.

Lisa and I extend our thanks to Linda Lee, who brought a welcome critical eye to the work during the editing process. Our editorial team at Routledge—Wendy Fuller and Grace Harrison—has provided us with the unique opportunity to share the work of many. Thank you for your support and wise recommendations during publication development.

And a special thank you to my family, Victoria, Sky, and Cole, who bring great joy and love to my life every day.

—Bryan Bell

This publication would not have been possible without the support of designers from around the globe who have used the SEED process to verify their public interest design practice. These individuals and organizations are responsible for building the field and in so doing generously allowed Bryan Bell and I to share the story of their successes and challenges. Thank you to the SEED Network—a membership community that includes professionals, students, educators and volunteers—your belief in the power of design to impact meaningful change is an inspiration that guides this publication.

Bryan Bell has my respect and gratitude: his ever-present optimism and vision over many years of evolving public interest design initiatives has driven our collaboration. Eric Field is a noted collaborator whose development of the SEED Evaluator software has been essential in our ability to document and assess projects. Thank you to Design Corps Fellow Marie Schacht, who was instrumental in supporting image collection for this book.

Thank you to Metropolitan State University of Denver, where my students and colleagues inspire me on a daily basis. Your enthusiasm and support surrounding this research effort is so appreciated. Special thanks go to Michaela Haluko and Drake Johnson for research assistance.

The encouragement of my family—my parents, Peter and Nancy, and my husband, Eric—has been my strength. Without your love and belief in me none of this would have been possible. This book is dedicated to my sister Katie, who I hold close to my heart.

The journey toward this publication began many years ago as design historian and educator Philip B. Meggs inspired me to understand the complexities of the world through the lens of design.

—Lisa M. Abendroth

Foreword

Scott Moore y Medina, Jon Red Corn

Perhaps one of the biggest favors practitioners of public interest design can do for themselves and for the communities they work with is to take a step back and understand what history has done and where healing must occur. In every corner of the world there are orphans of wars, victims of colonization, and refugees of social, economic, and environmental crises that need places to live and work. There are those for whom history has been more favorable than others: history is most often recorded by the victors of war and those who control the majority of resources. Nonetheless, we live in a world in which its inhabitants must increasingly acknowledge its origins and reassess what is and is not working any longer if it is to have a chance at survival.

In indigenous, rural, and disadvantaged communities across the world lies an embedded code for what public interest design strives to be. Within these populations lie deep connections to place, the limited resources that spur problem solving, and the thick fibers of culture, art, and tradition that bind people together in spite of staggering challenges. These are communities often misunderstood—pitied or treated like adornment—although they continue to exist, fascinate, and inspire, despite all odds. They do not need all-knowing experts or saviors but rather a functional exchange system that works in a larger context in which the overwhelming majority of Earth's known resources are controlled by a very small segment of the population.

This exchange system is based on the idea that the most effective way of creating adaptable, innovative, healthy, strong, resilient, and hopeful places to live, play, pray, and work is by taking simple action. This requires enough listening and learning to know a designer or architect does not know everything. This takes respecting the inherent knowledge of different worldviews. It means owning up to the fact you may not have all the answers. We must go about understanding who is not yet at the table and then invite them into the circle. It takes carving out valuable spaces for meaningful exchanges of ideas and knowledge to occur. After nearly two centuries of unprecedented transfers of wealth—and an ever-shrinking class of clientele able to afford design—the field of design may just now be finding itself waking up, groggy eyed, to a new reality.

The classical understanding of architecture and engineering are as languages learned and spoken by an elite few. These professions are generally accessible to those whose fortunate socioeconomic conditions have offered them the right mix of problem-solving, reading, and math skills at an early enough age to allow their creativity and confidence to blossom. Those who excel on standardized tests and can showcase their talents will be admitted into the established educational system, which largely focuses on the power structures, accomplishments, and traditions of the most effective colonizing powers and empires. Regardless, the space for other, but not necessarily "new," vocabularies is emerging. This is especially apropos given recent shifts in cultural awareness and changes in population demographics. There is much to be realized as this develops in the decades to come.

These other languages can teach us if we are open to listening. For instance, in the Lakota language, the words for "economy" and "environment" are a variant of the same word, symbolizing the deep connection between the continuation of life and the giver and sustainer of life—nature herself. What does this tell us about our own views of economy and the natural world? In most indigenous languages there are no words for "sustainable" or "regenerative," but there are words for "living life" and "respecting all of creation." How connected are we in our daily lives to the life-giving systems that sustain us if we must make use of nouns describing the type of world we *hope* to live in instead of how we are *actually* living? As one Lakota tribal elder once reminded a team of architects and planners at a community meeting where the topic was sustainable design: "You are funny with these ideas. We had self-sufficient, interconnected communities for thousands of years, and it worked. It has only been the last two hundred years we got off track. But if we did it before, we can do it again."

In fact, some of the more widely accepted tenets of human comfort, health, and prosperity come from this viewpoint. In research conducted among the Northern Blackfoot indigenous peoples of Alberta in 1938, psychologist Abraham Maslow discovered that certain ideals about human beings and their development that he had previously considered universal across cultures were erroneous (Newhouse 2006). In the context of the Blackfoot, Maslow realized that these truths (among them prosperity, power, and security) had to be understood through the specific framework of individual cultures and societies.

For example, Maslow encountered in his research on cross-cultural issues that the Blackfoot community's unique definition of prosperity was not based on the broadly accepted definition of amassing wealth but instead on generosity of spirit

(Newhouse 2006). Lateral associations to social power or dominance were similarly dispelled, and defined instead based on local identity. The issue of emotive, personally held security revealed the majority of the Blackfoot population, approximately 80 to 90 percent according to Edward Hoffman (1988), to be "rated about as high in ego security as the most secure individuals in our [own] society, who compromise perhaps 5 to 10 percent at most" (Hoffman 1988, 123; Newhouse 2006, 2). Maslow's research exposed the reasons why: personal accountability that promoted independence during childhood, along with the sense of security that accompanied deeply devoted relationships spanning across community and families, supported the prevalence for emotional security among tribal members (Newhouse 2006).

What does this tell us? The context of people and place matter. Stories and spirit matter. How can public interest design as a profession narrow the increasingly prevalent and pervasive divide that has isolated architecture and associated design fields from the communities they hope to engage? How can we reconnect in considerate ways that create space for clients and communities to be deeply understood at the level of design? Meaningful personal involvement may often be new or different in highly contextual ways that evolve and impact our profession profoundly. How do we establish a set of values and thus an ethic that respects our years of training as well as the many years of experience and wisdom held by those we hope to serve?

Although access to funding and political networks have become the key determinants and measure of wealth in much of today's world, we *can* maintain and strengthen the value of other factors at play. There is still much that can be accomplished with local resources mobilized by the grit and willpower of committed groups of people. In some of the poorest places with the greatest struggles there are still miracles and beauty—in songs, prayers, and community conscience. The outlook for communities challenged by poverty has changed after years of trying out systems that did not fit, and today more people are starting to believe in themselves again.

On the Rosebud Indian Reservation of South Dakota, a team of local leaders, tribal programs, public interest design professionals, and many others are working with interested local citizens, medicine people, families, and others to bring back Lakota language and values. Within a community called Keya Wakpala Waíçageyapi (Turtle Creek Development), its tribal citizens are implementing a resilient development master plan to re-embrace their culture and to become the best of what they wish to be. This is a movement to promote economic vitality that is firmly planted in the ecosystems of the prairie and in the cultural code of its people.

Resilience is the capacity to adapt to change or disturbance while maintaining or effectively rebuilding vitality. A resilient Lakota community, Keya Wakpala Waíçageyapi recognizes that familial interconnections are absolutely vital to the strength of the Nation, cultivating the health of the immediate family (*tiwahe*), extended family (*tiyospaye*), and wider relations of the Great Sioux Nation. Health is cultivated through the familial relationship of mutual help and support (*wokiye*), placing children—our sacred gifts—at the center, surrounded by the wisdom and guidance of elders (*wakanyeja*). A strong Lakota community embodies *nake nula waun*, which means "Ready for anything. Any time. Anywhere."

Part of the magic of this project has been the embedded nature of the planners, architects, and others who have been a part of the journey from the very first community conversations. These are people who come from poor, rural, tribal, or disadvantaged places themselves but have succeeded in getting an education and experience, vowing to come back and help. They remember the sacrifices of grandparents, parents, aunts, and uncles. They know the struggle. Others are new to this awareness, but have brought patience, humility, and respectfully shared alternative viewpoints. They have not looked away or put themselves above others but have chosen to stay and to become a part of something bigger than themselves. All of these people share a common passion to humbly give the best they have to offer, and in the process have created new extended families or been "adopted in" to circles of love, laughter, and prayer they could never have imagined before.

Good design is thrilling and should be shared liberally. It should be meaningful and reward us from time to time with moments of joy, such as a room full of young men and women grasping straw bale wall construction for the first time, or the tears of a community of elders who have watched their words transform into a new building. Public interest design is not only about sharing knowledge but ensuring that capacity is built and lives are made better. So often we hear from community members: "I don't know how. Who can help me?" If we can continue to search out the best answers and leave the know-how embedded within the community, then we are doing our work in a good way. And often it is the architect or designer who must acknowledge if he or she does not understand the community values and traditions. This is absolutely essential. In order to see what will otherwise remain invisible and to truly understand the unique requirements of social and cultural contexts, public interest designers must take a step back and immerse ourselves in the life and community of the people we serve.

There is a saying in the Lakota language, "We are all related." If we take this to heart and ask the right questions, we are opening up to the possibility that solutions come from many voices and viewpoints. Too often has mathematical certainty and mechanical precision obscured the amazing awareness that there is yet a Great Mystery unfolding in the universe. Knowing this, we must better embrace our intuitions and take journeys that teach us about ourselves as interrelated human beings on Earth. In this way, we can function more as interpreters between worlds. We become interpreters for those who have needs, translating responsive design that meets those needs at a deeper level.

Public interest designers have much to offer the world, but until we fully develop a language to express how much we care, people will not care about what we are capable of. As one Lakota grandma once quietly explained to a newly arrived planner who was boldly presenting his expert findings at a public community meeting on her Indian reservation: "You don't talk like us. Nobody is gonna listen to what you say, because it don't make sense. They can't hear you yet. You need to stay a little longer grandson. You'll figure it out then." Then she smiled, laughed a little, and nodded to him to continue.

It is time to continue. It is time to get more connected—with community, with cultures different than our own, and with the value systems found in each. It is time to keep learning and growing—but never forget to take time to celebrate the equitable outcomes created together. The contents of this book provide just that opportunity—to get more connected and reflect on design processes that support localized community-driven values.

May the themes and concepts in this book inspire you in ways that connect your mind and your heart at the nexus of your skills and abilities. May you too be ready for anything. Any time. Anywhere.

References

Hoffman, Edward. 1988. *The Right to be Human: A Biography of Abraham Maslow.* New York: McGraw-Hill.
Newhouse, David. 2006. "Editorial—From Woundedness to Resilience." *Journal of Aboriginal Health.* 3 (1): 3. Accessed May 19, 2014. http://www.naho.ca/jah/english/jah03_01/editorial.pdf

Introduction

Lisa M. Abendroth, Bryan Bell

This publication marks the formal recognition of public interest design as a distinct and valuable profession—one that envisions a community-centered approach in the design of buildings, environments, products, and systems. The publication of this first practice guidebook marks a significant benchmark in the development of the field. For the first time, this profession is defined through clear professional standards of practice and with tools and methods supported by best practices.

Defining a Field of Practice

What is public interest design? We recognize that public interest design is a practice that first and foremost engages people in the design process. We assert that it differentiates itself from other design practices because of its deep commitment to community engagement, public participation, and democratic decision making. This practice informs the results of design because it is derived directly from the community or audience—individuals who share a common quality—for whom the designs are created.

Public interest designers advocate for an issue-based approach to problem solving and in doing so are able to confront and resolve more than a single design problem during any given project. Connecting design problems to human issues (social, economic, and environmental) helps establish the value of design to a broader audience and provides designers with a much-needed platform for affirming the value of this work.

The requirement for assessing and then communicating results is mandatory in this field. In an effort to serve the entire spectrum of people in need—not simply those who can afford design services—the public interest designer is beholden to documenting results. Vulnerable audiences and underserved communities do not have the time for—nor can they afford—failed solutions. Our efforts advance a critical discourse on the evaluation of design outcomes so we can better demonstrate our capacity as a field.

Together these qualities help establish a framework for understanding the field as well as the content of this book. The following pages evince the value of design—the worth of design that serves all people. By presenting a broad range of issues addressed across the many design disciplines (specifically architecture, communication design, industrial design, landscape architecture, and urban planning), the book shows that every critical issue that challenges people can also be understood as a design issue. This makes a greater case for the relevance of design that serves a broad range of stakeholders in a variety of contexts and that demands accountability.

A Scaffold for Others to Build From

This book is composed of three parts that set the stage for pursuing an informed public interest design practice. Part 1, "Understanding Public Interest Design: Essays," introduces the tenets of this pursuit through a combination of practical, historical, and theoretical frameworks that unpack the complexities and demystify ways of working. This section is devoted to assessing where we have come from and where we are going as a field. It describes where more work is needed (ethical dilemmas and evaluation quandaries) and where there have already been successes (historical precedents and business opportunities). Featured contributors write from personal perspectives, reflecting on practice- or research-based endeavors in the field that reveal the fundamentals of public interest design.

Part 2, "Practicing Public Interest Design: SEED Methodology," offers best practices and methods by presenting Social Economic Environmental Design (SEED) (also known as the SEED Network), and the SEED Evaluator, a recognized standard for triple bottom line evaluation of design.[1] The SEED Evaluator is a system of assessment that positions sustainability not only as an environmental issue but also as social and economically driven concerns. The SEED Network is a principle-based group composed of design professionals and organizations that facilitates action by providing guidelines for pursuing a design process informed by inclusivity and participation as well as creating a community of knowledge for professionals and the public based on a set of shared values.

With the SEED methodology, this section addresses the need for a clearly stated and focused discussion of the professional standards of practice within public interest design—and offers a concrete framework for defining the professional standard. Part 2 integrates research and contemporary methods into one complete resource for both designers and those we serve. Because an analysis of methodology is sorely needed, a series of practical yet comprehensive essays from the field leverage SEED systems into easily applied ways of working with communities. These process "deep-dives" feature essayists who also share a related case study in part 3.

The final section, part 3, "Documenting the Value of Public Interest Design: Case Studies and Issues Index," presents a selection of international projects—distilled to process, goals, and results—prioritized based on primary and secondary issues. The topics presented in this section are not of interest to designers alone—they demonstrate the capacity to impact change at a systemic level. The Case Studies and Issues Index, also cross-referenced in the Appendix, is one way to show that human issues are problems ripe for tackling through a public interest design framework. Linking design to documented impact on everyday life, we provide evidence of the value that design has for all people.

Learning from the Past[2]

We humbly acknowledge public interest design's foundational history having grown from the community-design movement. In 1968 American civil rights leader, Whitney M. Young Jr., addressed the American Institute of Architects (AIA) convention in Portland, Oregon citing architecture's failure to impact social and civic culture in the communities that need design the most. This challenge motivated an enhanced recognition of the social significance of architecture and supported efforts within the field to inclusively address the needs of minorities—a drive which also propelled some of the first community design centers (CDCs) that focused on serving local problems. These centers provide a variety of design services toward community development outcomes often in the neighborhood where the center is located. The Association for Community Design, founded in 1977, is the professional organization supporting community-centered design practices.

In architecture schools the existence of CDCs and design/build programs provide outreach to meet local design needs to often underserved and low income communities. Among the most publicized design/build programs is the Rural Studio at Auburn University, cofounded in 1993 by D.K. Ruth and Samuel Mockbee. Completed in 1995, the Bryant Haybale House was built by university students for the Bryant family, addressing factors of affordability (the house was built for $16,500) and sustainability (The National Building Museum 2004).

Meeting localized, discrete needs of audiences and communities has not been isolated to architectural practice alone. In his book *Design for the Real World: Human Ecology and Social Change*, Victor Papanek (1971), industrial designer and educator, made a case for social responsibility in design while advocating for a balance in economy and environmental fitness of design outcomes. Papanek's vision for sustainability was one that included a moral obligation on the part of the designer to ensure appropriateness of solution and resulting impact on people and the environment—a sentiment that resonates with public interest designers today but was a somewhat unpopular opinion in the 1970s and 1980s.

Evidenced by the growing number of conferences, books, and exhibitions since the 1990s that showcase socially responsible design—and specifically socially responsible architecture—public interest design has enjoyed increased visibility. This is due in part to the growth of nonprofit design organizations providing design services to communities beyond the scope of university-based CDCs, which had greatly decreased in prevalence since their peak in the 1970s. Nonprofit organizations, including some featured in this book—MASS Design Group and Catapult Design— provide design services that serve a larger segment of the population than had been served by traditional design professions.

In 2000 the annual "Structures for Inclusion" (SFI) conference, organized by Design Corps, featured public interest design projects from around the world. This first SFI conference, "Design for the 98% without Architects," featured speaker Samuel Mockbee, who reinforced the conference theme asking how citizen architects could serve more and diverse people:

"I believe most of us would agree that American architecture today exists primarily within a thin band of elite social and economic conditions ... in creating architecture, and ultimately community, it should make no difference which economic or social type is served, as long as the status quo of the actual world is transformed by an imagination that creates a proper harmony for both the affluent and the disadvantaged." (Bell 2003, 156).

Other conferences in the last ten years, including "Gain: AIGA Design for Social Value" (2012) have evolved the sentiment expressed by Mockbee back in 2000, contributing to the momentum in the field of public interest design we see today.

The celebration of knowledge sharing through conferences is but one demonstration of the vibrancy of this growing field of practice. Organizations that provide service-learning opportunities, training, and fellowships specific to public interest design are on the increase. One example, the Enterprise Rose Architectural Fellowship, fosters leadership in architects eager to expand their public interest design practice in low- to medium-income communities where long term and sustainable community development is desired. Other organizations supporting unique fellowship opportunities include Code for America, Design Impact, Gulf Coast Community Design Studio, and IDEO.org.

Design Corps is known for expanding its non-profit scope of service to offer training for design professionals and others. The first "Public Interest Design Institute" (PIDI) was conducted in 2011 at the Harvard Graduate School of Design. Since then the PIDI has trained over 1,000 people using case studies of best practices in the field. Institutes are held regularly and throughout the world. The AIA has worked closely with the PIDI to endorse continuing education credits—a demonstration of the AIA's commitment to expanded learning. The AIA furthers research in architecture through competitive grants provided by its College of Fellows. One such award offered every two years, the Latrobe Prize, was given to Roberta Feldman, Sergio Palleroni, David Perkes, and Bryan Bell, for "Public Interest Practices in Architecture" (2011) (essay pages 45–55).

Exhibitions have played an important role in supporting the discourse around public interest design as a field of practice. "Design for the Other 90%" (2007) curated by Cynthia E. Smith at the Cooper Hewitt, Smithsonian Design Museum was met with great success leading to a series of thematically focused exhibitions including "Design for the Other 90%: CITIES" (2011). Over the next five years a number of exhibitions—both national and international in scope—helped propel the work of public interest design into publically accessible venues. Notable examples include "Small Scale, Big Change: New Architectures of Social Engagement" (2010), curated by Andres Lipek of the Museum of Modern Art, "Spontaneous Interventions: Design Actions for the Common Good" (2012), curated by Cathy Lang Ho and featured at the U.S. Pavilion of the Thirteenth International Venice Architecture Biennale, and "Public Interest Design: Products, Places, and Processes" (2012), curated by John Cary and Courtney E. Martin at the Autodesk Gallery in San Francisco.

These efforts parallel the energy and drive of public interest design with, for example, the Green Design movement, and suggest how public attention to a cause can motivate change within a field of practice. The Leadership in Energy and Environmental Design (LEED) certification program, started by the U.S. Green Building Council in 2000, provided a guide—a standard to achieving levels of sustainability certification within a system of quantified measurements that justified "Green Design". Around this same time, evidence-based design used in health care contexts started to effectively use data to show the impact of design.[3] Before the establishment of a common standard, specific professions and the affected public lacked ways to determine a project's performance, leading to widespread "washing" or misleading claims.

But neither LEED nor evidence-based design had considered the relationship between design and social and economic challenges that communities face on a regular basis. The SEED Network was founded in response to this imbalance. Adopting the term *SEED* coined by architect Kimberly Dowdell—to recognize the need for a social equivalent to LEED—the SEED Network was cofounded in 2005 by a cohort of community design leaders concerned about a balanced and inclusive approach to design. With the reinforcement of many SEED members and contributors, this book provides a concrete strategy for pursuing public interest design and a vision for systemic change across design disciplines.

In a recent (2014) and promising development, the USGBC has introduced into LEED certification a pilot social equity credit, "Social Equity within the Community," a credit which can be accomplished by using the SEED Evaluator or other social evaluation programs. This integrated and embedded nature of solving problems with an eye toward social, economic, and environmental factors means that public interest designers are simply doing more. They are working toward a balance of these and understand that in doing so they have a higher rate of success of addressing long-term, sustainable community-centered outcomes.

Achieving Systemic Change

The term *public interest design* represents an evolving history of struggle and progress. And yet, it also represents unification, the formation of a recognized professional practice for designers across disciplines. When designers share best practices, we all benefit. That shared knowledgebase underscores the purpose of this publication—to demonstrate a professional standard where tools, resources, and methods for accomplishing goals are proven by example and can be used as models to build from. Ultimately, the power of design remains in the hands of our "client"— our community or audience—and it is with them that we must prove our value.

Looking forward, we know that it will take more than individual designers or projects for this work to function at a level at which we can consider serving the whole spectrum of public need through design. It will take systemic solutions and a vision for the profession that is unified by a professional ethic, a code of conduct. While we have outlined the legacy of what we call "public interest design" today, we recognize we are in many ways still in the infancy of this field with room to grow. It is through the contributions of the many dedicated collaborators found in these pages that a collective action forms a systemic approach to this work. We greatly value their individual ideas and know that these are helping shape the standard of practice that is required in the field of public interest design.

References

Bell, Bryan. 2003. *Good Deeds, Good Design: Community Service Through Architecture*. New York: Princeton Architectural Press.

Elkington, John. 1998. *Cannibals with Forks: The Triple Bottom Line of 21st Century Business*. Gabriola Island, BC, Canada: New Society Publishers.

Papanek, Victor. 1971. *Design for the Real World: Human Ecology and Social Change*. New York: Pantheon.

The National Building Museum. 2004. "Samuel Mockbee and the Rural Studio: Community Architecture," organized by the Birmingham Museum of Art. Accessed on August 22, 2014. http://www.nbm.org/exhibitions-collections/exhibitions/samuel-mockbee.html

Notes

1   Author John Elkington coined the term *triple bottom line* in his book *Cannibals with Forks: The Triple Bottom Line of 21st Century Business* (1998). Elkington refers to social, economic, and environmental concerns in the context of corporate performance and business. The SEED mission—that every person should be able to live in a socially, economically, and environmentally healthy community—leverages a vision toward long-term and sustainable outcomes informed by a participatory practice, issue-based approach to problem identification, and evaluation of results.

2   Bryan Bell authored the first Wikipedia entry for public interest design on October 25, 2012 from which aspects of content in this section are derived. The entry was edited by Stephanie Hashagen under contract for services to Bryan Bell.

3   Steven A. Moore's essay in chapter 7 entitled, "Post-Occupancy: Implementation and Evaluation" provides discussion of evidence-based design in the context of post-occupancy evaluation.

Part 1

Understanding Public Interest Design: Essays

1

The State of Public Interest Design

Bryan Bell

The field of public interest design is quickly emerging. And while there has been growing momentum over the last fifteen years, much remains to be done. What we are now beginning to see is a realization of the full potential of design—the highest and best use of design to serve 100 percent of the population. We are seeing the emergence of what can rightly be called public interest design (Bell 2013, 52). While this relationship between design and the public interest has come more into focus during the last decade, we are still at the beginning of what needs to happen. We need to move past catchy names and rallying cries into a deeper understanding of how this potential can be fulfilled.

Evidence has been growing over the past fifteen years of the many designers engaging in projects of public benefit around the world. My own work in this sector began in 1990 when I left Steven Holl's office to design housing for migrant farmworkers, although I did not know what to call the work then—I was simply the "non-architect" or the "alternative career" person.

My research into this field of work started in 2000 when the nonprofit organization I founded, Design Corps, held the first "Structures for Inclusion" conference at Princeton University during which we made the challenge to "Design for the 98% without Architects."

Designing for the 98 percent has served since then as a rallying cry for this growing movement that is now becoming a profession.[1] This slogan, that so well illustrates that designers have only been serving the very few, symbolizes how much work we still need to do before we can use design to address the most critical challenges we face in the world.

1.1
Migrant Farmworker Housing Unit: In 1989, when Bell moved to rural Pennsylvania to design and build housing for migrant farmworkers, he did not know what to call his field of work. He now understands it is public interest design. Design: Bryan Bell, Model: Mathew Heckendorn.

The research and documentation of this work has focused on individual projects and individual people. But individual projects and individual people have a major problem—they can all go away. They lack the advantages of collective action. To reach its potential, this movement must become permanent and effect systemic change. This work must resonate at a deep cultural level. We must understand and make clear how these individual projects and people add up to a collective action that provides a value so deep the public will make sure that it does not go away. The challenge is to find a cultural basis for design that will provide value to 100 percent of the general public (Bell 2013, 52).

So to build a field of public interest design that can grow to serve 100 percent of the public, we need to make clear the public benefits of design. These are beyond the scope of the design professions as they are currently defined, which is largely based on the needs of individuals or private institutions that can afford to pay the professional fees for services. Similarly, the standards of practice that deliver these benefits are yet to be fully clarified. This clarity is essential to create the understanding and trust of service the public deserves.

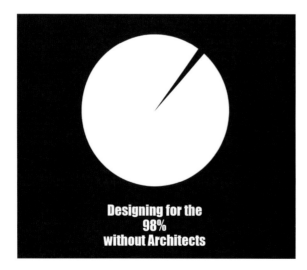

Designing for the 98% without Architects

1.2
In 2000 Design Corps held the first "Structures for Inclusion" conference at Princeton University called "Design for the 98% without Architects", which is now a rallying cry for public interest design.

Bell

What does it mean to be a profession? It means to profess a mission. With a mission, public interest design is an emerging field, like public interest health that arose from the medical profession. Without a mission, design can be seen merely as an advanced technical skill. While technical skill is certainly valuable to society, it does not serve the greater public good. "This is because more fundamental than the other defining features of a profession (a specialized body of skills and knowledge, a code of ethics, a community that controls who can practice, etc.) is its raison d'être: 'to serve responsibly, selflessly, and wisely'" (Gardner and Shulman 2005, 14).

Other professions that serve the public have resonating values deep in our culture. The United States Constitution states the ideal of equal justice that is the cornerstone of the legal profession. The Hippocratic Oath, which originates from fifth century BC, offers an ethical foundation for health care professionals. What is the collective mission of public interest design?

To understand what the mission of public interest design should be, I surveyed a representative sample of the national AIA membership as part of the American Institute of Architects (AIA) College of Fellows Latrobe Prize.[2, 3] I asked those surveyed whether a specific statement would be an appropriate mission if a profession of public interest design were to exist. Seventy-seven percent agreed with the following mission: "Every person should be able to live in a socially, economically, and environmentally healthy community." (This mission was originally determined through a democratic decision process in 2005, conducted among the two hundred founding members of the SEED Network.)

In the Latrobe survey I also sought to understand what principles could define the expected field of practice aligned with this mission. The question was posed: "If a profession of public interest design was to exist, would the following

1.3
A survey of the members of the American Institute of Architects showed a strong consensus for the SEED Mission and Principles as being a mission and principles for the practice of public interest design. Source: Survey conducted by Bryan Bell and the American Institute of Architects (AIA) for "Wisdom from the Field: Public Interest Architecture in Practice," by Roberta Feldman, Sergio Palleroni, David Perkes and Bryan Bell, 2013; Funded by the AIA College of Fellows 2011 Latrobe Prize.

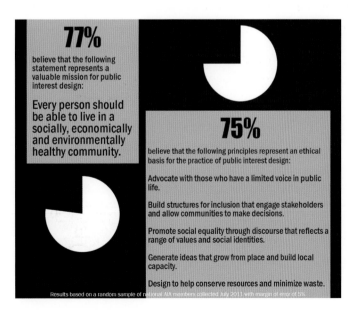

77%
believe that the following statement represents a valuable mission for public interest design:

Every person should be able to live in a socially, economically and environmentally healthy community.

75%
believe that the following principles represent an ethical basis for the practice of public interest design:

Advocate with those who have a limited voice in public life.

Build structures for inclusion that engage stakeholders and allow communities to make decisions.

Promote social equality through discourse that reflects a range of values and social identities.

Generate ideas that grow from place and build local capacity.

Design to help conserve resources and minimize waste.

Results based on a random sample of national AIA members collected July 2011 with margin of error of 5%.

be an appropriate mission?" Seventy-five percent agreed with the following principles:

- Principle 1: Advocate with those who have a limited voice in public life.
- Principle 2: Build structures for inclusion that engage stakeholders and allow communities to make decisions.
- Principle 3: Promote social equality through discourse that reflects a range of values and social identities.
- Principle 4: Generate ideas that grow from place and build local capacity.
- Principle 5: Design to help conserve resources and minimize waste.

These survey questions started to provide the needed clarity to define the foundation for the profession of public interest design. The principles set the stage for a *vision* of success and a way to *measure* success within the field. A review of these principles confirms the core relationship between design and democracy—the use of the democratic decision making process is clear in Principles 1, 2, 3, and 4.

The recognition of a clear and accepted mission and principles is an important step to defining a profession. The survey responses show the beginning of that collective understanding that public interest design is the practice of design, with the goal that every person should be able to live in a socially, economically, and environmentally healthy community. The research also showed that those practicing public interest design take a holistic approach, considering a broad range of social challenges not dissimilar to the field of public health that we draw much inspiration from. Public, interest design also seeks to provide services to the entire general public, as does public interest law. The ideals of democracy echo in the cultural foundation and values of public interest design. Design and democracy are linked in a deeply powerful way that is both idealistic and practical—and both can be strengthened by building the relationship within them.

The value of this relationship was given evidence through the Latrobe research done by Roberta Feldman, Sergio Palleroni, and David Perkes. They interviewed 118 public interest design practitioners. Ninety-three, or 78 percent, cited the value of stakeholder participation in the design process. This high percentage of interest in collective decision making supports a democratic design process in the practice of public interest design.

From these findings, we move to a "value proposition," a statement about what the democratic design process provides that is of value to the public. *Public interest design efficiently allocates public resources to address a community's highest priorities through a democratic decision making process that is transparent and accountable* (Bell 2013, 52).

Identifying a mission, principles, and value proposition starts the process of clarifying what public interest design can hope to contribute for the public good. Not only should a building provide shelter and meet basic functions but also, through design, it can meet the higher goal of providing a socially, economically, and environmentally healthy community while supporting a democratic and inclusive decision making process (Bell 2013, 52).

Growth with Caution

Every new field that has emerged to serve the public goes through an initial phase of defining itself. In addition to a mission, principles, and a value proposition, professional standards need to be defined. Professional standards determine the level of performance that people are expected to achieve in their work as well as the knowledge and skills they need to perform effectively in their field. Professional standards form the principles of conduct governing an individual as a part of a professional group. The reason for these to be clear is to assure the public what they can expect while holding practitioners accountable to established criteria.

When professions fail to make these clear, the value of a profession can be compromised and the public trust jeopardized. During the 1930s, pioneers like photographer Dorothea Lang created a public demand for social justice with her camera. However, this field had no clear professional standards, and writer Erskine Caldwell violated what is now an established code of conduct. Having a personal ethic that did not distinguish between fiction and non-fiction, Caldwell fabricated quotes for photographs of poor rural Southerners that were taken by his partner, Margret Bourke-White (Broadwell and Hoag 1982).[4] His fictitious captions were juxtaposed with photographs of real people without their consent, an act unimaginable today under current professional standards of journalism. Taking these photos would also be considered unethical by the standards that have come to define a profession with great public value.

A similar violation to professional trust happened during the early days of public interest health when standards of practice had not yet been established. In 1932 the U.S. Public Health Service conducted the Tuskegee syphilis experiment to study the effects of syphilis among poor rural African Americans in Tuskegee, Alabama. The six hundred men studied were not told what disease they had contracted and were intentionally untreated with penicillin when it was established as a cure in 1947. The experiment continued until 1972. The victims of the study included numerous men who died of syphilis, wives who contracted the disease, and children born with congenital syphilis. As a result of such misguided experiments, public health now has self-imposed standards of informed consent in any situation where human subjects are involved.

One key question raised by these two incidents is how these professionals could take actions that clearly violate what we now understand as the ethical foundation for journalism and public health. The answer is that they were acting under their own personal standards, not a set of professional standards. Professional expectations had not been determined yet, and there was no professional accountability.

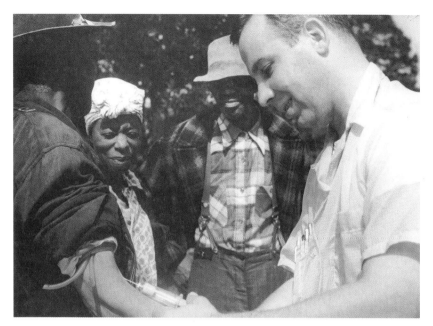

1.4
A doctor and patient of the Tuskegee Syphilis Study conducted by the U.S. Public Health Services between 1932 and 1972 to study untreated syphilis in rural African American men. The patients thought they were receiving free health care from the U.S. government and did not receive a cure when it became available. The study was conducted without the patients' informed consent. The U.S. National Archives and Records Administration.

How do we create accountability in public interest design? To do so, we must first determine if *public interest design* is a general term that anybody can use to describe any intention and any agenda or a specific standard that can be measured and verified. This moment in the development of public interest design strikingly parallels the moment a decade ago when many things were called Green Design. Because there were no standards for what constituted a "green" practice then, this term could easily be abused. Without accountability, public interest design could face a similar predicament in which design claims to be in the public's interest, but there are no standards to measure or uphold the validity of these claims.

I believe that the term *public interest design* means that the design is in the interest of the public; and if it is not, it should not misrepresent itself. Data from the AIA Latrobe Prize survey of the architecture profession address whether this should be a regulated profession that self-maintains standards. In the survey, 57 percent of architects said that an ethical violation should result in removal, which confirms that, at least as far as licensed architects are concerned, there is support for a professional field with accepted practices that should not be violated. *Public interest design* is not just a term to be freely used by anyone to describe anything remotely related. It is a profession, and the practitioners need to be held accountable.

Now Is the Time

We are now at the critical moment in time when public interest design is taking shape into this specific field of practice, a moment when the disparate activities of individual projects by individual people from across design disciplines are no longer just separate efforts. While design professions are ancient in many ways, from planning cities and designing buildings to shaping tools and creating lucid communications, ideas about the public benefit of design are just now being made meaningful.

If public interest design is to move from its current limited role to realize its greater public value, we must face our challenges. As a first step, public interest designers need to change our self-vision and the goals we set for ourselves in our work. We need to change the public perception of what and how we can contribute to the greater common good. This is already happening. The collective consciousness of design is changing. This shift gives us an opportunity to do more good work and to make a permanent change in our collective futures. The massive shift we need is not going to happen by supernatural forces. It will only happen when many of us become engaged—by the design community becoming activists for the human community.

The need for public interest is undeniable. We can design for 100 percent of the public. This is when we realize our full potential. We need to learn from the best practices presented in this publication. We need to show the public what value this field has for them by addressing their most critical issues. But while progress has been made, much more progress is needed. Public interest design is not set in stone and hopefully it never will be. The best of creativity is always about finding better ways. I challenge you to learn from the best and be part of the incredible and exciting potential of public interest design.

References

Bell, Bryan. 2013. "Towards a Cultural Value of Design and Democracy." *Oz*. 35: 52–57

Broadwell, Elizabeth Pell and Ronald Wesley Hoag. 1982. "Interview: Erskine Caldwell, The Art of Fiction." *The Paris Review* 62. Accessed on August 22, 2014. http://www.theparisreview.org/interviews/3098/the-art-of-fiction-no-62-erskine-caldwell

Gardner, Howard and Lee S. Shulman. 2005. "The professions in America today: Crucial but fragile." *Daedalus*. 134 (3): 13–18. doi:10.1162/0011526054622132

Notes

1　The Cooper Hewitt, Smithsonian Design Museum held a well-known exhibition in 2007 entitled "Design for the Other 90%" curated by Cynthia E. Smith.

2　The AIA College of Fellows awarded the 2011 AIA Latrobe Prize to Roberta Feldman, Sergio Palleroni, David Perkes, and Bryan Bell for "Public Interest

Practices in Architecture." Research from this award resulted in the report, "Wisdom from the Field: Public Interest Architecture in Practice." The full text is available at: www.publicinterestdesign.com/wp-content/uploads/2013/07/Wisdom-from-the-Field.pdf.

3   The 2011 Harvard Loeb Fellowship supported Bryan Bell's survey research. Dr. Patrick Moynihan of the Harvard Institute for Quantitative Social Science and Dr. Howard Gardner of the Harvard School of Education provided crucial survey support. Dasha Ortenburg provided valuable assistance in conducting the surveys.

4   *You Have Seen Their Faces* by Erskine Caldwell and Margaret Bourke-White was published in 1937 by Viking Press. It documents the authors' journey through rural southern America among some of the country's poorest sharecropper communities.

2

What Social Justice Movements Can Teach Us about Public Interest Design

Barbara Brown Wilson

What can public interest designers learn from past social movements, including civil rights, disability rights, and environmental movements? What critical aspects of these influential social movements codify their values into the built world? Professional movements like public interest design (PID), which want to alter urban form, need to make sure that they are 1) amplifying traditionally unheard voices to express a shared set of big-picture goals, 2) nurturing many avenues to grow the knowledge base, 3) helping talented resource mobilizers craft their messages appropriately to express authentic movement aspirations and build collective funding and media opportunities, and 4) nurturing coalitions with (at times unlikely) allies that can widen the movement's base and create new venues for innovative problem solving.

At a few critical moments in modern history, society successfully adopted previously underrepresented values into urban forms. Social movements provide a venue for such paradigmatic change, especially when the movement's collective vision is paired with tangible strategies to implement this change in built form and within the industries influencing it.

In order to understand how we might better democratize contemporary built form—the question underlying this exploratory inquiry—we must first understand how it has been done in the past. Since the 1960s, the United States has experienced waves of civil unrest that inform the ways in which its cities grow, the process through which policies are made, and correspondingly, the perspective from which the collective built world is understood. The civil rights movement (CRM) arguably began this tidal wave of social movements, introducing a language of rights into modern U.S. activism that empowered generations of citizens. Unprecedented successes, including the Montgomery bus boycotts and the March on Washington, led a well-organized CRM to the Civil Rights Act of 1964, which banned discrimination in public facilities and employment and became the legal basis on which many other identity and rights-based movements drew their strength. This inquiry investigates patterns found in the CRM and two other U.S. movements that drew from the CRM's radical platform for urban change: the disability rights movement (DRM) and the environmental movement (EM).

Precedents presented here provide historic context to inform one specific emerging social movement, public interest design, to discern the characteristics of democratic design processes that lead to new patterns of urban form. This study analyzes the three U.S. movements in terms of their origins, the claims made, strategies employed, and outcomes achieved. Patterns are then extrapolated to identify qualities of collective action that contribute to the democratization of built form.

Social movements in the United States require a myriad of different activist organizations—radical and mainstream, professional and grassroots—employing diverse strategies through an integrated frame of collective action to institutionalize new types of civic urban form. The study illuminates four critical roles contributing to the development and sustenance of collective action: 1) democratic claim making, 2) knowledge brokering, 3) resource mobilizing, and 4) alliance building. When movement actors build these four critical activities around a shared vision that co-evolves with relevant socio-technological change, lofty public interest values, like equity, can influence the otherwise obdurate built world. This chapter will first briefly summarize each role as it might apply to PID before fully describing the social movements in which they arose.

Democratic Claim Makers: If the most important aspect of a successful social movement is its democratizing power—providing a platform for previously unheard voices—then the organizations helping to define democratic claims and also maintain the centrality of these claims within the movement play a critical role in its success (Tilly 2004). In the CRM, for instance, the Southern Christian Leadership Conference maintained a connection to the African American church networks that precipitated and reified the movement tenets. Without grassroots activists validating the integrity of the claims made by the movement as it evolves, the authenticity of a movement may not remain intact. But this internal auditing system, although critical to the substance of the movement, must focus on advocating for and empowering the previously underrepresented while other organizations focus on education, alliance building, and resource mobilization (Melucci 1996). For professional movements, like PID, identifying the best grassroots partners to represent the evolving concerns of underserved populations remains a major challenge. Making professional language accessible and relevant to the larger public is a huge cultural hurdle for any professionally driven movement, and finding grassroots partners that see the benefits of helping craft the larger vision is critical to sustaining widespread and positive change.

Knowledge Brokers: Knowledge brokers assist with the translation of a movement's identified needs and theoretical understandings to the public with tools that also provide innovative practical solutions. Knowledge brokers are essential to any process of socio-political change that connects emerging research and technological innovation to practical policy applications (Rogers 2003). Serving as the cheerleader for important ideas that might otherwise get lost in the political negotiation process, a knowledge broker provides a platform for public discussion regarding policy innovations as they are proposed, refined, and adopted across the political landscape (Thompson, Estabrooks, and Degner 2006). Because knowledge brokers have the power to frame the discourse as it enters the public domain and to disseminate this new knowledge widely, they are exceptionally influential. The U.S. Green Building Council (USGBC), for example, is a primary knowledge broker for the environmental movement and trains professionals all over the world on how to best use the tools inherent within its building-assessment system to integrate new value-based technologies and practices into the culture of the building industry (Kioski 2010). There are several important knowledge brokers within the constellation of PID— groups like the Detroit Collaborative Design Center (chapter 11, pages 109–14) and the Center for Urban Pedagogy in New York City are important knowledge brokers focused on community-design issues salient to their community partners, while Public Architecture and the SEED Network both strive to create national systems for knowledge dissemination that influence various larger professional spheres of PID.

Resource Mobilizers: Resource mobilizers use their national or international media relationships to help smaller grassroots organizations leverage outside funding and media attention to more effectively implement local change. The Congress of Racial Equity (CORE) often led the resource-mobilization efforts of the CRM. Established by Caucasian intellectuals in the movement with a talent for demonstration organization, CORE often recruited African American students from local universities to participate in its events. Although CORE's founding members were not racially representative of the oppressed minorities, it skillfully organized several national demonstrations, such as the Freedom Rides and the lunch-counter sit-ins of the early 1960s, that brought the plight of the CRM to the attention of media outlets and wealthy foundations across the country (Stanley 1982; McAdams 1999).

When appropriately paired with grassroots organizations and aligned with the vision guiding the movement, both resource mobilizers and knowledge brokers can transform a growing movement. For instance, John Cary launched the website and blog, PublicInterestDesign.org[1], which has become an important resource mobilizer in attracting media attention and potential funding toward best practices in PID, while the Surdna Foundation has become a critical leader in the funding community, driving the field toward innovation through their focus on community-engaged design. In order to successfully co-evolve with technological change, however, an urban-focused social movement must also continue to forge alliances that broaden the boundaries of its vision and the base of its constituencies.

2.1
CORE demonstration, Phyllis
Twachtman, 1964.

Alliance Builders: In order to develop an integrated, inclusive frame of collective action that influences the development of the built world, alliances must be constructed among seemingly divergent groups. For instance, the unlikely alliance between DRM activists championing visitability standards and the Congress for New Urbanism (CNU) expanded and benefited both groups. The CNU previously upheld the front-porch stoop as the quintessential iconic image of the home. But when DRM activists redefined the front stoop as a barrier to accessibility, the two groups worked to find an innovative solution that honored both perspectives. This particular collaboration yielded the zero-step entryway—a fully accessible, covered portico that requires no change in elevation from the walkway but maintains the feel of a front porch and a nuanced rhetoric of "lifelong communities." Without the openness to coevolve while staying true to the primary values, these new alliances cannot contribute to the creation of positive spatial change. In PID, for instance, MASS Design Group's partnership with health care professionals building hospitals in Africa (chapter 23, pages 167–71) engaged an international social-service industry without knowledge of how design might benefit their building practices. This recent alliance is already re-creating the professional boundaries of both groups and building new capacities to better serve their clientele and their missions.

PID has amassed an impressive constellation of organizations working toward its general goals. Nevertheless, it is not likely to fully mature into an impactful social movement until it finds community advocates outside of the design profession, who see the benefits in articulating and refining a national frame for collective action on

Brown Wilson

which meaningful alliances with underserved populations can be built. For example, at the time of this publication the SEED Network is in discussions with Partnership for Working Families, a labor-union-driven base-building umbrella network for local advocacy organizations across the country, about potential synergies. If a shared and inclusive vision can be built and maintained with both organizations' larger constituencies involved, alliances like this one have the potential to ensure the relevance of the emergent PID-movement goals to the broader public.

In what follows, the methods used by the CRM, DRM, and EM to affect the urban form will be briefly discussed to exemplify the importance of each of these four roles in such an effort. Although none of these movements fully embodies the perfect constellation of movement organizations and networks to achieve systemic change, each has contributed something unique to the understanding of how social justice movements can positively alter the patterns of the built world.

Community Development as a Claim to Civil Rights

The CRM drew from the energy of countless organizations within its constellation; however, four specific groups contributed most significantly to the trajectory of the movement. Often referred to as the Big Four, this group includes the National Association of the Advancement of Colored People (NAACP), the Student Nonviolent Coordinating Committee (SNCC), the Southern Christian Leadership Conference (SCLC), and CORE. Each played a distinct role—the NAACP was the litigious brain trust as well as the historical base; the SNCC was the source of youthful activism that animated many of the most important protests; the SCLC represented the spiritual, grassroots base; and CORE was a formidable resource mobilizer. Often, these groups worked in partnerships of two or three, but rarely did all four major organizations agree on the trajectory, mission, and language to best represent the cause. This infighting would eventually dilute their collective impact and become a cautionary tale for other movements.

The Big Four did agree on one critical thing—the rights-based frame on which the movement built its foundation—and collectively adopted a persuasive rhetorical frame that fundamentally altered the political climate in the United States. The language of *rights*, which drew from the country's founding rhetoric and served as constitutional leverage in the NAACP's early court cases, was a novel and phenomenally effective frame through which this movement made its claims (Tarrow 1998). Many of these litigious successes, however, were ineffective in altering the spatial patterns that embodied the prejudices that the movement was attempting to eradicate.

When it became clear that minority–majority neighborhoods regularly did not receive the same level of municipal service provision as other parts of town (e.g. daily trash pick up), the Community Development Corporation (CDC) organizational model was created to give disenfranchised community members a voice in the development of their neighborhoods. The "primary characteristic of these early groups was their broad-based community involvement," with goals of engendering small business, utility provision, or affordable housing depending on community interests (Sahd 2004, 86). With the hopes of institutionalizing the empowerment-based ethics of the CDCs into federal policy, CORE presented several versions of the Community Corporation Act to Congress between 1968 and 1971 that failed because of the infighting. Within this legislation was the Community Self-Determination Act, which would have provided CDCs with the autonomy they needed to remain staunch advocates for municipal change. The act would have created a nationwide Community Development Bank as a secondary financing institution, favorable tax status for CDCs as well as "turnkey" tax incentives for cooperating outside businesses, tax credits for local hiring, and managerial and technical assistance money for CDCs through the Small Business Administration (Faux 1971, 114).

Between five hundred and one thousand housing-development-focused CDCs emerged during this early period, with an explicit interest in gaining agency over deteriorated inner-city neighborhoods under siege from outside forces. But without autonomy from local governments, CDCs could not pursue their advocacy missions, which were supplanted by the interest of maintaining the city financing necessary to develop much needed affordable housing (Thibault 2007).

Although the value of community-oriented affordable housing produced by CDCs cannot be underestimated, the original goals of community control and resident empowerment have been abandoned out of necessity by most CDCs (Vidal and Keating 2004; Stoecker 1997). Because the Big Four could not identify shared basic tenets for the legislation, CDCs were left without the tools to retain their fiscal autonomy. The rights-based foundation of the CRM movement, however, was a legacy on which many social movements built their own platforms—and the DRM may be the most direct descendent. When civil rights leaders began to protest the Vietnam War alongside disabled veterans, the rhetoric of rights for disabled people gained enough momentum to become its own political force. The DRM borrowed many phrases, techniques, and even members from the CRM, but strove to maintain a collective frame of action defined by inclusion and self-representation.

Architectural Barriers as an Alliance Building Strategy

The DRM, even in its earliest days, fought to shift the public's perception of disability from a medical condition (and thus public burden) to an environmental limitation (Imrie 1996). Movement leaders became remarkably talented at integrating their own constituents into leadership positions and finding ways to work with like-minded activist from other strands of the movement.

In the early 1960s, Ed Roberts, paralyzed by polio as a teenager and dependent on an iron lung, became the first severely disabled student to enroll in the

2.2

As early as 1919 the Red Cross Institute for Crippled and Disabled Men, prompted by WWI, created a series of posters like this one attempting to dispel the stigma that persons with disabilities were inherently less capable.

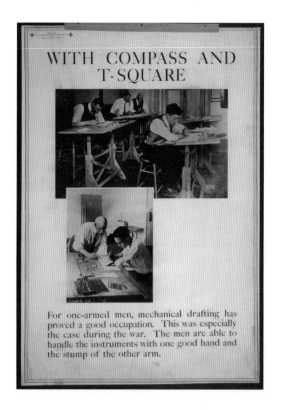

WITH COMPASS AND T-SQUARE

For one-armed men, mechanical drafting has proved a good occupation. This was especially the case during the war. The men are able to handle the instruments with one good hand and the stump of the other arm.

University of California at Berkeley. At Berkeley, Roberts honed his organizational skills and learned the importance of alliance building between the various disabled communities—a lesson that pervaded the ethics of the entire movement: "None of us wanted this to be simply a wheelchair crusade. We enlisted the support of deaf students, blind students, and students with epilepsy and others. We quickly learned the value and strength of coalition politics" (Roberts 1980). Roberts became a strong voice for the mantra of inclusion and self-representation that defined the DRM. During a speech at a rally the same year he cofounded the World Institute on Disability, Roberts asserted a concept that became critical to the movement's success: "One thing we learned from the civil rights movement in the U.S. is that when others speak for you, you lose ... We are not begging for our rights, we're demanding our rights. We're not going to sit out and wait for them; we're going to sit in the streets if that's what it takes" (1983). Later this concept of self-representation would be further popularized on an international scale by the slogan "Nothing about us, without us, is for us" and would lead to the passing of the Americans with Disabilities Act in 1990. This empowered mantra helped popularize the growing movement in the 1980s, but it was the increased visibility of Vietnam War heroes with disabilities that first began to open up a public dialogue about the rights to which disabled persons might be entitled.

As waves of injured veterans returned from World War II ready to take advantage of the educational benefits promised by the G.I. Bill, university campuses first began grappling with the issue of architectural accessibility as a human right. Nevertheless, an attempt to add the disabled population to the interests groups protected under the Civil Rights Act failed in 1972. In the next piece of DRM legislation, the 1973 Rehabilitation Act, the issue of disabilities was still treated as a medical concern in every section of the bill but one—Section 504 (Roberts 1978).

When President Carter stalled the signing of the "Section 504" regulations, because of its huge potential impacts on the marketplace, the American Coalition of Citizens with Disabilities, a newly formed "coalition of coalitions," made the signing of these regulations the focus of their efforts (Pelka 1997, 10). There were multiple occupations of federal buildings involving hundreds of protesters, but historian Joseph Shapiro refers to the occupation in San Francisco—the nexus of the DRM—as the "political coming of age of the disability rights movement ... a mini-Woodstock" in which people with different disabilities were forced to not only join together, but also to actually live in close proximity for a month and survive together (1994, 68). The collective identity that had only been discussed in theory was created through practice during their occupation (Moore and Wilson 2013). On April 28th, Health, Education, and Welfare Director Robert Califano signed the regulations, and two days later the newly solidified DRM marched in the streets chanting, "We Have Overcome."

Initial backlash against these regulations by the business community was profound. Enforcing disability rights legislation meant higher costs, which was very different from the cost-saving measures resulting from integration during the CRM. The DRM successes were few during the Reagan administration, with several scholars claiming during those years that 1978 was the peak of the movement (Scotch 1984). Yet, thanks to the efforts of the 1970s DRM participants, the next generation of disabled activists was educated in a public school system to which their predecessors never had access. These children grew up in a world where ramps, curb cuts, and accessible bathrooms were civil rights to which they felt entitled. By the late 1980s, these young activists reenergized existing advocacy groups to push their rights further by enacting the watershed legislation of the movement.

The comprehensive Americans with Disabilities Act (ADA) bill—which first failed to pass in 1988—was signed into law by President George H. W. Bush on July 26, 1990, in part as a result of the coordinated efforts of leading advocacy groups and national lobbying organizations with grassroots demonstrations in civic spaces around Washington D.C. by their more radical allies (Pelka 1997, 20). The ADA "prohibits discrimination in private employment, public accommodation, and telecommunications" (Scotch 2001, 384). The ADA definition of disability is based on the one provided in Section 504 and draws language—almost verbatim—from the Civil Rights Act of 1964 (Scotch 1984, 52). The ADA regulatory structure was socially constructed over decades—some were the bricks of past triumphs in the state legislatures and some were issues still plaguing the daily life of thousands of citizens. This incremental legislation fundamentally altered the urban form of the United States, with accessible design standards, such as curbs, ramps, sidewalks, workplace accommodations, and restrooms, now mandated for all publicly funded commercial spaces. The architectural design and construction industries now consider these accessibility standards to be commonplace, and the costs of building more accessible places have decreased as building habits have changed.

The most effective strategies to draw from the DRM are related to the movement's aptitude for coalition building. Although the DRM were originally harsh critics of the CNU for its glorification of the front stoop, the two are now unlikely allies. Disability advocates argued for the inclusion of visitability standards as an option in CNU rhetoric, focusing on the zero-step entrance and an accessible half bathroom on the first floor of any multistory residence as easy, inclusive alternatives to the CNU aesthetics. CNU leaders responded positively to the critique, and within a few years an antagonistic relationship transformed into an alliance against sprawl—a pattern of development not suited for people who do not drive. This alliance highlighted the importance of developing "lifelong communities" and educating practitioners interested in the ethics of either group on the importance of "designing for a pluralist population" (*New Urban News* 2004).

Not to say that every project built in the style of New Urbanism is now fully accessible and well conceived—even those that attempt to do so. But by resisting the hubristic urge to essentialize the movement into one or two specific disabilities, such as deafness or paralysis, and remaining open to new, if difficult, advocacy partnerships around shared goals, disability rights advocates cast their inclusive web so broadly that it touches every citizen's sensibilities. Through the engagement of grassroots radicals and savvy lobbyists, of militant protests and persuasive rhetoric, of right-wing economists, social-service providers, and liberal clergymen, a richer platform to argue for paradigmatic change has been built. DRM activists drew from their daily struggles—climbing a set of stairs or using public transportation—to articulate their assertions for spatial change and an accessible built world through dynamic coalitions. This inclusive approach to movement politics allowed for the redefinition of disability from a physical handicap to an environmental limitation.

Sustainable Development and its Knowledge Brokers

The EM has not always been as well unified as the DRM, and its relationship with the marketplace has been fraught with contradictions. Yet, among its varied successes lays the development of the most influential voluntary building-assessment systems yet accepted by the industry. Recent government reports estimate that the building industry is responsible for 50.1 percent of the annual energy consumption in the United States (Rawlins and Paterson 2010), for roughly half of the greenhouse gas emissions each year (Roodman et al. 1995), and for the use of 12.2 percent of all potable water (Solley et al. 1995) and 40 percent of raw materials globally (Roodman et al. 1995). Thus, any alteration in the practices of the building sector has the potential to greatly mitigate environmental degradation.

Green building rating systems are voluntary, market-driven metrics, but they have been so well indoctrinated into the practices of the building industry that many thought leaders predict their eventual assimilation into regulatory building codes. Although even the leading building-assessment systems fail to integrate the full cadre of environmental ethics into the built world, the organizations that continue these systems have enormous value as knowledge brokers for the institutionalization of green building tenets.

Rating systems, which are now an international craze, come from humble, local beginnings. In response to wide gaps in sustainable-building regulations, progressive municipalities, homebuilders associations, utility providers, and local environmental organizations sponsored green building-assessment systems that often focused on energy and resource conservation in building. The city of Austin, Texas, pioneered one of these programs in 1990, with Denver, Colorado, and Santa Barbara County, California, adopting similar systems in the subsequent five years (Green Building Comes Home 2004, 34). By 2006 the National Association of Homebuilders counted more than sixty-one thousand homes certified under local green building systems—with the numbers having begun to rise exponentially around 2005 (Williams and Bourland 2008, 108). Today, many metropolitan areas have adopted some sort of green building certification system in their building codes, but most of them are a combination of national standards like Energy Star, the USGBC's Leadership in Energy & Environmental Design (LEED) rating system and the Enterprise Community Partner's Green Communities Initiative.

The USGBC was founded in 1993 as a "national-reaching council, one that was comprehensive, open and included bankers, builders, architects and designers, manufacturers, environmentalists, government and utilities all in the same conversation" (USGBC Annual Report "The First Council Meeting," 2008). With the help of the American Institute of Architects, the first USGBC council meeting in April 1993 attracted sixty organizations and architecture firms. They proposed an "open and balanced coalition of the entire building industry that [would] manage its own green building rating system," which would be funded by membership fees (USGBC Annual Report 2008). Fusing elements of the Austin Energy Green Building rating system with Britain's national model, the Building Research Establishment Environmental Assessment Method, the USGBC industry membership created LEED. Their intent was to foster the premier U.S. national green building certification system.

In the LEED certification system, a building accrues points based on the implementation of energy- and resource-saving features in site planning, water management, energy management, material use, indoor-environmental air quality, and innovation and design process. By 2014 LEED standards certified more than one hundred thousand buildings in the United States, estimating that every day over 1.5 million square feet of space is certified using LEED. Although originally created to solely regulate new commercial construction, LEED's expanded system now accounts for existing buildings, commercial interiors, neighborhoods, site-development projects, schools, health care facilities, building core and shell, and residential structures.

Many critics argue that this system has become too abstract, too point driven, too time consuming, too prone to green-washing, and too expensive (Schendler 2005). Citizens often complain that the buildings produced are unattractive and/ or out of character for the context. Because USGBC is composed of contributing membership organizations and firms—most primarily from the building industries— environmental groups argue that many of the requirements favor industry prerogatives over environmental benefits (Moore 2003). Many environmental-justice advocates push the critique further, finding fault in the lack of a focus on equity in the rating system (Oden 2010). Leslie Moody, executive director of the Partnership for Working Families, worries that LEED could significantly reduce the carbon footprint of developments, but leave the workers and community members affected by these developments behind if their well-being is not considered. "Because who has access to the jobs?" she asked. "And who helps maintain these systems once they are built? There is definitely a push from all of our organizations that environment without equity is green-washing poverty" (2009, pers. comm.).

What USGBC has done well in the equity realm is to develop strategic alliances with organizations that create multidimensional hybrid codes. For example, USGBC helped to develop the Green Communities Criteria (GCI) with Enterprise Community Partners that assesses sustainable, integrated design processes of affordable housing developments alongside a powerful suite of tailored knowledge brokering services. Enterprise birthed this hybrid code in partnership with the USGBC, the Natural Resource Defense Council, American Planning Association, Global Green, American Institute for Architects, Southface, as well as a few influential banks and foundations. Dana Bourland, a primary Enterprise champion for the creation of this effort, attributes GCI's effective knowledge brokering to its vigilance in learning from the struggles of early adopters and then adapting the program to help bridge the "disconnect between green building consultants and the affordable housing sector ... including the creation of a database of qualified green building practitioners, a series of manuals, and a funding mechanism to ensure that the integrated design process was privileged up front" (Dana Bourland 2014, pers. comm.).

Together, these two checklists formed a new standard for development and a new learning community to support it. Although many cities have mandated that publicly funded buildings comply with these two standards, Washington D.C.— with the D.C. Green Building Act of 2007—became the first city to require private developers to meet LEED standards for commercial projects and GCI standards for residential ones. Through these partnerships and educational programs, the two organizations have become incredibly effective knowledge brokers for environmental values.

Both the LEED and GCI standards advocate for integrated design processes that acknowledge the limitations of the tools as creative guides, allowing participants to "agree on a vision that affirms their values, on a process for employing the tool, and then a path to look beyond it" (Gail Vittori, pers. comm.). Many leaders in the USGBC governing structure argue that LEED need not bear the burdens of the entire

EM and that it might not even be the best venue to represent some of its values (Moore and Wilson 2013). Gail Vittori, co-creator of the Austin Energy Green Building rating system and former chair of the USGBC Executive Committee, argues that although it is the point of entry for many architectural professionals, the movement must stretch well beyond the boundaries of LEED to grow. This turn in the building trades toward the triple bottom line ethic pushes the industry beyond the status quo (now perpetuated by LEED), is a main driver of much of the work happening in PID, and serves as inspiration for the creation of the SEED metric and its associated network of practitioners.

In fact, the SEED Network (full disclosure: I am a SEED Network founding member) engaged Gail Vittori and other thought leaders in building assessment systems early on in its development, and maintained critical relationships with Vittori and other USGBC leaders like John Quale as both metrics evolved. While SEED remained critical of LEED's silence on social equity, its leadership also continued to engage in constructive dialog about how the two could collaborate. In 2014 the USGBC codified its growing interest in equity with the launch of a new social equity pilot in LEED certification. This first draft allots 1 possible point to "Social Equity within the Community," which can be achieved through one of three means. The point can be earned through the collaborative performance of a Community Needs Assessment, the results of which must be incorporated into the design and/or programming of the project. Or, the point can be earned by receiving GCI or SEED certification, or another USGBC equivalent. Partnerships like these, embedded into this ubiquitous system, create hybrid codes that foster new paths for innovation.

The SEED Network's emerging cadre of tools includes a member pledge, training programs, online metric, award program, and catalog of case studies that empowers designers to think about process and well as product. After a summit SEED convened to reflect on the past, present, and future of the network, SEED founding board member Jess Zimbabwe, who is the Executive Director of the Rose Institute for Public Leadership, stated the aspirations of the network well, "the next phase of SEED will look to establish community driven design as the rule, and not the exception in global design practice, and will look to increase SEED's influence beyond the existing community design sector, and extend membership to include citizens, policy makers, corporations, and other stakeholders." This suite of knowledge broker services could be incredibly influential for PID, especially if PID can continue finding new ways to make its work relevant to grassroots community-development advocates, resource mobilizers, and alliance builders, who can broaden PID's purview and impact outside the professional design sphere.

Pushing Beyond the Profession for PID

This historical analysis suggests that movements attempting to codify their values in built form need to expand their impact and relevance to the general public.

2.3
The ecosystem of actors needed to develop hybrid codes that embody democratic values serves as a powerful set of checks and balances toward positive change in the built world.

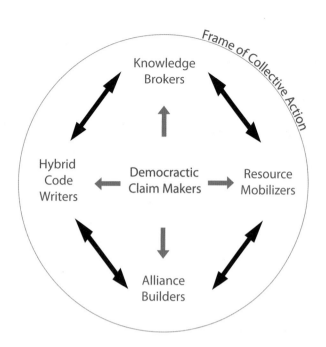

Movements must negotiate the agendas of various entities to translate grassroots claims into a collective vision, to broker knowledge with outside forces, to mobilize resources that support the ongoing work of those underserved communities advocating for themselves, and to make alliances with often seemingly opposed outside groups.

The constellation of organizations within a social movement must find venues to integrate divergent values into a frame of collective action that coevolves with social and technological change. Today's built systems and the social movements must dialectically coexist and productively support one another to successfully grow as a collective force. PID is poised to become such a movement and a force for positive change within its associated professions, if its constellation of actors agrees upon a shared vision for collective action that allows the grassroots values of the populations it hopes to serve to play a substantial role in shaping its trajectory.

References

Faux, G. (1971). *CDCs: New Hope for the Inner City.* New York: Twentieth Century Fund.

"Green Building Comes Home" (2004) In *Building Design and Construction, Supplement: Progress Report on Sustainability.* November.

Imrie, R. (1996). *Disability and the City: International Perspectives.* New York: St. Martin's Press.

Kioski, C. (2010). Greening America's Skylines: The Diffusion of Low-Salience Policies. *The Policy Studies Journal*, 38(1), 93–117.

McAdams, D. (1999). *Political Process and the Development of Black Insurgency, 1930–1970*. (2nd edn). Chicago, IL: University of Chicago Press.

Melucci, A. (1996). *Challenging Codes: Collective Action in the Information Age*. Cambridge: Cambridge University Press.

Moore, P. (2003). Sustained by Science. *Architecture*, 92(9), 112.

Moore, S. A. and B. B. Wilson (2013). *Questioning Architectural Judgment: The Problem of Codes in the United States*. London: Routledge.

Morris, A. (1984). *The Origins of the Civil Rights Movement*. New York: The Free Press.

New Urban News (2004, October, November). Search is Underway for Accord on "Visitability". *New Urban News*.

Oden, M. (2010). Equity: The Forgotten E in Sustainable Development. In S. Moore (Ed.), *Pragmatic Sustainability*. New York: Routledge.

Pelka, F. (1997). *The ABC-CLIO Companion to The Disability Rights Movement*. Santa Barbara, CA: ABC-CLIO.

Rawlins, R. and R. Patterson (2010). Sustainable Buildings and Communities: Climate Change and the Case for Federal Standards. *Cornell Journal of Law and Public Policy*, 19, 335–382.

Roberts, E. V. (1980, May 19). *The Emergence of the Disabled Civil Rights Movement*. Disability Rights and Independent Living Movement Archive, Berkeley, CA: The Bancroft Library.

———. (1983, January). *When Others Speak for You, You Lose*. Disability Rights and Independent Living Archive, Berkeley, CA: The Bancroft Library.

Roberts, S. (1978, June 19). *The Handicapped are Emerging as a Vocal Political Action Group. New York Times*.

Rogers, E. M. (2003). *Diffusion of Innovations* (5th edn). New York: Free Press.

Roodman, D. M. N., K. Lenssen, and J. A. Peterson (1995). *A Building Revolution: How Ecology and Health Concerns are Transforming Construction*. Washington, D.C.: Worldwatch Institute.

Sahd, B. (2004). Community Development Corporations and Social Capital: Lessons from the South Bronx. In R. M. Silverman (Ed.), *Community-based Organizations: The Intersection of Social Capital and Local Context in Contemporary Urban Society*. Detroit, MI: Wayne State University Press.

Schendler, A. (2005). Top Green-Building System is in Desperate Need of Repair. *Grist*, October 27.

Scotch, R. K. (1984) *From Goodwill to Civil Rights: Transforming Federal Disability Policy*. Philadelphia, PA: Temple University Press.

———. (2001). American Disability Policy in the Twentieth Century. In P. L. a. L. Umansky (Ed.), *The New Disability History* (pp. 375–392). New York: New York University.

Shapiro, J. P. (1994). *No Pity*. New York: Three Rivers Press.

Solley, W. B., R. R. Pierce, and H. A. Periman (1995). *Estimated Use of Water in the United States in 1995*. Washington, D.C.: U.S. Geological Service.

Stanley, A. K. (1982). Oral History Interview. On GreenboroVOICES Collection. Greensboro, NC: University of North Carolina at Greensboro.

Stoecker, R. (1997). The CDC Model of Urban Redevelopment: A Critique and an Alternative. *Journal of Urban Affairs*, 19(1), 1–22.

Tarrow, S. (1998). *Power in Movement: Social Movements and Contentious Politics*. Cambridge: Cambridge University Press.

Thibault, R. (2007). Between Survival and Revolution: Another Community Development System is Possible. *Antipode*, December.

Thompson, G. N., C. A. Estabrooks, and L. F. Degner (2006). Clarifying the Concepts in Knowledge Transfer: A Literature Review. *Journal of Advanced Nursing*, 53, 691–701.

Tilly, C. (2004). *Social Movements, 1768–2004*. Boulder, CO: Paradigm Publishers.

USGBC Annual Report (2008). *15 Years, 15 Stories*. Accessed at http://www.usgbc.org/about/annual-reports on May 10th, 2014.

USGBC (2014). *U.S. Green Building Council Certifies 50,000th Green Housing Unit Under LEED for Homes*. Accessed at http://www.usgbc.org/articles/us-green-building-council-certifies-50000th-green-housing-unit-under-leed-homes/

Vidal, A. C. and W. D. Keating. (2004). Community Development: Current Issues and Emerging Challenges. *Journal of Urban Affairs*, 26(2), 125–137.

Williams, S. and D. Bourland (2008). Green Affordable Housing: Enterprise Green Communities Initiative. In E. Birch and S. Wachter (Eds), *Growing Greener Cities: Urban Sustainability in the Twenty-First Century*. Philadelphia, PA: University of Pennsylvania Press.

Note

1   Although John Cary founded the blog publicinterestdesign.org, it now goes under the name of impact design hub and is owned by Autodesk.

3

Professional Responsibility and Ethics

Thomas Fisher

As the economy has become more global, designers have increasingly found themselves working in cultures very different from their own. This has become even more of an issue for public interest designers, whose work largely occurs in less affluent communities and in more diverse cultures than most mainstream designers encounter. With cross-cultural public interest design projects come new kinds of ethical dilemmas. Conflicts can arise not only as a result of individual actions but also because of misunderstandings resulting from cultural assumptions, differences in social mores, and contrasts in religious beliefs. This, in turn, requires that public interest designers remain attuned to the ethical dilemmas that can arise from their work. It also shows the need for these designers to have ethical tools at their disposal that differ from those needed by most mainstream designers, who, while they may work in another country or culture, often serve those in their same socioeconomic class.

Ethics has sometimes offered designers too blunt a tool. Historically, ethicists have tended to seek one, all-encompassing way of assessing the right or wrong of a situation, judging everything according to its intentions or its consequences. In contrast to these "monists," other ethicists have offered so many specialized tools that it becomes difficult to know when to use what. These "relativists" have emphasized cultural difference to the point where they claim that we cannot make ethical judgments about a culture if not already a part of it.

For public interest designers—and indeed for anyone working in another culture—both of these extremes do little good. The monist's singular approach often gives too little credence to cultural differences, and the relativist's emphasis on particulars often gives too much. A relatively recent development in ethics offers a more useful middle ground. Called Moral Foundations Theory (MFT), its advocates argue that there exist a relatively small number of foundational ideas—five or six—that guide people's judgments about right and wrong across many different cultures (Graham et al 2012).[1] Whatever other merits this approach may have, MFT also offers those who work in other cultures a set of tools that they can use to assess the ethics of situations that may differ dramatically from what they might encounter in their own culture. As such, it seems perfectly suited for public interest design.

Developed by the social psychologist Jonathan Haidt and his colleagues Craig Joseph and Jesse Graham, MFT stems from an architectural analogy. As Haidt, Graham, and several of their colleagues describe in a recent paper on MFT, they

> chose the architectural metaphor of a 'foundation' ... [because] the foundations are not the finished buildings, but the foundations constrain the kinds of buildings that can be built most easily ... Similarly, the moral foundations are not the finished moralities, although they constrain the moral orders that can be built. Some societies build their moral order primarily on top of one or two foundations. Others use all five ... MFT is a theory about the universal first draft of the moral mind, and about how that draft gets revised in variable ways across cultures. (Graham et al. 2012, 10)

In other words, this approach to ethics acknowledges that there exist certain universal or foundational notions of right and wrong that occur across all human communities and that different emphases and interpretations of those notions vary from one culture to another. For the public interest designer, this requires the weighing of both universal principles and cultural differences in any particular situation. When confronted with a conflict or a condition that may not seem right, a designer working in another culture needs to ask what foundational issue applies to the situation and what relative value the particular culture places on that issue. In that way, MFT provides a check on making inappropriate assumptions about morality in another culture, without making the equally inappropriate assumption that we can never judge the ethics of a situation if not already a member of that culture.

The Five Foundations

MFT can also help us apply the SEED principles discussed elsewhere in this book in appropriate ways across diverse cultures. The SEED principles do an excellent job in articulating universal ethical ideas, but MFT can help us navigate moral assumptions that can vary widely among Western and non-Western societies. In Western cultures, two foundational values—fairness and caring—typically dominate ethical discussions, and we hear those two values coursing through the five SEED principles:

1) Advocate with those who have a limited voice in public life.

2) Build structures for inclusion that engage stakeholders and allow communities to make decisions.

3) Promote social equality through discourse that reflects a range of values and social identities.

4) Generate ideas that grow from place and build local capacity.

5) Design to help conserve resources and minimize waste.

Every culture, of course, values fairness and caring. In many non-Western parts of the world, however, three other foundational values—loyalty, authority, and sanctity—also matter greatly. SEED principle 1 urges designers to advocate for those who have a limited voice in public life, but what if that conflicts with values of authority and sanctity widely held in, say, a conservative Muslim country? Follow our principles or honor a culture's traditional values? MFT can help navigate such dilemmas.

The following five sections will take each of these five foundational values and explore their relevance to public interest design, drawing from projects that have also won SEED awards, many of them featured as case studies in this book. The analysis will answer the pragmatic question of what use and relevance MFT has for those working in other countries. The value of any ethics lies in its ability to help solve problems and resolve conflicts and the following shows how MFT meets that test in addressing people's needs.

Fairness/Cheating

Fairness or justice remains a core value in every society, according to MFT, because without them, society itself cannot function. Haidt and his colleagues note that "those whose minds are … highly sensitive to evidence of cheating and cooperation … [have] an advantage over those who had to figure out their next move using their general intelligence" (Graham et al. 2012, 13). This evolutionary advantage exists across cultures, and so every person, whether working within their own culture or in another, can safely assume that others value fairness and decry cheating as well. How that moral foundation gets interpreted or acted out, however, may vary widely from one culture to another, evident in the following examples.

Consider the Towns Association for Environmental Quality (TAEQ) Green Building Headquarters (case study pages 222–5) in Sakhnin, Israel. Established by Israel's minority Arab community, which makes up 20 percent of the population, the TAEQ provides information and education about sustainable development to six communities in its region. The project suggests that humanity's common interest in the well-being of our planet can overcome the political and religious conflicts that have occurred in places like Israel. Here, the foundational value of fairness transcends other values, such as loyalty to one's ethnic group or the sanctity surrounding one's beliefs.

That may vary, though, from one person to another. As critics of the moral-foundations idea have noted, MFT tends to overlook the role that interpersonal relationships play in a person's behavior, with peer pressure from the group overpowering an individual's sense of fairness. That does not mean that prejudice always trumps justice. But it does mean that when working in a country in which internal conflict prevails, one has to appeal constantly to people's sense of fairness in the face of political and personal differences. In that context, the heavy masonry walls and fortresslike form of TAEQ's building not only have environmental benefits but also symbolic value.

Design's ability to enhance fairness can extend beyond buildings. The Impact Detroit Community How-To Guides (case study pages 194–7), created by Impact Detroit and a number of local nonprofits, show how well-designed graphics on a series of colorful, easily carried cards can help underprivileged people access the resources and information they need. The very fact that the citizens of Detroit required such an aid shows that, in a supposedly egalitarian country like the United States, there remain profound inequalities. One project cannot singlehandedly change that condition. But these how-to guides are a reminder that we have an ethical responsibility, as well as a largely untapped opportunity, to use design to help empower the disadvantaged.

This might seem easier to do in one's own community, but that is not always the case. Haidt and his colleagues recognize that "intergroup moral conflicts are particularly intractable" (Graham et al. 2012, 27), and that people in the same culture—or, in the case of Detroit, the same city—can become blind to the injustices around them. Design, in this framework, not only seeks out dilemmas and solves problems but also reveals prejudices and reminds those in public office of their duty to attend to the needs of every constituent.

Care/Harm

The foundational value of care seems obvious: a baby cannot survive long without the care of an adult, and those parents who care well for their offspring have a distinct advantage over those who do not. This relates to a growing body of work expounding that ethical behavior has evolutionary benefits, suggesting that care for—and prohibitions against harming—others remains a universal human value that cuts across cultures.[2] But, again, what constitutes care and how that manifests can vary considerably across cultures, and designers need to know how to distinguish between the universal and the contingent when dealing with care in different countries.

The Comunidad Ecológica Saludable (healthy ecological community) (case study pages 230–3) program in Lima, Peru, shows the difficulties of making this distinction between the universal and the specific. Located in Lomas de Zapallal, an informal settlement, the project involves the condensation of water from the fogs that frequently blanket the area, initially providing a group of twenty-nine families with clean water for domestic use and for their gardens as well as for local parks and reforestation efforts.[3] This is an extraordinary accomplishment for people who have little access to the formal economy of Lima or to the water infrastructure of the rest of the city. Since the government or utilities do not care enough to deliver water to the Eliseo Collazos neighborhood, the residents, with the help of the University of Washington, have successfully wrung water from what they have.

But care, as a foundational value, cuts more than one way. For example, the residents of informal settlements occupy land that they frequently do not own, which raises the question of whether or not ownership is relevant. Governments sometimes point to the illegality of these settlements as a reason for not supplying them with basic infrastructure, so how does care for the rule of law compare with care for the people of a place? Public interest designers might side with the latter, although one would do well not to ignore the former. In such situations, it seems advisable to remain personally helpful and politically neutral regarding the ethical conflicts that can arise between the formal and informal sectors of countries.

Such neutrality becomes harder to justify in a country like the United States. Its persistent problem of homelessness stems more from public-policy decisions, such as those that led to the closure of many homeless shelters and the end of funding for many support services. In a country as wealthy as the U.S., such decisions seem both careless and harmful, and cities have only now begun to recover from the effects of these politically motivated decisions. New Orleans just recently built its first supportive housing project, the Rosa F. Keller Building, designed by HCI Architecture, which offers on-site services and facilities—such as a gym, community room, computer room, and garden—to its low-income and once-homeless residents.

Here, the ethics of care comes through in the building designer's attention to the particular needs of this population. Too often, the public sector seems to serve the poor begrudgingly, if at all, with buildings that seem to flaunt their inadequate budgets and the insufficient attention paid to materials and details. The Rosa F. Keller Building shows how, even with modest budgets, owners and architects who care about the people who occupy a place can make something extraordinary. The building's courtyard, with its open corridors overlooking the outdoor space, offers a protected place that simultaneously feels inviting and inclusive. It reinforces the foundational idea that when it comes to people in need, we have no excuse for not caring.

Loyalty/Betrayal

Haidt's research shows that, in the United States, political liberals often place more emphasis on fairness and care, while political conservatives favor loyalty, authority, and sanctity. That same divide can occur in other countries, where many people may value cultural traditions and religious practices more than in some Western democracies. When public interest designers from the West work in more conservative countries, respect for the values of other cultures must be weighed against the recognition that some principles pertain to all human beings—e.g., loyalty to a particular community versus a shared humanity.

Wherever one's ultimate loyalty resides, resolving such conflicts requires a great deal of respect. The new housing on the Puyallup Tribal Reservation in Tacoma, Washington, demonstrates the good that can happen when a design team shows proper deference to the loyalty that people have for their cultural traditions. Referencing the historical longhouses of the Puyallup Tribe, this project features ten townhomes (with another ten anticipated in the second phase) that face a central space, where the residents can gather for communal activities. Tribal members, many of whom have struggled with unemployment, participated in the design process and worked on aspects of its construction. Loyalty to cultural traditions can occur in the means and methods of design and construction as well as in the end result.

Projects like this, though, also reveal the different loyalties that designers must navigate. While the Puyallup Longhouse recalls the tribe's traditional form of housing, it also meets modern building codes and exceeds Washington's current energy code, employing technologies that have nothing to do with the tribe's past. In a country like the United States, that coexistence of modern technology and cultural tradition has become the norm. In other nations, the use of unfamiliar technology, however well meaning, can strap people with equipment they cannot operate or maintain, and in these situations, respecting a community's historical accommodation of its climate and traditional energy strategies represents the wiser choice.

Loyalty can also create a community where one did not already exist. Haidt and his colleagues have argued that sports teams and their fans represent a modern version of group loyalty, and this is the case in more traditional cultures as well. In Africa, the Football for Hope Movement has established a series of sports centers, in Manica, Mozambique, for example, that combine football pitches with indoor spaces used for promoting community health and education. This program remains loyal to its host communities, employing many locals to construct their buildings. It also uses the community's loyalty to sports and teams as a way of informing people about issues, such as AIDS prevention and children's rights—sensitive topics related to people's lack of fidelity.

Clearly, navigating the ethics of such situations can be tricky. Public interest designers have a responsibility to involve communities in the design of their facilities, such as the Manica Football for Hope Centre (case study pages 242–5). But where does one draw the line between global and local values? In cultures where children are expected to work at a young age or women are not allowed to work outside the home, for example, where do the loyalties of designers from the West lie—with the values of the community in which they work or with their own? Maybe the answer lies with education: accepting people as they are and at the same time helping them see how else they might live.

Authority/Subversion

After a century of suffering as a result of people's loyalty to ideologues on the political left—Stalin, Mao—and on the political right—Hitler, Mussolini—many in the West have become wary of authority figures in general. The same does not always hold in non-Western countries. Public interest designers might find themselves working in places where authoritarian leaders hold sway, and dealing with authorities while also addressing the needs of communities can lead to situations fraught with ethical dilemmas.

In some places, the authorities can seemingly ignore the plight of their own people. In South Sudan, a new country struggling with civil war, the government has not had the ability to meet the needs of many of its people, and nongovernmental organizations have stepped in to fill the void. This can be hazardous work, especially in locations where armed conflict can put everyone in harm's way, but public interest design can bring tremendous benefits to such places.

The South Sudan Jalle School (case study pages 254–7), created with the help of the nonprofit Rebuild South Sudan for a remote area in South Sudan's Jonglei State, is a clear example of this. As the region's first school and the only permanent structure within seven miles, the building, raised above the flood plain, provides a safe haven for the community and serves as a primary school and a welcoming place for people of all ages, with a computer lab, library, and gathering space. Rebuild South Sudan sees the school as a prototype for "improving literacy rates, promoting equality, and offering the next generation of children a future for themselves and generations to come" (Rebuild South Sudan 2014). In the absence of an effective government authority, projects like this help give people authority over their own lives.

If education offers one way of giving a future, economics offers another. In efforts like Yayasan Kota Kita's design of Firm Foundation (case study pages 190–3), a community center, market place, and port for an impoverished waterfront community in Banjarmasin, Indonesia, or the work of a group of community leaders and U.S. universities in developing an "aquaponics" system to bolster the economy and reduce hunger in the Bondo District of Nyanza, Kenya, public interest designers can help people achieve a degree of autonomy by creating spaces for economic opportunities.

This may seem responsible and ethical from a Western perspective. Depending on the country, however, it can also appear subversive to those in power, undermining their authority, which shows why an understanding of the context in which the work occurs remains so important. A public interest designer needs to involve community members for this very reason: they have a much better sense than outsiders of how a well-intentioned project might appear to those with the ability to oppose or stop it. The real authority for all of this work exists with those most affected by it at the local level. They have the wisdom to know what they need and what the context will allow, with public interest designers playing the part of facilitators rather than the traditional Western role of professional experts. Humility, always an important virtue, has particular value in this work.

Sanctity/Degradation

The final foundational idea is sanctity and its opposite, degradation. In the West, sanctity is often linked to religious and other ceremonial practices—this is true in many non-Western cultures as well. But in the latter especially, sanctity extends beyond religion to include the sacredness associated with a culture, a community, a family, and even one's body. As a result, sanctity remains an area where public interest designers can encounter some of the greatest cultural dissonance, since, unlike government authority or political loyalties, sacred topics are often unspoken and unwritten parts of a culture. Public interest designers need to tread carefully when building on this foundation.

An example of this discord exists in the sanitation project for the resettlement area of Savda Ghevra in New Delhi, India. While sanitation remains a central problem in many informal settlements around the world, it presents a particular challenge for women who often have little or no sanitary privacy. The Potty Project (case study pages 302–5) provides a decentralized way of providing private sanitation for the residents of this community, while offering a safe, private place for women to use. The need for sanitary privacy, of course, remains nearly universal, but in a country like India, where the female body, in particular, remains sacred and women's bodily functions are a taboo topic, public interest design has to address those values and make extra effort to accommodate them.

Haidt and his colleagues recognize that differences *within* classes or castes of a single culture can trump the differences that exist *among* cultures, something evident in this project. In a country like India, the provision of public toilets that few women will use allows a government to appear as if it has accommodated the needs of its people, while actually serving only the male half of its citizens and furthering the difficulties of women. Infrastructure can, in other words, enforce oppression in the name of sanctity.

The ethical dilemma faced by Western designers in such situations involves determining what takes priority: the authority of those with power or the sanctity of those without. While the answer may differ depending on the culture and context, ethics generally falls on the side of the underserved and the disempowered, suggesting that public interest designers can play an important role in respectfully revealing the contradictions that can arise in a community.

Such contradictions occur in countries like the United States as well. Haidt and his colleagues have acknowledged a possible sixth moral foundation that concerns liberty and oppression. In the Owe'neh Bupingeh Preservation Plan and Rehabilitation Project (case study pages 202–5) for the Ohkay Owingeh pueblo in New Mexico, the Native American tribe took liberties with the federal guidelines for preserving historic buildings in order to pursue a path more appropriate to its culture. Rather than making visual distinctions between new and old parts of the pueblo, as the federal guidelines require, the tribe used this rehabilitation project as an opportunity to train its members in traditional building methods. Liberty took the form of reinterpreting what people saw as an oppressive federal guideline that does not apply to this community, suggesting that freedom is, to some extent, in the eye of the beholder.

Foundations for the Future

MFT offers a useful way of navigating the ethical challenges that can occur when working in another culture, providing a middle path between a single answer to every ethical dilemma and a relativistic position that makes finding any answer almost impossible. Like design itself, this approach to ethics recognizes that life occurs not in black and white but in shades of gray. Haidt and his colleagues continue to investigate additional foundational ideas, including ownership/theft, efficiency/waste, and honesty/deception, all of which have connections to public interest design—whether that involves property ownership, building efficiency, or the honesty of contractors and government officials.

Indeed, the built environment provides a kind of test case for MFT. As I hope the preceding has shown, this approach to ethics can sensitize us to the nuances of right and wrong in diverse cultures and prepare us for working in places with values that may differ from our own. While ethicists have often made universal claims for the validity of their positions, MFT shows how much ethics—like public interest design—remains highly contextual in nature. What may look like oppression from one cultural perspective can look like sanctity from another, and public interest designers need to know which is which and where.

MFT can also help public interest designers see their own work from the perspective of others. In contrast to the aesthetic bias of designers when assessing each other's work, MFT shows how ethics provides a better way of evaluating public interest design. While the completed work of public interest designers certainly matters a lot to those who have so little, the process of designing and constructing this work—by engaging, employing, and empowering people in new ways—may matter more. Both the SEED principles and MFT provide public interest design with a stable foundation on which to construct not only good buildings but also strong communities.

References

Graham, Jesse, Jonathan Haidt, Sena Koleva, Matt Motyl, Ravi Iyer, Sean Wojcik, and Peter Ditto. 2012. "Moral Foundations Theory: The Pragmatic Validity

of Moral Pluralism." *Advances in Experimental Social Psychology*. 55–130.
http://papers.ssrn.com/sol3/papers.cfm?abstract_id=2184440

Haidt, Jonathan. 2012. *The Righteous Mind: Why Good People are Divided by Politics and Religion*. New York: Penguin.

Rebuild South Sudan. 2014. www.rebuildsouthsudan.org/. Accessed on August 15, 2014.

Notes

1   The quotes from Jonathan Haidt and his colleagues related to Mortal Foundations Theory come from www.moralfoundations.org and from the paper "Moral Foundations Theory: The Pragmatic Validity of Moral Pluralism," written by Jesse Graham, Jonathan Haidt, Sena Koleva, Matt Motyl, Ravi Iyer, Sean Wojcik, and Peter Ditto for *Advances in Experimental Social Psychology*, posted on December 4, 2012 and available at http://papers.ssrn.com/sol3/papers.cfm?abstract_id=2184440

2   You can find an excellent summary of this work in Richard Joyce's book *The Evolution of Morality* (Cambridge: MIT Press, 2006).

3   The case study presented in this book details a related project in the same community focused on developing twenty-nine household gardens.

4

Learning from Public Interest Practices[1]

Roberta Feldman, Sergio Palleroni, David Perkes

The American Institute of Architects (AIA) College of Fellows awards the Latrobe Prize every two years for research in architecture. The 2011 call for research proposals offered the following challenge to address changes in the profession:

> Many of the assumptions that have long guided the field of architecture no longer seem relevant to the challenges we now face not only as a profession and discipline, but as a civilization ... Nor can we assume that the practices that have guided architectural practice in the 20th century will serve us in the 21st. (Feldman et al. 2013, 12)[2]

The Latrobe research team, Bryan Bell, Roberta Feldman, Sergio Palleroni, and David Perkes, was pleased to be awarded the 2011 Latrobe Prize to support the proposed research, "Public Interest Practices in Architecture." The goal of the research was to describe current innovative efforts within architectural practice that strive to address community needs and to recommend ways to increase the impact of these types of practices. The 2011 Latrobe Prize is not only significant because it funded research to bring public interest work to light but also because the prize shows the profession and the public that the AIA values community service work, even when it does not follow conventional practice models.

The team interviewed 118 practitioners and fifty of their community partners. The interviews provide detailed accounts of the motivations and operations of a wide range of practices. The overarching tone from the interviews is determination, which is well stated in the words of Gail Vittori, co-director of the Austin-based Center for Maximum Potential in Building Systems: "You used every mechanism that was possibly available to you to keep doing what you're doing" (Feldman et al. 2013, 51).

Public interest practitioners work at overcoming the obstacles that get in the way of meeting the needs of the community. Some of these obstacles are inherent to architectural practice; others have a more basic cause—the limitations of market-driven development. In some way, all of the obstacles stem from the uneven distribution of power, wealth, risk, information, opportunities, etc. Vittori's observation was a bellwether of what we would find through the interviews: the mechanisms to overcome these obstacles are as varied as the particular working contexts and show a wide range of innovation and experimentation. Public interest practitioners are pragmatists, creatively pushing the boundaries of conventional practice. Nevertheless, independent of their distinct methods and business models, they follow typical strategies. Therefore, even with the variety in methods, there is considerable overlap in the strategies employed. The seven strategies that follow introduce how the field is operating.

Strategy 1: Focus on Social, Economic, Political, and Environmental Impact

Public interest practitioners address challenges in the communities in which they work. Such challenges include chronic problems of poverty as well as acute humanitarian crises resulting from disasters. To engage effectively in these complex challenges, public interest designers consider the social, economic, political, and environmental conditions of the places in which they work.

Buildingcommunity WORKSHOP (bcWORKSHOP) was, in the words of its founder Brent A. Brown, "incubated" out of his private architectural practice, which he had established in Dallas. Even in his earlier conventional practice, Brown already provided public design services without receiving compensation. "Public design work was of ever-increasing interest to me, and I felt the need to expand my practice's activities beyond facilitation and move into a position of direct community advocacy" (Feldman et al. 2013, 42). His first step in the shift toward public interest was made possible by creating a donor-advised fund with a local community foundation. This allowed Brown to receive donations for nonprofit work through a foundation as he began the process of setting up bcWORKSHOP as its own nonprofit entity.

The first project was the Holding House, completed in 2008, a single-family residence built for families that live on Congo Street, a one-block street that was a historically marginalized community in the heart of Dallas. The families took turns staying at Holding House while their run-down homes were being renovated as part of a community redevelopment project. Keeping families in the neighborhood while improving the value, livability, and energy efficiency of their homes allowed bcWORKSHOP to address both the individual homeowners and to maintain the cohesion and social fabric of the community. But the success of Congo Street and its role in launching the work of bcWORKSHOP also occurred because of the nonprofit structure of the practice. Brown explains:

> No money had been raised, and no donor was identified for this house. What I knew was that in order for the project to be successful, the structure of how we went about working had to be beyond doubt. The decision to formally establish the nonprofit and no longer take private commissions was a personal choice and one that was based on an ethical intent to not confuse private benefits with the public good. (Feldman et al. 2013, 51)

Even though operating a pro-bono design program within the activities of a conventional for-profit practice could have worked, Brown decided to create a nonprofit practice that makes clear its mission to serve the community. bcWORKSHOP offers a successful example of a practice that is defined in its mission as well as its legal structure to completely focus on community needs.

Strategy 2: Engage the Community

Collaboration with community stakeholders is a hallmark of public interest design. Such collaboration is facilitated by the continuity of relationships over time and by building trust. Community participation improves the project's social outcomes and its financial viability. And, importantly, participation can also support community empowerment; that is, the ability of the community to act on its own behalf in current and future projects.

Christine Gaspar, executive director of the Center for Urban Pedagogy (CUP) in New York City, explains that the goal of public interest work is not simply the resulting design, it is the organizing of the people using the design. CUP creates visualization tools to demystify design, development, and public policies to "improve public participation in shaping the city and shaping the places we live." Gaspar continues:

> For us at CUP, it's not just about having the designer work on this project. It's about making sure the people that are on the ground in the community, who are really struggling with that issue, come to the table and bring their knowledge of the issue and the challenges they've seen. It's about making sure that their constituents are going to look at the project and give us feedback, about making sure it's doing the thing it's meant to do and it's going to meet the needs on the ground. (Feldman et al. 2013, 54)

Linda Baird, the program coordinator for the Youth Justice Board at the nonprofit organization Center for Court Innovation, initiated a project with CUP to use innovative design to advance Youth Justice Board's mission to help the youth in the New York justice system. CUP worked with a graphic designer to create a comic book illustrating how "Chris," a fictitious teenager in trouble, negotiates the complicated system. Baird commented that the project was an "incredibly successful way to communicate with young people" (Feldman et al. 2013, 83). Strategies that build on an understanding of the culture and the means of communicating with the client community are parts of the work of many of the practitioners interviewed.

Strategy 3: Identify Projects

Public interest design projects generally do not come to practitioners through marketing efforts, as is the norm with conventional firms. Most projects originate from relationships that practitioners have with the community and nonprofit organizations. Other projects come from grant programs or are initiated by practitioners themselves in response to their understanding of community needs.

The Detroit Collaborative Design Center (DCDC) at the University of Detroit Mercy School of Architecture receives projects from its successful long-term involvement with the community. Dan Pitera, the center's director and faculty at the School of Architecture, explains that being involved in the community is a successful means of identifying projects:

> Our philosophy is we have to be invited to do the projects, so 99 percent of our projects come to us. But we need to be known before we can be invited to participate, so we sit on boards, we give talks, we are constantly in the community. Because of our presence, people come to us and ask us to work on this or that project. We call it social marketing. We don't have brochures; we don't advertise. By getting ourselves out there and talking about these issues, people come to know who we are. (Feldman et al. 2013, 55)

The community views university-affiliated nonprofit design firms, such as the DCDC, as having a public-service mission. Therefore, other nonprofit partners feel comfortable working with them, knowing the work is in the interest of the public. One common strategy for university-based design centers is to forge community partnerships during the grant-making process. Even if they are not compensated directly, DCDC, for example, places a financial value on their services and uses a part of that value as an in-kind match. Pitera states:

> We're funded … about 50 percent through philanthropy and about 50 percent through project fees. In essence, our project fees are about 50 percent of what a typical professional would charge. You could say that as a traditional practice we may not be sustainable, but we figured out how to be sustainable in a nonprofit environment. (Feldman et al. 2013, 89)

The nonprofit, university-affiliated business model functions as a framework for long-term community engagements. Outreach activities and the service-oriented business model work together to build trust, which not only leads to new projects but also shapes the relationships between the architect and their community partners during the project. An example is the relationship between the DCDC and the Harry Thompson Center in New Orleans, a nonprofit organization affiliated with the Jesuit Order that provides daytime support services to the homeless. After Hurricane Katrina the number of homeless people in New Orleans grew to more than ten thousand, and the Catholic Church, in partnership with the Harry Thompson Center, decided to place a day facility in the parking lot behind the church building.

Because the DCDC is part of the University of Detroit Mercy, a Jesuit institution, they were asked to provide architectural services for the project. Don Thompson, the executive director of the Harry Thompson Center, describes the partnership with Pitera and the other people at DCDC: "Our religious connections brought us together, but it's not what kept us together. What kept up together was their skill set" (Feldman et al. 2013, 89). He described the design process as "very relational." He praised the DCDC designers for being great listeners, asking a lot of questions, striving to find out what the client wants, and showing a real enthusiasm for the work. Thompson said of DCDC: "It was a real pleasure to be a part of it and to spend time with people that love what they do" (Feldman et al. 2013, 89).

Strategy 4: Expand Disciplinary and Professional Boundaries

Most practitioners find they need to expand beyond the conventions of their professions and the services they typically provide to meet the requirements of a project that goes outside the scope of the building's program. This requires cultivating new skills and strategies and working in collaboration with community partners and experts in other fields.

Peter Landon and his partners, of Landon Bone Baker, have sustained the firm he founded by focusing a considerable percentage of their work on affordable housing and community-based projects. From the onset, Landon intended to do community design in the context of a for-profit firm. He explains the firm's business model and their flexible approach to fees:

> What we try to do is to approach these jobs as a business, with the business model that we get paid for what we do….We do the best we can. We try to get a reasonable fee, and we try to make sure that the whole process works….It might be that somebody can't really afford a $100,000 project, but they can afford a $50,000 project. The fees that would go along with that. That's kind of the way we think of it. (Feldman et al. 2013, 38)

In some instances, the firm may start a project pro-bono or at a reduced fee to assist in getting a project off the ground and then follow with a fee if the project moves ahead.

In addition to their building projects, Landon Bone Baker was instrumental in creating two community service programs: Archi-treasures, an arts-based community-development organization that creates partnerships between artists and low-income community residents to design and build public spaces; and Shade Lab, an educational program that teaches high school students about environmental sustainability. Landon explains that these programs not only educate community residents and students but also inform them about the community in which they live.

By expanding the boundaries of their practice programmatically and by operating a business model that is responsive to the client, the firm is more able to address the needs of the community. Angela Hurlock, the executive director of one of the community non-profits the firm has served, Claretian Associates, praised partner Jeff Bone for his ability to work with the community and to understand Claretian Associates' mission. She said: "They get it. They get who we are and know what is important to us." Angela summarized Landon Bone Baker's understanding of their vision: "They are almost an extension of who we are" (Feldman et al. 2013, 81).

Strategy 5: Overcome Funding Limitations

Approximately half of the practitioners interviewed offer their services free of charge; the other half receives full, reduced, or delayed payments. In all cases, providing professional services to those that cannot afford to pay requires some sort of supplemental contributions. Even though much of public interest work is accomplished with professionals donating their time, sustained public interest practices depend either on external funding or on compensation from internal business profits.

Perkins + Will's Social Responsibility Initiative is a leading pro-bono program within the for-profit architectural firm and provides professional services to clients who cannot afford them. According to Perkins + Will's corporate website:

> Since 2007, Perkins + Will has more explicitly committed our resources to serve society through an extensive pro-bono program. Through our public interest work, we seek to address basic human needs—food, shelter, health, education, and empowerment. Since our initial experience working hands-on in New Orleans after Hurricane Katrina, our Social Responsibility Initiative has expanded our pledge to Public Architecture to commit 1 percent of our billable resources to support pro-bono initiatives. (Perkins + Will 2012)

> Every year, Perkins + Will contributes the equivalent of a fifteen-person firm working full time to provide pro-bono services to organizations in communities

that would otherwise not have access to such skills. We have empowered all of our offices to engage in their communities on a local level. With a global perspective supported by local engagement, social responsibility is a core value of our firm and integral to everything we do. (Perkins + Will 2012)

To accomplish their goals, Perkins + Will has formal criteria for selecting projects. Staff members of the initiatives in Perkins + Will's various offices regularly meet to vet projects identified by employees of the firm or through the 1% Program. Many members of the firm are on community and nonprofit-organization boards and have relationships with communities in need.

Mark Jolicoeur, principal at Perkins + Will's Chicago office, explains that once a project is selected, they provide indispensable professional services:

We're working with [the communities] each step of the way. It's not uncommon … [when we first] come in that we will do programming. We will take a look at facilities as possibilities: we will vet opportunities with them, complete schematic level design work, and do some marketing material for them. Then they'll go out and do their fund-raising. (Feldman et al. 2013, 31)

These types of projects can take years, according to Jolicoeur:

We [Perkins + Will] have a project we're doing for Erie Neighborhood House, a new immigrant resource center in Little Village of Erie, Pennsylvania. It was originally planned as a complete gut renovation of a building, but when the economy tanked the way it did, that possibility really waned. It went away. Erie needed to re-evaluate. Subsequently, we were going to be taking on a long-term lease at a facility on Twenty-Sixth Street. We are now doing a complete interior build-out for the project. However, on each of these projects, we are not only doing the design work but also all the permitting work with the city (Feldman et al. 2013, 31).

In the Erie project, Jolicoeur explains the assets of the professionals that can be called upon: "The team working on the project extended itself well beyond professional services to assure the success of the project." Jolicoeur encouraged team members to challenge the building industry and to step up as well:

So the staff starts calling our suppliers. The next thing you know, we're getting all the vinyl base provided. We've got all of our high-quality, sustainable, renewable, rubber flooring provided gratis. There was that big green show, a sustainability show in Chicago last fall. I can't remember the manufacturer or which furniture line—[they] had their display there—so one of our team members asked them: "The furniture—what are you going to do with it?" They said, "We don't really know what we're going to do with it." We inquired,

"Would you give it to Erie House?" They replied, "Yes." The next thing you know, we've got furniture for our [Erie House] entry lobby.

It's interesting how it can start to blossom. We're providing typical professional services, and then we're able to provide this value added by going to these different organizations and looking for materials. (Feldman et al. 2013, 31)

Strategy 6: Advocate for Equity

Public interest practitioners are advocates for the underserved and address public needs with the partnerships they choose, the collaborations they build, the resources they bring to a project, the projects they accomplish, and programs they set up specifically to advocate for equity in design resources and decision making. Almost half of the practitioners stated that they engage in advocacy practices to educate and promote democratic values through publications, events, and even theater pieces that assert the rights of the community to meet, gather, and express their opinions.

An example is the work of Teddy Cruz at the U.S.–Mexico borderlands on issues of migration, housing, and the environment, which involves the San Diego and Tijuana communities, local nonprofits and city officials, as well as international foundations. His work and that of his newly established Center for Urban Ecologies, formed in partnership with local organizations, most importantly Casa Familiar, has installed a set of local funding sources that support families and communities in the San Diego region. Cruz's collaboration with Casa Familiar includes other stakeholders and leaders, among them Oscar Romo, a local environmental-issues leader, who focuses on the impact of a local estuary on poor nearby communities. Their combined efforts have led to a series of proposals that explore new housing strategies and political and social scenarios for making them possible. These have helped Casa Familiar rethink its mission from service to advocacy through its new role as a developer.

With the last series of elections, new political leaders in both San Diego and Tijuana have asked Cruz to help them set up offices within both municipal governments that would address the larger-scale issues faced by what is now essentially a transnational metropolis with two distinct political governances but a shared set of conditions. Cruz describes:

Our projects primarily engage the micro scale of the neighborhood, transforming it into an urban laboratory of the twenty-first century. The forces of control at play at the most trafficked checkpoint in the world has provoked the small border neighborhoods that surround it to construct alternative urbanisms of transgression that infiltrate themselves beyond the property lines in the form of nonconforming spatial and entrepreneurial practices—

a migrant, small-scale activism that alters the rigidity of discriminatory urban planning of the American metropolis and searches for new modes of social sustainability and affordability. The political and economic processes behind this social activism bring new meaning to the role of the informal in the contemporary city. (Feldman et al. 2013, 49)

This rethinking of the civic and political discourses that architects are capable of promoting has caught the attention of international foundations, principally the Ford Foundation. Through his Center for Urban Ecologies, Cruz has promoted a series of exchanges addressing the issues faced in this border region. These conversations are framed as dialogues of a *Political Equator,* based not on latitudes but on the global north–south political division. These dialogues have brought designers and activists from worldwide to this transnational metropolis to contribute their thoughts and ideas and to share their experiences in their own areas of conflict. Ford Foundation has funded these exchanges, which have brought participants in direct contact with the social, political, and environmental conditions that define this region by immersing the participants in intervention sites on both sides of the border.

Strategy 7: Educate the Profession

Educational opportunities for professionals and students to learn about public interest design have, until recently, been limited. To fill this gap, public interest design professionals are working to educate professionals, nonprofits, service organizations, and foundations. Practitioners are acquiring practical skills through participation in initiatives, such as the Public Architecture's 1% Program; through donated hours spent on specific projects or initiative, supported by the employees firms; and through internships and continuing-education programs.

The Rose Fellowship adopted a long-immersion strategy with a paid three-year internship awarded by Enterprise Community Partners, a national affordable-housing supporter. The fellowship provides an opportunity to work in a community development corporation or a public interest design firm for three years. The length of the residency was strategically planned to allow young practitioners enough time to foster necessary skills and to potentially see a project through from start to finish. The Rose Fellowship draws from a highly competitive pool and each fellow, reflecting his or her promise, is charged with a significant amount of responsibility. As Katie Swenson, the director of the program, describes:

> For the Rose Fellows, many of whom apply and certainly the ones who are selected, there is not just a generalized desire to take an abstract architectural concept and apply it to an abstract community concept. That's not going to make it over the line in terms of being a Rose Fellow. That's a nice idea,

but there has to be a sincere connection to a place and the issues about place, plus a skill set to deploy creative solutions to make that match. (Feldman et al. 2013, 65)

Conclusions

The Latrobe research team is inspired by the innovation and commitment of the practitioners who we interviewed. The support shown by the AIA in awarding the Latrobe Prize to research public interest practices is encouraging. The creativity and diversity of methods to address community needs and to overcome the limitations of conventional practice are sources of optimism for the future of design professions. The momentum of these works allows us to make the hopeful claim that public interest practices play a key role in the transformation of the architectural profession. These practices should not be seen as marginal but as a model, growing from within the profession. They have the capacity to help change the field, making it more diverse, socially engaged, and responsible—to fundamentally transform the practice of architecture. We hope for a shift that compels collaboration with the community to build public values, such as democracy, environmental stewardship, equity, service, opportunity, and other aspirations, that help society and apply the skills of design to their best use.

References

Angela Hurlock, interview by Roberta Feldman and Sergio Palleroni, assisted by Deidre Colgan, 2011–12.

Brent Brown, interview by Roberta Feldman and Sergio Palleroni, assisted by Deidre Colgan, 2011–12.

Christine Gaspar, interview by Roberta Feldman and Sergio Palleroni, assisted by Deidre Colgan, 2011–12.

Dan Pitera, interview by Roberta Feldman and Sergio Palleroni, assisted by Deidre Colgan, 2011–12.

Don Thompson, interview by Roberta Feldman and Sergio Palleroni, assisted by Deidre Colgan, 2011–12.

Feldman, Roberta, Sergio Palleroni, David Perkes, and Bryan Bell. 2013. "Wisdom from the Field: Public Interest Architecture in Practice." 2011 AIA Latrobe Prize Research. Accessed July 17. www.publicinterestdesign.com/wp-content/uploads/2013/07/Wisdom-from-the-Field.pdf

Gail Vittori, interview by Roberta Feldman and Sergio Palleroni, assisted by Deidre Colgan, 2011–12.

Katie Swenson, interview by Roberta Feldman and Sergio Palleroni, assisted by Deidre Colgan, 2011–12.

Mark Jolicoeur, interview by Roberta Feldman and Sergio Palleroni, assisted by Deidre Colgan, 2011–12.

Perkins + Will corporate website. 2012. "Social Responsibility Initiative Annual Report No. 4." Last modified July 2012. http://perkinswill.com/search?s= purpose%20social%20purpose.

Peter Landon, interview by Roberta Feldman and Sergio Palleroni, assisted by Deidre Colgan, 2011–12.

Teddy Cruz, interview by Roberta Feldman and Sergio Palleroni, assisted by Deidre Colgan, 2011–12.

Notes

1   All quotes originally appeared in "Wisdom from the Field: Public Interest Architecture in Practice," by Roberta Feldman, Sergio Palleroni, David Perkes, and Bryan Bell—a result of the 2011 AIA Latrobe Prize Research. Quotes were transcribed from telephone interviews conducted by Roberta Feldman and Sergio Palleroni, assisted by Deidre Colgan, 2011–12. The full text is available at: www.publicinterestdesign.com/wp-content/uploads/2013/07/Wisdom-from-the-Field.pdf

2   See also the American Institute of Architects, Press Release, July 17, 2013, Washington, DC, http://www.aia.org/press/releases/AIAB099588.

5

Designers Engaging in Business Development

Heather Fleming, David Kaisel

As leaders of Catapult Design, a nonprofit design consultancy working in global development, we got our start in the international development sector with philanthropic engagements. There has always been demand for free consulting from professional designers and engineers. However, it did not take long to see that there was a real need for professional and integrated product development services, particularly with organizations developing market-based solutions to poverty. In fact, the philanthropic model has ultimately had an opposite effect to what we as designers and on-the-ground organizations needed—the lack of skin in the game has led to fickle objectives, and the lack of on-the-ground context has left United States–based engineers and designers without a real understanding of the challenges. We began to understand that working with organizations that did not have the capacity to pay for services are typically not the organizations that have a lasting impact. In order to reach the organizations that have the capacity to implement market-based solutions to poverty, we needed to break out of the philanthropic nights-and-weekends mindset of a volunteer. We needed to be an integral part of their development story.

Catapult Design, though a nonprofit organization, operates on a fee-for-service consulting model. We cofounded Catapult Design in 2008 to work with organizations that are using technology to alleviate poverty and make positive change in their communities. We started with what we knew, product development, and then expanded and tuned our services to the marketplace—to the global development sector, including small, on-the-ground social enterprises as well as large international development institutions. Based on our philanthropic experiences, we knew it was critical that both types of entities be a part of our portfolio. Small social entrepreneurs break new ground and push the boundaries of what is possible, but often with limited capacity to scale their ideas; large international development institutions have vast capacity but often design programs that are counter to producing innovative results. Small organizations may not have the capacity to afford market-rate design services; larger organizations do. Call it a subsidy or call it a sliding-scale rate structure, the reality for our success is the ability to remain flexible in how we cover our costs.

But how do we find the right social enterprise to work with? How do we get in with large international development institutions? We did not start Catapult Design with a large Rolodex. It took persistence, and a willingness to network and learn the art of tactfully badgering people in order to secure meetings. Above all, it took a readiness to sell design to an audience that typically never works with designers. Catapult entered into its sixth year in business in 2014. While we are often regarded as a "success," the more we learn, the more we realize that we have much more to learn. We view our experience and model as not one to replicate but one to build on.

Achieving Financial Sustainability

It took us a few years to really embrace new business development. During our initial years, we were a reactive organization: we primarily waited for new business to come to us in the form of a meeting request with a potential client or responding to a request for proposal (RFP) or request for application (RFA) opportunity. We frequented local industry events and spoke at conferences, and while we did not think of these activities as new business development, it was these kinds of word-of-mouth occurrences that provided reactive opportunities.

Being reactive was not enough to grow Catapult Design in the way it needed to grow to attract larger clients. This was the tough lesson we learned in year three, and we began to fundamentally change our approach and attitude toward new business development. First, we reorganized. We identified one team member as the "champion" of new business development. Making the champion accountable for meeting quarterly new business financial goals was the backbone of what would become a strategic plan for new business development.

Thanks to a board member, we also secured a sales coach who donated her time to train the team on new business development tactics. Our coach taught us about the importance of a sales funnel (Figure 5.1) (a tool with which to track our new business efforts), how to set one up, and how to move potential clients through it. Our first sales funnel was simple, visual, and interactive. We used our weekly new business development meetings to physically move potential projects through the funnel. As our sales coach instructed us, the goal is always to drive potential clients to being either a YES or NO opportunity for us, but never MAYBE—advice we follow to this day.

With goals, financial targets, and a visual way to track our progress in place, we grew increasingly strategic and proactive. Suddenly, we viewed conferences

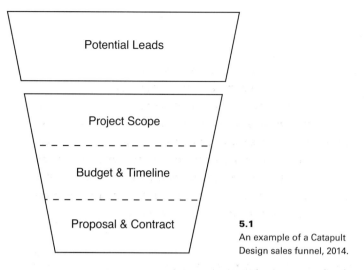

Potential Leads

Project Scope

Budget & Timeline

Proposal & Contract

5.1
An example of a Catapult
Design sales funnel, 2014.

and local industry events as opportunities to find potential clients or people who are connected to potential clients. We actively brainstormed about organizations we wanted to work with and projects we wanted to work on.

We became accustomed to cold emailing and adept at delivering our pitches, and, by repeating these actions, we came to understand what types of marketing materials we needed to sell our services. We were beginning to embrace the mindset of new business development and being a service-driven company. Emails from potential clients never went unanswered for longer than twenty-four hours. Phone calls from potential clients were always prioritized. Meetings were promptly arranged and confirmed. Intentional or not, we began to professionalize our infrastructure.

Client Segmentation

Our sales funnel is divided into three primary columns indicating client size and defining project size: small, medium, and large projects. The funnel enables us to visualize activity within each column and helps us prioritize where we need to allocate our time. For example, we knew that historically, large organizations take longer for us to move through the sales funnel than small ones due to our lack of relationships with the former.

Creating these three divisions was our initial and rudimentary way of classifying potential clients. Over time, as we grew to know the market, we were better able to segment potential clients: academic institutions, social-enterprise clients, local governments, nonprofit clients, multinational corporations, development contractors, bilateral agencies, and large nongovernmental organizations (NGOs). Each has different ways it engages with external contractors, a different appreciation of the value of design in its programs, and different methods for structuring a project. For example, working with United States Agency for International Development (USAID) required learning how to track the status of their RFPs through their federal business- and grant-procurement systems, and the entire lingo that goes along with that. In contrast, engaging with social entrepreneurs typically entails a Skype call directly with two decision makers. We can often codesign a scope of work in one meeting, whereas the scope of work and outcomes are often predefined with government RFPs/RFAs.

Tracking the movement in our sales funnel during a year, it became obvious that our team was comfortable having business-to-business conversations with potential clients but lacked understanding of how to navigate what we called "DC-culture," or the international development institutions. This included bilateral and multilateral agencies as well as larger development contractors who might subcontract work to Catapult. We were still designers playing the role of sales people.

It became critical for us to attract team members that understood this culture, who knew the language, and who had the necessary contacts to build business and relationships. In other words, as we matured we began to add people to the team who had different skills that would enable growth.

Fee Structures

From the beginning we knew that different-sized clients had different capacity to pay for United States–based design-consulting services. But what was the appropriate rate for each type of client? How would we base our estimates? What if we undersold ourselves?

We still regularly debate these questions. For opportunities that come with a predefined budget, the answer is simple. You can either afford to work within the budget or you cannot. It is as straightforward as understanding your costs to do business and your cash flow. But Catapult—more often than not—is asked to put together a budget based on a day rate, a task list, and a deliverable timeline. We are often asked to negotiate, to remove tasks from an already lean budget, and to reduce our day rate. The back and forth can take a significant amount of time with less-than-desirable results, so we began to set boundaries. We implemented project-budget minimums and accepted that there are simply budgets, and therefore a segment of potential clients, that we could not afford to work with.

Besides the price tag for services, there are also different contract mechanisms by which to structure payment. We have used a fixed-price fee structure and time- and-materials fee structure; and we have tried, unsuccessfully, to employ a value- based fee structure. Most clients are familiar and comfortable with fixed-price fee structure. There are pros and cons to each, and a variety of other flexible payment structures that we have not explored. The bottom line is to achieve the desired margin. Ideally, you cover your business costs and achieve a margin that enables growth. Margin targets vary from consultancy to consultancy and industry to industry.

Ebb and Flow of the Consulting Model

Catapult Design was built on the consultant-for-hire model, which can have a highly variable revenue stream. Many consultants do not have the luxury of a regular source of revenue. Fee schedules are often tied to milestones or deliverables, resulting in a large chunk of revenue one month and then nothing until the next milestone is reached. You will need to be constantly aware of that buffer if you are going to thrive.

There are exemplary consulting groups that have flipped this model to earn consistent revenue, but they are the exception. We encourage groups pursuing an earned-revenue consulting model to think about ways they can secure a consistent source of income.

Sourcing Clients, Securing Work

Recruiting Potential Clients

Most often whoever is paying the bill is the client. Clients, however, can resemble customers when seen through the lens of design practice, because the work will need to address the expectations and requirements of various stakeholders—a group that may extend well beyond the immediate employer.

When first engaging with the world of international development, it soon becomes clear that while the project contract may be with one person or organization, the real task is often to help the client to satisfy the goals of the organization actually funding the work. At Catapult, it is not uncommon for our direct clients to be second or third in a line of organizations that pass along funds from the original source, which may be a philanthropic organization, such as the Rockefeller Foundation or the Bill & Melinda Gates Foundation, or a bi- or multi-lateral development agency, such as USAID, the Department for International Development, or the World Bank.

The consequence of this layer-cake scenario is that having a good sense of the ecosystem of funding—who are the sources for development funds, what organizations specialize in administering those funds, and who in turn are the organizations that specialize in doing on-the-ground implementation—will help identify potential clients. At Catapult, we do not have the resources to directly manage the scale of project commonly funded by a bi- or multi-lateral agency, but we are aware of the existing programs and RFPs that these agencies publish. We identify the next tier of organizations that specialize in administering these large programs to seek out opportunities for collaboration.

It is at the next, the third, layer of implementation organizations, where we focus our recruiting efforts. We use a whole quiver of tools and strategies to do this. Among these are:

Active networking. This includes making liberal use of social-networking tools like LinkedIn as well as customer relationship management (CRM) software such as Salesforce. But most significantly, it consists of building personal contacts. This can only result from getting physically in front of potential clients—at conferences, at workshops, at discussions, talks, and industry social events. The more familiar you become, the more likely you will come to mind when someone decides they need help with a project.

Referrals. By far the most compelling incentive for someone to contact you regarding a project is the recommendation of a previous client. Do not be afraid to ask satisfied clients to write an endorsement, which you can share with potential customers. Developing a steady stream of work is about building long-term relationships with your customers—think beyond the immediate project to understand how you can support your client's broader organizational objectives in the long run.

Actively scan industry blogs and interest groups for RFPs. There are a myriad of blogs, list servers, websites, and mailing lists for every possible public interest topic. Websites for the Global Alliance for Clean Cookstoves, AgTechXChange (USAID Feed the Future Program), and USAID WashPlus, for example, list past, current, and upcoming RFPs in their respective industry sectors. Most funding agencies and larger development contractors have to follow established procurement rules, including publishing and evaluating proposals through a formal system. Thus, tracking these procurement portals is important. However, often by the time the opportunity has been released for bidding, the competition and potential collaboration opportunities are limited so it is helpful to get in front of these opportunities before they are released.

Understand trending topics in philanthropy and development. Funding for development sectors follows clear trends and shifting priorities. At one point, significant investment was going toward improving cookstove designs and reducing indoor air pollution. Funder interest shifted toward clean drinking water, then tacked toward improved sanitation and toilets. Currently, there is growing investment in a second green revolution in agriculture of emerging markets. Knowing which topics are generating the most interest from funding agencies, and why, is a key criterion for identifying potential clients.

Getting the Work Funded

Getting in front of a potential client is the first win. Unless you were referred, then it is the second win. In the first meeting, your success hinges on a variety of factors, such as:

Learning the needs of your customer. Often times we have clients who are not able to articulate their needs in a way that leads to a clearly defined scope of work. The first meeting is an opportunity to uncover the biggest challenges by determining what they want to achieve and what is preventing them from achieving it. Understanding where your skills fit will help turn a big-picture conversation into a concrete scope of work.

Understanding your value and communicating it well. Design-speak is sophisticated and is foreign to most organizations serving the public sector. We have found that sharing stories of design impact through case studies that include video or photographs of our methods produce best understanding of what we offer. Never assume your potential clients know what a prototype is, much less what design is. If a potential client is meeting with you, it means they have already been sold on the idea that design has something to offer them. It is your job to make it concrete for them without shortchanging yourself.

Educating your audience on the value of design. Not everyone sitting at the table will embrace what you have to say. Design is often perceived as a luxury, too focused on aesthetics, or too expensive. We often get asked about return of investment for design, about the measureable impact of the work, if we can skip several rounds of prototyping, and so on. This makes sense, particularly in the global development sector, which is dominated by data-driven professionals working with finite resources. Have your answers ready. Navigating these issues requires finesse, confidence, and concrete case studies that illustrate the pitfalls of skipping steps.

Building a strong brand. Most potential clients who meet with you will have done their research. They will have Googled your firm or asked their colleagues about their experiences with you—this is your brand. A tidy website that provides information about your services and previous experience is essential.

Also consider how they might come to know you. For example, some of our early connections came through social media activity. We started Catapult with a clear point of view on every public-facing media tool we used. Engaging the community through avenues like Facebook and Twitter, hosting public workshops, and curating local design events all contributed to building the brand.

The Qualities of a Good Client

Thinking through Vetting...

We are often asked who our ideal client is. Describing the ideal client is an exercise worth going through. Create a wish list. We have had less-than-positive experiences that have allowed us to identify the characteristics of the types of clients we are cautious about. When you are just getting started, it is difficult to be strategic or selective about who you work with. Your goal is to build your portfolio and pay rent. But here are a few vetting questions to consider when you are approached with a project opportunity:

1)   Do they value your services enough to pay you what you are worth?
2)   Have they demonstrated the capacity to implement their idea?
3)   Is the issue they are addressing a real one? Having a solution-in-search-of-a-problem project in your portfolio does not make the case for design.
4)   Is the relationship beneficial to you? Focus on clients that will validate you and your brand, not the other way around.
5)   Will project failure leave the end user or customer in a worse situation than before you engaged?

As you build your portfolio, you will develop your own vetting mechanisms, like budgetary minimums and alignment with strategic goals. Keep this information in a public place for your internal team to access.

...And Impact

Your impact is defined by your ability to: 1) define what effect you want to have, 2) develop a mechanism for measuring it, and 3) stay focused on achieving your goal. Catapult has various methods for measuring impact, but none is tied to the end user. This is primarily due to the fact that we are not implementers of solutions but the consultants that help enable the realization of the solutions. We look at impact through a lens of the value we add to our clients. Unfortunately, most funding agencies and potential clients would rather see quantitative data than qualitative data or anecdotes, such as client testimonials. Understanding how both forms of data support impact goals and measurement is most important to a well-balanced approach.

Closing Words

It is important to disclose that no one at Catapult has a degree in business administration or claims to be a business guru. Our advice in this section about margins, fee structures, impact, and sales funnels was gathered through trial, error, and emulating people whom we respect and admire. We have never been afraid to borrow models and strategies from other industries, to read books and blogs on business development, and, most importantly, to ask for help. While we adopted the traditional consultant model, there are a variety of new ways to fund public interest work via crowdfunding and strategic partnerships, and we encourage you to explore a range of avenues. Any success Catapult has achieved during the first six years of business is due to a supportive board of directors, a team that is willing to learn and fail, and a community of people who want to see Catapult achieve its mission.

Good luck!

6

Evaluating Impact without Evidence

Michael A. Cohen

This chapter addresses the question of whether aid works and if so, how. It suggests that in reality there is little or no serious assessment of the impact of development assistance. And most significantly, there is no assessment of the medium- to long-term impact of aid. The key point in this argument is that development agencies monitor and evaluate the "outputs" of aid—e.g., whether money was spent, whether the school was built, or whether the water supply network was constructed—but not the outcome—e.g., whether the students attending the school were well-educated or whether the water improved the health status of people using the network. Outputs can be defined as the physical and financial results generated by a project, while an outcome is the consequence of that output. The difference between output and outcome is fundamental.

An important dimension of this difference is the issue of design itself; that is, how aid projects are designed so as to have significant development impacts. Indeed, for the purposes of public accountability and assuring the efficiency of resource allocation and use, implementation and impact should be the key objectives of design rather than beautiful design and feasibility drawings. In this sense the process of implementation itself should be designed ahead of time, based on local institutional capacity, in such a way as to assure positive and sustainable development impacts.

One of the major social experiments of the post–World War II period was the extensive provision of development assistance to developing countries. One of the key tenets of this time began with the establishment of the International Bank for Reconstruction and Development, aka the World Bank, in 1945, whose name reflects the dual objectives and mission of the organization. This mission was further articulated through the Marshall Plan of 1947, with which the United States helped European countries rebuild after World War II. The subsequent transition from colonial status to independent states for nearly fifty countries in Africa and Asia starting in the mid-1950s led to many bilateral and multilateral programs to provide assistance of many kinds: from the construction of infrastructure, such as roads, electric power plants and transmission lines, and water supply systems, to social services, such as schools, clinics, hospitals, and a wide variety of public facilities. The conclusion of the Pearson Commission in 1968 that the United Nations' Development Decade encouraged economic growth but not equitable development led to a reorientation of the policies of the World Bank under President Robert McNamara and a substantial increase in the level of official development assistance (ODA) provided by both multilateral and bilateral institutions (Pearson Commission 1969).

The expansion of ODA, however, needs to be understood in terms of the actual amounts of aid provided and what share of the gross domestic product (GDP) it represented in donor countries. Until the substantial increases of ODA provided by the Bush Administration in 2003, when U.S. aid alone reached 0.14 percent, the target established by the Organisation for Economic Co-operation and Development (OECD) for donor countries had been 0.7 percent of the GDP. Norway exceeded targets at .92 percent, and only Denmark and the Netherlands followed closely behind, reaching .84 and .81 percent, respectively, in 2003 (OECD 2004). In contrast, surveys by the University of Maryland revealed that most U.S. citizens believed that "foreign aid" accounted for about 25 percent of the U.S. budget, while in fact it is about 1 percent of the federal budget (PBS 2010). This gross exaggeration demonstrates the failure of the media to educate the American public.

Another incorrect "factoid" about ODA is that it does not work; that its objectives to create infrastructure and facilities for basic needs and social services are not achieved. The media continue to portray an image of aid as wasteful, badly delivered help, paid for with taxpayers' money. This factoid, when combined with the claims by opponents of development assistance to developing countries, suggests that aid has no significant positive development impact. Indeed, it suggests a negative impact.

There are two scales of this alleged negative impact that are frequently highlighted. The first is the nation itself, i.e., whether the population of developing countries has improved their conditions in areas such as health, education, or water supply as a result of the aid. The second is who among these people have benefitted. Here the argument is that the poor have been left aside and goes back to the assessment of the Pearson Commission, which argued that there was growth but not development and that the essential distributive dimension of economic and social change had been neglected. Both of these scales require re-examination.

The Urban Aid Portfolio—Frequently Contradictory and Confused

Scale

Given the scale of the development assistance effort in more than 150 countries, it is useful to circumscribe the portfolio, which this chapter discusses. Between 1972 and 2000 urban assistance projects were undertaken in more than 11,000 cities and towns in the developing world. This includes projects in housing, water supply, sanitation, urban transport, social services—such as education and health—environmental management, and municipal strengthening (Cohen 2001, 37–60). About 7,000 of these efforts were supported in part by World Bank financing, the remaining 4,000 by other multilateral and bilateral agencies such as the United Nations (UN) organizations, UN Habitat, United Nations Development Programme (UNDP), World Health Organization (WHO), United Nations International Children's Emergency Fund (UNICEF), or the International Labour Organization (ILO), the United States Agency for International Development (USAID), the regional development banks, and many bilateral agencies from France, the United Kingdom, Germany, Sweden, Denmark, Canada, and the Netherlands. In addition, there are many nongovernmental organizations, such as Habitat for Humanity, Save the Children, Oxfam, and others, that also worked in this field.

Features

This portfolio of urban assistance has several interesting features. First, it embodies a wide diversity of objectives and intentions. Some donors wanted to support cities in developing countries to help address the growing issue of urban poverty, while others defined their objectives more narrowly, such as providing clean water supply for children, increasing local municipal capacity to manage urban infrastructure, or increasing local revenue to sustain urban services. Policy objectives as well as operational strategies differed significantly. Moreover, some donors allocated funds and turned them over to local institutions and then left the scene, while others sent their own staff to work on the ground in collaboration with local agencies. This varying approach to aid is reflected in the frequently contradictory and confused policy objectives and design of aid in a specific city.

An example of these contradictions is Manila, the largest city in the Philippines, where the World Bank alone had twenty projects under implementation in 1980. These included low-cost housing, water supply, sanitation, transport, municipal strengthening, and many social services, such as schools and clinics. The World Bank worked with many different municipalities in the Manila Metropolitan Region, with various national government ministries, and a large number of sector agencies, such as the Water and Sewerage Management Board. Within the World Bank there was insufficient coordination among its own project officers and this lack of coordination was clear in Manila itself. Different jurisdictions had different mandates and responsibilities as well as political interests. When the activities of many other donors are added into this mix, it is not surprising that the management of aid itself took much of the energy of local professionals. Aid had become a development fact, and not always a good one.

Twenty years later this example had been replicated many times over around the developing world. Cities including Bangkok, Delhi, Jakarta, Nairobi, Lagos, Abidjan, Mexico City, and São Paulo had become vast spaces of urban experimentation, with new approaches to urban problems, some local but many initiated by international actors. Aid diverted local institutions from their local responsibilities, transforming them into local aid bureaucracies and leaving them with little energy and political motivation for implementation, much less the evaluation of development impact. The international agencies themselves were required to report on the disbursement of funds and on the achievement of key performance indicators within a reasonable time. The more important achievement of development impact was far off in the distance and in time, because, in reality, development impact was only visible after many years of operation.

The Results of Urban Aid

Many of these efforts were successful in that they contributed to improvements in urban living conditions. Physical improvements, often with low-cost designs, were relatively easy to build and to launch. Large slum improvement programs in Calcutta, Chennai, and Jakarta demonstrated that providing water, sanitation, footpaths, and some modest housing improvements was feasible and affordable, even by asking poor local residents to contribute toward the cost of these programs. Housing programs in African cities, such as Nairobi or Abidjan, also made a difference, but they faced institutional difficulties with the lack of trained staff to carry out projects. Latin American countries, such as Argentina, Brazil, or Mexico, were relatively stronger in technical and institutional capacity of municipalities, but they frequently faced changing political landscapes that disrupted project implementation.

Nonetheless, despite regional, country, and city variations, the general evidence is that the outputs of urban aid were generally positive results of an often unnecessarily arduous process of development assistance. What has proven much more difficult to determine, however, is whether longer-term outcomes have been positive or not. Here the real, as opposed to the rhetorical, agendas of the development agencies become evident. Extensive efforts had been made to assure that money had been properly spent, that cement had been poured, bricks assembled, and desks delivered. But the opportunity costs of those efforts have been that few resources remained to study the longer-term impacts of that aid, i.e., the assessment of the outcomes of the efforts on people's lives.

6.1

The vertical axis represents staff weeks, while the horizontal axis represents the steps in the project cycle, from project identification, preparation, and approval to implementation and evaluation. The typical allocation of resources from the World Bank took the shape of a bell curve, with the highest point at the moment of loan approval. The lower sides of the bell curve reflected lower levels of staff input in the framing or identification of the project and its implementation.

Diagram 1: Banker's Curve

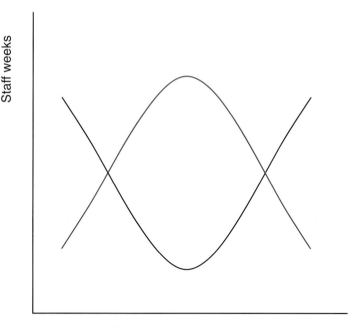

Staff weeks

Steps in project cycle

The scale of this experience and the evidence from many countries and cities suggests that this confusion between outputs and outcomes was not random. Rather it is a consequence of the faulty planning of the assistance process from the outset. While each aid agency and donor has its own project cycle, there are some common features that suggest that the real agenda of these agencies was to demonstrate outputs while not really addressing the more important issue of outcomes.

This difference is captured in the diagrams showing the difference between what might be called a "banker's curve" and a "development curve." Diagram 1, the curve was essentially a banker's curve, much like the allocation of staff required to process a mortgage in a commercial bank in the United States. The startling features of this curve are that relatively little attention is devoted to getting the initial framing correct—i.e., deciding which problem is being addressed, what are alternative solutions, and what kinds of consultative and due diligence processes, such as assessment of environmental or social impacts—might be required before project preparation proceeds. And critically, few resources are devoted to solving the myriad problems that arise during implementation. An allocation of resources intended to assure positive development outcomes would have the shape of a U-curve as shown in Figure 6.2.

The difference between these two curves reflects the schizophrenic character of the design of international development assistance. Is the objective of urban aid to produce outcomes that reduce urban poverty, or is the objective to demonstrate

Diagram 2: Development Curve

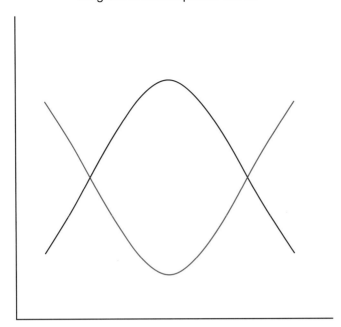

Staff weeks

Steps in project cycle

6.2
An allocation of resources intended to assure positive development outcomes would have the shape of a U-curve as shown in diagram 2. This curve might be called a development curve, because it devotes most of its resources to the framing of the problem, appropriate consultations, and to implementation. It allows for more attention to local knowledge and feedback loops.

that aid institutions have provided resources to produce outputs, which in turn demonstrates that they have met their mandates?

Outputs versus Outcomes: The Senegal Project Experience

The confusion in objectives is well reflected in the experience of the Senegal Sites and Services Project, the first loan for an urban development project financed by the World Bank, which was approved in June 1972 (Cohen 2008). The interest-free loan for fifty years was for US$8 million for the construction of a sites and services (*parcelles assainies*, in French) project in Dakar, Senegal's capital city of 500,000 people. The project involved providing 14,000 plots of land (150 square meters each) with minimal infrastructure services (water supply, sanitation, unpaved dirt roads, and social services). The project for low-income households was to be implemented by the government's Office de Habitations à Loyers Modéré (OHLM) on 400 hectares in a vacant site in Pikine to the north of Dakar. The project was the responsibility of a central housing agency and was not institutionally connected to either the Ministry of Interior or any municipality under its supervision (*tutelle*).

This project was the first of hundreds of urban projects financed by the World Bank since 1972 and represented a milestone for the international community because it signaled the World Bank's entrance into this complex and relatively unknown sector and the introduction of a new approach to the provision of shelter and infrastructure services for the urban poor. At the board discussion of the Senegal Sites and Services Project, the then president McNamara and the staff readily admitted that the Bank's first effort in this sector should be called "learning by doing." While the amount of financial assistance was small, the intellectual and policy stakes of this project were high. The biggest question posed at the time was whether low-income households, when guaranteed land tenure, would actually invest and build their own homes while paying modest amounts over fifteen years at 7 percent interest for the land and infrastructure services. The challenge was to reduce the costs of the project (by lowering standards) and thereby increase its affordability for low-income households. Density was the variable that could make that possible. Reducing costs meant increasing the number of plots per hectare, and in so doing, increasing the density and the numbers of households per hectare. Residential densities increased, and public spaces and additional spaces for social facilities sacrificed.

The basic hypothesis of project design was that poor people would invest in their housing if they had tenure. This hypothesis was based on studies and experience in cities around the developing world, best typified at the time by the field experiences of British architect-planner John F. C. Turner, whose influential work in Peru in the 1960s had established the empirical basis for the sites and services policy and project approach (Turner and Fichter 1972).

After 1972 the major debate in Washington D.C. and Dakar was focused on the slow pace of project implementation. The original implementation schedule had assumed that 14,000 plots could be constructed and services provided in six years, with households beginning to build their self-help housing as soon as they received ownership of the plot. The loan was to come into force when the government fulfilled several basic conditions, such as amending the building code and obtaining Supreme Court validation of the loan agreements and legal modifications to OHLM. This process was to have been completed by March 1973; it was not completed until 1975.

While the World Bank staff had badly underestimated the time for such institutional changes, the delays also reflected more profound second thoughts on the part of the Senegalese government. By the late 1960s, government housing programs were largely subsidizing civil servants in metropolitan Dakar while at the same time systematically bulldozing squatter settlements (*bidonvilles*). Public agencies justified this strategy with the contention that squatters were illegally occupying public and private lands. Sites and services projects legitimating access to land and urban infrastructure for poor households represented an abrupt departure from existing urban policy. Senegalese government officials were at best ambivalent about a project destined for the poor, preferring instead to continue a policy of bulldozing slums (Vernière 1977, 278).

Despite its misgivings, the government was legally bound by agreements it had signed with the World Bank, and the implementation of the project continued and the government temporarily stopped its policy of forced evictions (*déguerpissement*). By 1976 the first phase (*tranche*) of 3,500 households had been allocated plots (*parcelles*), and the roads, water supply, and sewerage system were slowly being built. There was growing concern in Washington that the project would never be completed and that the "first urban project" would be an embarrassing failure.

By 1978, three of the four *tranches* of *parcelles* (10,500 total plots) had been allocated and most of the project's infrastructure had been built. Delays, inflation, and physical contingencies had absorbed the remaining funds, resulting in a decision in 1976 to drop the fourth *tranche*. But the biggest problem was that selected households were not constructing their houses nor occupying the plots. By May 1978 only seven households had moved to the site out of 10,500 plots allocated. A vast area with completed infrastructure was vacant, with households wary of the lack of security, others unhappy about the lack of public transport to their employment, and others unable to afford to pay their rents downtown while investing in construction in the new neighborhood. In addition, other households were likely holding on to the land for speculative purposes. These initial results demonstrated that the project designers in Washington had a different, unrealistic view of what constituted success.

To accelerate occupancy the World Bank and OHLM agreed on a series of measures, including construction loans, more flexible building codes, and simplification of settlement procedures. The latter was very costly, with selected households required to make eleven visits to seven institutions in order to obtain certifications costing less than US$20. Unmarried recipients had to make sixteen visits to nine different institutions. The World Bank and OHLM adopted the target of 1,500 households occupying plots by December 31, 1978, but by November 1979, only 300 households had moved to the site. It is interesting to note that despite this slow progress, some 25,000 Senegalese households had applied for plots in the sites and services project.

Eventually households began to move to Parcelles Assainies. In 1982 the World Bank and the Senegalese government agreed that the project had been completed, as the momentum of occupancy and construction had increased considerably. Each wrote a report on the experience, with the World Bank staff noting that, despite the delays, the concept of the project had been validated by the fact that for every US$1 of public funds, some US$8.2 of private funds had been invested in housing in the neighborhood (Tager 1982). The World Bank staff calculated the economic rate of return for the project to be 19 percent, easily falling within an acceptable range for projects in Senegal—and Africa in general. The World Bank staff had commented that one of the most important contributions of the project had been the training of more than one hundred professional staff at OHLM as provision for the low-cost urban infrastructure and housing.

While the time for implementation had been seriously underestimated, the most significant impression of the project in Washington was its bad reputation for delays, disagreement, and stigma of failure. These perceptions were neither accurate nor informed by the contextual factors that had affected implementation on the ground. In 1980, I observed that the World Bank had tried "to make the context conform to the project rather than the project conform to the context," with the resulting delays for mediating the differences between the World Bank and the government (Cohen 1980, 35).

One conclusion of a World Bank urban staff member who had visited Dakar in the period from 1972 to 1982 was that the Dakar project had been too big. This was not an unreasonable insight: with 10,500 plots with ten persons per plot, Parcelles Assainies was the second largest city of Senegal and a project unrealistically expected to be built in six years! The experience of the project also led to the perception that sites and services projects were too complicated to implement efficiently, particularly in terms of the difficulty of achieving cost recovery (Cohen 1983, 55). The experience of one project seemed to have a worldwide impact, as subsequent projects in southern Africa, East Asia, and Latin America were designed with fewer components and different approaches to cost recovery.

Looking for Outcomes: Thirty-four Years Later

In 2006 a group of students from the New School University in New York City spent two months in Dakar, to study the outcome of the project. Their evaluation of longer-term impact generated many surprising findings, some that contrast sharply with earlier assessments, including the following:

- By 2006 the population of Parcelles Assainies was home to somewhere between 350,000 and 500,000 people, or from three to five times the originally projected population and density per hectare.
- The neighborhood had been built since the mid-1980s, with most plots housing two- or three-story brick-and-concrete buildings. These buildings housed extended, polygamous households of from twenty to thirty people, many younger than twenty-five years old.
- Parcelles Assainies was a neighborhood of many female-headed households. With few job opportunities in Dakar, many Senegalese men left to find work in Europe, North America, and other African countries, regularly sending remittances to their families living in Parcelles Assainies. Remittances covered daily consumption as well as investment in housing.
- The neighborhood had begun to change in the mid-1980s, when low-income households began to sell their land and houses to middle- and upper-income families. The absence of opportunities for investment in housing or even for speculation in the 1980s led to rapidly rising prices for plots in Parcelles Assainies. By the 1990s there were very few of the original households from the project's intended low-income population.

This process had its roots in the original design of the project. By providing land, secure tenure, and infrastructure, project designers believed that the necessary conditions existed to stimulate investment in housing. In fact, these features were necessary but not sufficient. In the absence of loans for construction, poor households were unable to start, much less sustain, the construction process. The costs necessary to move to a vacant site, with new construction and transportation costs, as well as more expensive food, meant that poor households could simply not afford to move to the site. Even when a loan program was finally established, the terms for the loans were not sufficiently favorable to the poor. Delays in the completion of infrastructure further increased the carrying costs for poor households. That construction loans were essential components of this housing solution for the poor was a lesson not lost on the World Bank and other governments.

This result of gentrification is more complicated. Parcelles Assainies was in a good location and a good place to live, but a visitor to Parcelles Assainies in 2006 would have been hard pressed to describe the neighborhood as rich, with a few exceptions of relatively luxurious houses near the beach or in a few of the blocks. Its sandy streets, lack of shade, and unfinished buildings hardly suggested privilege. In fact, the often half-finished appearance of buildings masked the sharp contrasts in the lives of the people living in these buildings. These households were actually house poor, with their homes not providing accurate pictures of their socioeconomic status.

Regardless of the changing profile of the population, the project proved the desirability of opportunities for housing investment. Indeed, despite the dire economic straits of Senegal since 1972, households have continued to invest, albeit slowly, room by room, floor by floor, and have created a medium-sized city—Parcelles Assainies—of about 500,000 people. If the economic rate of return of the project was 19 percent in 1982, it was certainly much greater in 2006. Indeed, in an economy with so little investment capital, so little employment, and a great premium placed on location near downtown Dakar, it was surprising why more housing had not been built closer to the center of the city.

A central market and peripheral markets complement the many smaller stores and a wide range of goods and services available in the neighborhood. The high density of residential buildings left little room for production of anything except clothing.

One immediate negative consequence of the increased density of the area was the lack of sufficient numbers of schools and clinics. Given the crowded condition of primary schools, many Islamic schools, which are not public, had been established. Also there was only one clinic and no hospitals for the population.

If the density of economic activity was a healthy indicator of neighborhood life, the quality of infrastructure was more problematic. The originally designed water supply system had provided for one water faucet for one hundred families in order to keep costs affordable. However, neither the quantity of service nor the lack of individual household connections was deemed sufficient by the residents. By the mid-1980s they began to lobby the public water company, and starting in the late 1980s private water connections were extended house by house throughout the neighborhood.

A positive aspect of the consolidation of the neighborhood has been the proliferation of religious organizations and community organizations. One observer noted that while public space was limited and many social services relatively neglected in project design, at least one mosque was built in each of the twenty-six *unites* (Marusek 2006). The vitality and importance of Islam in this neighborhood reflects its central social and economic roles in Senegalese society. Administrative and real estate pressures had reduced public space in Parcelles Assainies, but religious and social pressures had nevertheless carved out spaces—and frequently large spaces—for this important religious facility.

Conclusions

Outputs and Outcomes: Assessing Development Impact

Looking back at the Parcelles Assainies project, the following key conclusions are clear:

- The sites and services project responded to a large unsatisfied demand for housing.
- Despite implementation delays, it has provided one of the largest public-sector housing solutions in Dakar.
- The sale of plots by low-income households to middle- and upper-income buyers reflects the need for income by the poor, the lack of well-located housing-market alternatives for wealthier Dakar households, and the behavior of households who simply sold their plots by choice.
- The increases in density from 350 people per hectare to between 1,000 and 1,700 people per hectare reflects the lack of alternative serviced sites in metropolitan Dakar (World Bank 2004, 16).
- The popularity of Parcelles Assainies reflected its location and relatively easy access to employment in central Dakar.
- Increased density of the area also signals a shift from owner-occupied housing toward a growing market for rental housing.
- Increased density could be seen as an indicator of project success—the existence of the neighborhood has accounted for about 15 percent of the Dakar population, assuming a metropolitan population of approaching 3 million people.

These observations hint at larger conceptual and policy problems of contextualizing the project within metropolitan Dakar. In fact, there are additional issues that have greater significance for the urban economy and the Dakar metropolitan area, including:

- The World Bank and the government explained the slow pace of implementation as a result of the project's complexity and its scale, concluding that the project was *too big and too ambitious*. This view, however, contradicts the fact that the increased density of Parcelles Assainies over time suggests that the project was probably *too small* when placed in the context of growing effective demand.

- Delay and controversy frightened off both the World Bank and the government from sites and services projects, thereby eliminating the possibility that sites and services projects could be considered as options for the national housing policy in Senegal. This occurred despite the fact that sites and services proved to be the only likely successful large-scale housing solution seen in Dakar during the past forty years.

- In place of sites and services, the government reverted to its old policy of subsidized apartments for middle and upper classes, to the extent that public finance was available to cover the costs of subsidy. This was complemented by support for scattered private-investment projects that attracted remittances from abroad. The policy of bulldozing of slums and relocation was continued until 1985, when large public demonstrations against the policy forced the government to stop (World Bank 2004, 6).

- The result of this combination of policies was the continued rapid and extensive growth of squatter areas lacking infrastructure services. By 2006 more than 60 percent of the metropolitan population lived in *bidonvilles*. A 2004 study of ten squatter settlements in Dakar showed that 82 percent of the population lived below the poverty line (World Bank 2004).

To conclude, the Dakar experience showed that evaluation requires evidence of medium- and long-term outcomes, not just assessment of short-term outputs. This is a matter of planning of policies and projects as much as post-hoc evaluation.

References

Cohen, Michael A. 1980. *The Senegal Sites and Services Project*. Washington DC: World Bank.

———. 1983. *Learning by Doing: World Bank Lending for Urban Development, 1972–1982*. Washington DC: World Bank.

———. 2001. "Urban Assistance and the Material World: Learning by Doing in the World Bank." *Environment and Urbanization* 13 (1) (April): 37–60.

———. 2008 "Aid and Density." *Built Environment*. 145–56.

Marusek, Sarah. 2006. "Focus on Islam." Unpublished paper. Global Urban Studio West Africa Field Report. September.

OECD (Organisation for Economic Co-operation and Development). 2004. "Modest Increase in Development AID in 2003." Organisation for Economic Co-operation and Development website. http://www.oecd.org/general/modestincreasein developmentaidin2003.htm.

PBS (Public Broadcasting System). 2010. *PBS NewsHour.* December 6.

Pearson Commission. 1969. "Partners in Development: Report of the Commission on International Development." London: Pall Mall Press.

Tager, Carolyn. 1982. *The Senegal Sites and Services Project, Project Completion Report.* Washington DC: World Bank.

Turner, John F. C. and Robert Fichter, eds. 1972. *Freedom to Build: Dweller Control of the Housing Process.* New York: The Macmillan Company.

Vernière, Marc. 1977. *Dakar et son double Dagoudane Pikine. Volontarisme d'état et spontanéisme populaire dans l'urbanisation du tiers-monde. Formation et évolution des banlieues dakaroises. Le cas de Dagoudane Pikine* [Dakar and its double Dagoudane Pikine. State voluntarism and popular spontaneity in the urbanization of the third world. Establishment and evolution of suburban Dakar]. Paris: Bibliothèque nationale. (Comité des travaux historiques et scientifiques, Mémoires de la section de géographie, 7,) [(Committee on Historical and Scientific Work: Annals of the Geography Section,7)].

World Bank. 2004. *Upgrading of Low-Income Settlements in Sub-Saharan Africa— Assessing the Impacts of Formal and Informal Interventions,* Draft TF No. 024943, August, Annex II.

———. 2004. *Upgrading of Low Income Urban Settlements: Country Assessment Report: Senegal,* Draft TF No. 024943, August, Annex II.

7

Post-Occupancy: Implementation and Evaluation

Steven A. Moore

There may not be a single designer alive who would not claim to serve the public interest. This universal claim, however, leaves us with three interrelated questions: 1) who defines *public interest*? 2) how do we implement the preferred definition? and 3) how do we evaluate our projects in a manner that informs the ever-evolving definitions of public interest? In this chapter I briefly consider the first two questions, because they are prerequisites for consideration of the third. I, however, emphasize the third in order to provide practical suggestions concerning post-occupancy implementation and evaluation of how public interest has, or has not, been served.

Question 1: Who defines *public interest*?

Who gets to define public interest is the primary content of politics. In a society as diverse as that of the United States, there are inevitably multiple and competing interests—our "public" is, in fact, not singular but comprised of many social groups, or communities, with differing values and preferences (Trenz 2007). Should we, then, make design decisions based *only* on the values of the dominant social group? This is the concept of majority rule that is commonly accepted, if only by the dominant social group itself. I quickly dismiss this option because it leads to the suppression of valuable knowledge produced by minority groups, who have different experiences of the world (Haraway 1995).

But does dismissing the tyranny of the majority require that design should do exactly the opposite—serve only the values of the social group most directly affected? The notion that a nation is comprised of multiple distinct societies, each with its own self-defined rules, is roughly consistent with the politics of multiculturalism. Although multiculturalism may be appropriate in some contexts, this approach avoids a fundamental aspiration embodied in the Constitution of the United States: to recognize as equal the values and practices of others, not simply because it is ethical to do so, but because their knowledge is useful in the fashioning of a hybrid society, or melting pot. Our melting-pot logic suggests that the whole of society is greater than the sum of its parts—that we can imagine how social diversity contributes to the coproduction of a common future that will be different from any of our individual pasts (Rorty 1998). If our Constitution is understood to be a political strategy for conflict resolution, then public interest is best defined, and continually redefined, by creatively managing those conflicts that inevitably emerge between diverse social groups (Mouffe 1996).

Question 2: How do we implement the preferred definition?

An answer to the second question necessarily follows from the first. If conflict, creatively managed, works to define public interest over time, we must recognize that our collective interests can never be fixed by some well-intended political agreement or timeless theological pronouncement. Rather, our interests are constantly changing in response to the rational conflicts that derive from ever-changing social, technological, and environmental conditions (Moore and Wilson 2013). But how might we keep track of and anticipate the consequences of such complex and dynamic conditions?

Some readers will recognize that this is a question also asked in the natural and social sciences. Although far from perfect, the kinds of empirical research conducted in those disciplines are the best methods we have yet found to better understand our problems and propose solutions to them. So the answer to the second question is twofold: first, we need more and better interdisciplinary designer-researchers to collect empirical data documenting the past performance of our projects; and second, we need more and better designer-researchers to assist communities in the interpretation of empirical knowledge to influence the future (Fischer 2009). The implementation of the public's interest best relies then on empirical, or evidence-based design (Verderber 2005; Hamilton and Watkins 2008; Nussbaumer 2009; Kopec et al. 2012).[1]

Question 3: How do we evaluate our projects in a manner that informs the ever-evolving definitions of public interest?

I offer slightly more thorough guidelines to the third question. The fact that conditions, and the conflicts caused by them, are ever changing suggests a need for new methods of evaluating the consequences of what and how we build. In traditional post-occupancy evaluation (POE) researchers expect that conditions documented at one time and place will reoccur similarly in future cases, with the assumption that all other conditions remain the same.[2] We know, however, that change is constant. Nothing remains the same as it once was—not the climate, the technologies we use, the people who use them, building regulations, or the definition of public interest.

This qualification does not mean, however, that empirical knowledge derived from case studies is useless. Rather, it means that empirical knowledge of the past must be tempered by, and fused with, knowledge of its future context. The ability to reason in this way is what American philosopher Charles Sanders Peirce (1931) called "abduction," the designerly ability to anticipate how multiple conflicting systems might combine in the future as a single complex. Or as researchers Wolfgang Preiser and Jacqueline Vischer (2005) put it, we need a method to "feed forward" the knowledge gained in making the world a better place.

If the definition of public interest changes over time in response to constantly evolving contexts, the practice of POE can be improved by using methods more sensitive to the context in which design decisions were made and subsequent changes to that context (Flyvbjerg 2006). In other words, we need to know the intentions of the design team—which includes the architects, engineers, owners, and any participant who influenced any substantive decisions—before we can evaluate the efficacy of the decision (Holub 1984). Did decisions result in intended consequences or were some consequences unintended, be they positive or negative?[3]

Another way to approach this question is to consider the term *benchmark*, commonly understood as the standard against which the performance of any project is judged. In traditional POE, benchmarks are typically determined by industry organizations, such as the American Society of Heating, Refrigerating and Air Conditioning Engineers and the American Concrete Institute, and applied universally (Busch 2011). One problem of this practice is found in measuring energy consumption. For example, British thermal units per square foot per year (Btus/sf/yr) measured in Texas and in Munich are not commensurable *once put in a social context*. The point of this observation is that energy is *always* consumed in a social context that influences consumption rates. This observation suggests that collecting quantitative measurements of energy or water consumption, for example, is necessary but insufficient to evaluate building performance (Sovacool 2014; Kolarevic and Malkawi 2010). To evaluate building performance more holistically, we need to know: 1) what the intention of the design team for any given unit of evaluation was, 2) how that unit of evaluation was received by the community of users, 3) what the actual rate of consumption or use was, and 4) how social, technological, and environmental contexts of that unit changed after occupancy.

A simplified matrix to record performance data might look something like Figure 7.1.

7.1 Raw Data Matrix

Unit of Evaluation	1) Intention	2) Reception	3) Actual	4) Context
Fossil fuels	25 K Btus/sf/yr	Staff: "We couldn't reset the controls, so we just left them on high."	50 K Btus/sf/yr	Very low salaries and high staff turnover rate
Water	25 gal/p/day	Mgr: "Gaskets are impossible to maintain, so they leak."	60 gal/p/d	Plumbing fixtures were a bid alternate and project was over budget, so cheap fixtures were used
Reception desk	Reduce patron waiting time to 4 min.	Staff: "We love the f2f communication system."	2 min.	Communication system was reset with staff input after a month of use
Office area	Provide office workers with individual control of natural light and ventilation	Worker: "Once I learned to control the floor vent, I was completely comfortable; and having daylight at my desk helps me relax."	Not every worker has learned to make themselves comfortable	Additional staff and management training is recommended

Variations of this matrix might include different categories of data, depending on the purpose of evaluation, but should not separate quantitative and qualitative data because valid interpretation depends on relating them.

Methods of Data Collection

The financial and human resources available for any given project will influence the methods that can be used to collect data. Yet, even in the most elementary evaluation, multiple sources of data are required to reasonably ensure validity, in what is known as *triangulation*.[4] With this process, social scientists can acknowledge that each method of data collection and interpretation is effective at producing only one kind of knowledge. For example, analyzing monthly fuel bills in the context of climate data from the U.S. Weather Service can tell us a great deal about how energy consumption in a particular building relates to exterior weather patterns. However, interviews with building staff and operational contexts might show us why the correlation is not consistent. Collecting data using at least three different methods or data sources provides a check on the bias of any one method—there are multiple realities that inform each other. If they all converge on a single interpretation, findings are "robust"; but even if findings are not consistent, all is not lost. In fact, contradictory findings derived from different methods of data collection and interpretation may demonstrate how projects embody differing views of reality.

The kinds of data collection methods generally appropriate for post-occupancy evaluation of design projects include: interviews, focus groups, surveys, visual sorts, microclimate sensors, and archival sources, such as newspapers, correspondence, and consumption records.[5] Each method requires some amount of preparation, but most design professionals can use them effectively.

Methods of Interpretation

Once data are collected, they must be interpreted. Comparing rates of fuel and water consumption before and after production is a rather straightforward process. The comparison is made far easier by installing submeters within systems that measure specific spatial-use areas. However, comparing before-and-after descriptive texts by respondents, written correspondences, or archival material is more difficult and time consuming. The most reliable method available to analyze texts is *content analysis*, "a quantitatively oriented technique by which standardized measurements [of language] are applied to metrically defined units...[which are then] used to characterize and compare documents" (Krippendorff 2013, 112; see also Manning and Cullum-Swan 1994, and Moore and Wilson 2013).[6]

There are several digital softwares, including HyperResearch, Lexalytics Salience, and Smartlogic, that make content analysis much faster and more reliable.[7] These tools can help the analyst quickly identify recurring themes, or codes, that exist in the raw data. Coding a transcribed interview, text, or set of visual materials is a creative sense-making process that helps the analyst to reconstruct conditions or events as respondents perceived them. Comparing how different respondents or social groups interpreted conditions helps the analysts reconstruct how successes, conflicts, or misunderstandings unfolded.

A Note on Ethics

Because human subject research has had a controversial history, all universities and most other institutions have created Institutional Review Boards, or IRBs, to monitor the ethics of researchers (Kimmel 1981). IRB proposals require detailed descriptions of how respondents will be protected from unintended consequences of any proposed research. In the case of design professionals, who depend on their reputation in the marketplace to attract new commissions, firms have understandably been very reluctant to conduct, let alone make public, critical analysis of their projects. Unlike law or medicine, which have long-established procedures for empirical case-study evaluation and the management of data derived from evaluation, the discipline of architecture has no common data archive or published standard of ethics in the POE of projects, buildings, or landscapes. Other evaluation, or certification systems, such as LEED or Building Research Establishment Environmental Assessment Method

(BREEAM), will help to fill the void of building-performance data; but to date, it is only the SEED evaluation process that begins to measure the ethical dimension of how production of all kinds affects public interest.

Conclusion

The three questions investigated in this chapter provide minimal direction to undertake the POE of design projects—the resources cited throughout provide more. How public interest is defined, and how that definition is implemented, will depend on the quality and quantity of knowledge that designers can feed-forward from our collective experience. Properly understood, a POE is not a practice conducted by social scientists in white lab coats that is distinct from design; rather, a POE is a tool to serve the public interest by integrating new kinds of knowledge into design decision making.

References

Barbour, Rosaline. 2008. *Doing Focus Groups*. Thousand Oaks, CA: Sage.

Blair, Johnny, Ronald F. Czaja, and Edward Blair. 2014. *Designing Surveys: A Guide to Decisions and Procedures* (3rd edn). Thousand Oaks, CA: Sage.

Busch, Lawrence. 2011. *Standards: Recipes for Reality*. Cambridge, MA: MIT Press.

Calabrese, Raymond. 2009. *The Dissertation Desk Reference: The Doctoral Student's Manual to Writing a Dissertation*. Lanham, MD: Rowman & Littlefield.

Coxon, Anthony P. M. 1999. *Sorting Data: Collection and Analysis*. Thousand Oaks, CA: Sage.

Elder, Glen H., Eliza Pavalko, and Elizabeth Colerick Clipp. 1999. *Working with Archival Data: Studying Lives*. Thousand Oaks, CA: Sage.

Fischer, Frank. 2009. *Democracy & Expertise: Reorienting Public Inquiry*. New York: Oxford University Press.

Flyvbjerg, Bent. 2006. "Five Misunderstandings about Case-Study Research." *Qualitative Inquiry* (12): 219–45.

Hamilton, D. Kirk, and David H. Watkins. 2008. *Evidence-Based Design for Multiple Building Types*. New York: Wiley.

Haraway, Donna. 1995. "Situated Knowledges: The Science Question in Feminism and the Privilege of Partial Perspective." In, *Technology and the Politics of Knowledge*. Edited by Andrew Feenberg and A. Hannay. Bloomington, IN: Indiana University Press, 175–94.

Hill, Michael R. 1993. *Archival Strategies and Techniques*. Thousand Oaks, CA: Sage.

Holub, Robert C. 1984. *Reception Theory: A Critical Introduction*. London: Methuen.

Kimmel, Allan J., ed. 1981. *Ethics of Human Subject Research*. San Francisco, CA: Jossey-Bass.

Kolarevic, Branko, and Ali M. Malkawi, ed. 2010 [2005]. *Performative Architecture: Beyond Instrumentality*. New York and London: Spon Press.

Kopec, Dak, Edward Sinclair, and Bruce Matthes. 2012. *Evidence-Based Design: A Process for Research and Writing*. Boston, MA: Prentice Hall.

Krippendorff, Klaus. 2013. *Content Analysis: An Introduction to its Methodology*, MA (3rd edn). Thousand Oaks, CA: Sage.

Manning, Peter K. and B. Cullum-Swan. 1994. *Handbook of Qualitative Research*. Thousand Oaks, CA: Sage.

McCracken, Grant. 1988. *The Long Interview: Qualitative Research Methods*, 13. Newbury Park, CA: Sage.

McLaughlin, Thomas. 1996. *Street Smarts and Critical Theory: Listening to the Vernacular*. Madison, WI: The University of Wisconsin Press.

Moore, Steven A. 2001. *Technology and Place: Sustainable Architecture and the Blueprint Farm*. Austin, TX: University of Texas Press.

Moore, Steven A., and Barbara B. Wilson. 2013. *Questioning Architectural Judgment: The Problem with Codes in the United States*. London: Routledge.

Mouffe, Chantal. 1996. "Democracy, Power, and the 'Political'." In *Democracy and Difference: Contesting the Boundaries of the Political*. Edited by Seyla Benhabib. Princeton, NJ: Princeton University Press, 245–56.

Nussbaumer, Linda L. 2009. *Evidence-Based Design for Interior Designers*. London: Fairchild.

Onset: Data Hobo Loggers. 2014. Accessed 28 June. http://www.onsetcomp.com/.

Peirce, Charles S. 1931. *The Collected Papers of Charles S. Peirce*. Cambridge, MA: Bellknap Press of Harvard.

Preiser, Wolfgang F. E., and Jacqueline C. Vischer. 2005. *Assessing Building Performance*. Oxford: Elsevier.

Punch, Keith F. 2003. *Survey Research: The Basics*. Thousand Oaks, CA: Sage.

Rorty, Richard. 1998. *Achieving Our Country*. Cambridge, MA: Harvard University Press.

Rose, Gillian. 2012. *Visual Methodologies: An Introduction to Researching with Visual Materials* (3rd edn). Thousand Oaks, CA: Sage.

Roulston, Kathryn. 2011. *Reflective Interviewing: A Guide to Theory and Practice*. Thousand Oaks, CA: Sage

Sovacool, Benjamin K. 2014. "Where Are We Going Here: Analyzing Fifteen Years of Energy Scholarship and Proposing a Social Science Research Agenda." *Energy Research & Social Science* 1 (29): 1–29.

Trenz, Hans-Jörg. J. 2007. "Reconciling Diversity and Unity." *Ethnicities* 7 (2): 157.

Verderber, Stephen. 2005. *Compassion in Architecture: Evidence-Based design for Health in Louisiana*. Lafayette, LA: Center for Louisiana Studies.

Wang, David and Linda Groat. 2013. *Architectural Research Methods* (2nd edn). New York: Wiley. Original edition, 2002.

Notes

1   *Evidence-based design* is a term that emerged first in health care but has gradually been adopted by designers in several related fields (architecture, landscape architecture, industrial design, and engineering) after the turn of the twenty-first century. Although the authors cited each provide partial definitions, I will suggest this one: Evidence-based design for the built environment requires the use of empirical data, derived from case-study analysis of existing environments, in the making of design decisions for new ones. The application of context-dependent data is necessarily modified by the design team on the basis of thorough research of new biophysical and social conditions. The existing literatures of post-occupancy evaluation and building-performance evaluation are related resources.

2   This is the assumption that scientists refer to in Latin as the *ceteris paribus* clause (all things being equal). Conventional "bench science" laboratories filter out confounding variables, such a temperature swing, wind, or air quality, that might interfere with experimentation. But in the research of artifact design, buildings, cities, or regions, no such method is available. Topics must be studied in the context of their use.

3   Although not discussed in any SEED documents, the assumptions of the SEED evaluation process and the doctrines of reception theory are practically identical. The advocates of reception theory argue that the meaning of any work cannot be understood by interpreting the intentions of the author. Rather, meaning lies in the gap, or the degree to which there is one, between the intentions of the artist and the reception by the community. For a general discussion of reception theory, see Holub (1984). For an application of reception theory to architecture, see Moore (2001).

4   According to Calabrese (2009), "Triangulation describes the use of multiple data sources and/or research methods in a study. This apparent overlap by the qualitative researcher seeks to address threats to validity and reactivity … and researcher bias."

5   Interviews are a good method with which to reconstruct subjective interpretations of reality. By categorizing individuals with similar views, the identity of social groups and their common interests, or conflicts with other groups, can be identified. Interviews are, however, time consuming. See Roulston (2011), McLaughlin (1996), McCracken (1988). Focus groups can be understood as a group interview through which conflicts can be identified. Managing focus groups so that reluctant speakers are heard can be difficult. See Wang and Groat (2013), Barbour (2008). Surveys can reach many more people than interviews or focus groups. They are, however, difficult to construct. See Blair et al. (2014), and Punch (2003). Sorting of visual material can be a particularly appropriate method for designer-researchers. By ordering visual materials into categories and naming the categories, respondents can

construct subjective interpretations of reality via visual rather than linguistic means. See, Rose (2012), and Coxon (1999). Climate Consultant, Hobo Data Loggers, and RayMan softwares can provide accurate macroclimate data by measuring actual microclimate conditions. These can be compared with design intentions and/or digital models. See, Onset (2014). Archival materials of many kinds provide the raw material from which to reconstruct focal events and conflicts. See, Elder et al. (1999), and Hill (1993).

6   Manning and Cullum-Swan (1994) hold reservations concerning the validity of content analysis for two reasons: first, what the researcher brings to category making will influence findings; and second, focusing on small units of text tends to lose the context of the narrative as a whole. For these reasons, I recommend that multiple researchers conduct content analysis together as a form of researcher triangulation. In this process, meaning is negotiated in a social context related to and knowledgeable about the case. This triangulated method of content analysis was conducted as chapter 1 in Moore and Wilson (2013).

7   For a brief review of thirty available content-analysis softwares, see http://www.predictiveanalyticstoday.com/top-30–software-for-text-analysis-text-mining-text-analytics/.

Part 2

Practicing Public Interest Design: SEED Methodology

8

Social Economic Environmental Design Methodology

Lisa M. Abendroth, Bryan Bell

Learning from Best Practices

From our investigations, including the 2011 Latrobe Prize research, we have learned that current public interest design practitioners operate in the United States and internationally at a range of scales: from meeting the needs of long-standing underserved communities to addressing humanitarian crises of individual clients and those of large geographic regions. This broad spectrum reflects a growing trend taking place in design practice in the United States as we adapt to a shifting definition of the client and to changing economic conditions. Within this framework, the public interest design profession continues to evolve to meet new required standards and practices. The SEED methodology addresses this need.

Practices in the public interest are far reaching, and they are more interdisciplinary than the current prescribed model of design practice. Public interest design practices are more innovative in their protocols, procedures, economic models, and relationships, which fosters a vibrant and diverse discipline. Most of the skills necessary to be successful in this new line of work have not been learned in the academy or on the job; instead, skills have and are being learned in the field and in the context of working. New methods, educational models, curricula, and professional training courses are needed to provide a standard for these required competencies. This book, and specifically this chapter, contributes to this growing knowledge base. The following methodology is derived from the best practices of current successful models, curated with the guidance and input of SEED Network members.

How to Undertake a SEED Project Step-By-Step

The SEED methodology converts the SEED mission and principles into clear actions. Through its nine steps, the methodology guides locally based collaborations of design professionals and stakeholders who best know their community and their needs.

Step 1: Engaging Community Participation

An inclusive and transparent process is a critical element of public interest design. When supported and provided with the right set of engagement tools, communities can proactively contribute to a design process of participatory decision making to build consensus, establish priorities, and define goals.

    The question of how the community and relevant stakeholders have been involved in defining project challenges and setting specific goals is significant. Examples of participatory input or field research verified by the community may include the following: community charettes; interviews; discussion groups; photo or video ethnographies; asset-based development; asset-based design; public forums; local, regional, state, or national government support; stakeholder advisory groups; coordination with local comprehensive plan; and priority set by local government. (See projects about community participation on pages 105–32, chapters 10–12 and chapters 13–15.)

Step 2: Identifying Critical Issues

Critical issues are the challenges that define life's struggles, both day-to-day and during crises. They can be categorized and defined by societal, economic, and environmental considerations—categories that help clarify the unique priorities of every community or audience. These issues provide a bridge between design and people, a catalyst for opening a dialogue for defining needs that direct the purpose of the design project. An issue can also be the call to action that prompts the project and brings vested parties together for collaboration. Design teams and stakeholders should define their own distinct project issues in an effort to solve problems across social, economic, and environmental divisions. (See projects about critical issues on pages 133–46, chapters 16–18.)

Step 3: Defining Goals

Goals define the broad purpose toward which a project is directed. Goals address the big picture and what the project should achieve in relation to community needs. The process—which includes timelines, tasks, methods, and activities—defines how goals will be accomplished and affects project results. Project planning and preparation require that tasks with aligned goals and processes be stated and

Nine Steps of the SEED Process
Step 1: Engaging community participation
Step 2: Identifying critical issues
Step 3: Defining goals
Step 4: Research and data collection
Step 5: Setting benchmarks
Step 6: Defining performance measurement
Step 7: Developing a timeline
Step 8: Documenting and reporting results
Step 9: Evaluation and reflection

Abendroth and Bell

defined in advance of initiating a project. It is recommended that these be identified through collaboration that allows feedback and communication from all of the project participants. (See projects about defining goals on pages 121–32, chapters 13–15.)

Step 4: Research and Data Collection

Documentation gathered through a defined research process is necessary. Both quantitative and qualitative research methods are encouraged. Quantitative research is based on empirical evidence, quantities and numeric references, and subsequent evaluation or measurement of these data to establish broad connections. Qualitative processes tend to include in-depth analyses through a variety of other means, including observations, interviews, photography, video, and written or oral documentation.

The SEED process offers a framework for research and data collection in order to demonstrate the specific quantitative and qualitative approaches used in the project. The method used and the data gathered, as well as any participants involved, should be clearly described: results must be documented if success is going to be claimed. The reflections of a stakeholder, casual observations, phone conversations, or discussions may qualify as forms of research, so consider the scope of relevance when assessing opportunities for research and data collection. (See projects about the role of research on pages 105–32, chapters 10–15 and on pages 147–61, chapters 19–21.)

Step 5: Setting Benchmarks

Benchmarks are reference points or standards that establish performance goals for purposes of evaluation, measurement, or comparison. Example benchmarks for modular classrooms may include affordability, health and wellness, and design for productive learning environments. (See case study pages 270–3.) Benchmarks can be used within a project to define direction and indicate ideals. Design indicators are set during project planning, when the inclusion of community input can prove significant to project development and in meeting goals. (See projects about setting benchmarks on pages 147–61, chapters 19–21.)

Step 6: Defining Performance Measurement

Performance measurement involves the regular quantifying of benchmarks built into a project plan. These measures document and verify accomplishment of incremental goals toward social, economic, and environmental results (not just what it took to accomplish them) while providing a common language for the communication of strategy. The SEED process creates a framework for the identification of benchmarks and the regular documentation of accomplished goals. These verifications support the requirement for evaluating the success of met goals relative to designated project benchmarks. (See projects about defining performance measures on pages 147–61, chapters 19–21.)

Step 7: Developing a Timeline

A timeline is an essential tool that should communicate incremental progress throughout the phases of the project. It provides evidence of the anticipated schedule and criteria for project planning, development, implementation, and post-implementation assessment. A timeline that references dates and aligns with goals and benchmarks can aid in accomplishing project intent and demystify the process when working with stakeholders. It is recommended that the timeline and benchmarks be considered together and be established early in the life of the project. (See projects about the importance of timelines on pages 147–61, chapters 19–21 and on pages 163–77, chapters 22–24.)

Step 8: Documenting and Reporting Results

The act of documenting results is essential to any project: using the SEED process can help achieve the desired outcomes while ensuring a seamless and thorough process that supports a public interest design practice. Because documentation is an important step toward project assessment (step 9), it is critical that documented data be accurate, support project goals and processes, and offer analysis of project impacts.

Reporting results bring us closer to understanding how goals were accomplished, why they were not, or which outcomes were different than expected. When reporting results, accuracy in recording details, such as time, place, participants, context, methods used, and numeric documentation (as appropriate), is critical. Broad generalizations are of little help; instead, be prepared to verify the results of research or design processes. The inclusion of images that document results can help provide necessary evidence for analysis. (See projects about documenting results on pages 163–77, chapters 22–24.)

Step 9: Evaluation and Reflection

Accountability is what we strive for in our work to provide evidence of success. In order to demonstrate accountability in the work public interest designers produce, we must critically assess and evaluate what was accomplished and how it was accomplished. Our process embraces evaluation and integrates it into our working methodology. Understanding what we did well and what challenges remain in the work produced—and how it met or missed defined goals and benchmarks—is vital not only for the practice of public interest design but for those we work with and the public broadly. (See projects about evaluation and reflection on pages 163–77, chapters 22–24.)

Accountability can be achieved through evaluation. Evaluation measures successes, challenges, and failures—and these can be used strategically in a variety of contexts, including funding applications or in attracting new projects or partners.

Reflection allows us to critique and assess what could have been done differently in order to improve a given result. A practice of evaluation and reflection helps ensure best practices are embraced over the life of a public interest design practice.

The SEED process lays out a clear and principled approach to a public interest design practice that emphasizes communication between parties and promotes informed participation from the ground up during the project, from concept through implementation, scaling, and post-occupancy. The five topics below are discussed in depth in part 2 and translate the SEED process into easy-to-use techniques that span the life of a project. These strategies provide a way to measure successes and challenges in which transparency and accountability are vital ingredients to a healthy process and fully realized outcomes.

- Starting a Project: Public Participation and the Feedback Loop (Step 1, chapters 10–12)
- Sustaining Collaboration: Extended Engagement (Steps 1 and 3, chapters 13–15)
- Doing More: Issue-Based Design and the Triple Bottom Line (Step 2, chapters 16–18)
- Assessing Results: Defining and Measuring Success (Steps 3–7, chapters 19–21)
- Scaling a Project: Uniting Diverse Stakeholders (Steps 7–9, chapters 22–24)

9

The SEED Evaluator and SEED Certification

Lisa M. Abendroth, Bryan Bell

The SEED Evaluator

It is valuable to define a mission and principles for public interest design. However, it is equally important to have a clear process and tools to make the mission and principles actionable and to ensure that their value is realized as public benefit. (See pages 13–15 for the SEED mission and principles.) The SEED Evaluator is an online communication tool, software that supports and translates the SEED process. It allows communities, audiences, and designers to define goals for design projects and then measure the level of success in achieving these through a third-party review. Using the SEED Evaluator allows communities to develop their leadership and decision-making skills from within while using a proven method and recognized standard of success—this can also lead to SEED Certification, discussed in detail below (pages 101–3).

The SEED Evaluator can assist individuals, groups, designers, communities, project planners, and participants achieve like-minded goals that are focused on the triple bottom line of social justice, economic development, and environmental conservation. The SEED methodology responds to the questions many designers face today:

- How does this project create positive change in the face of social, economic, and environmental challenges?
- How does the design answer the short- and long-term needs of a community that validates ethical and sustainable approaches to design through a triple bottom line approach?

- How can the design team directly engage the client and other vested parties in every step of the project process so that the outcome is informed from the ground up?

A tool developed for architects, industrial designers, landscape architects, communication designers, urban designers, and aligned fields, the SEED Evaluator provides guidance through a strategic matrix of questions that critique the social, economic, and environmental viability of each phase of project development. Using a guided approach broken down into understandable and manageable steps, the SEED Evaluator creates a platform for collaboration and consensus building between design teams and stakeholder groups. Completion of specific phases of the SEED Evaluator can lead to SEED Certification, which can validate and provide the needed "proof" of a project. Progress and challenges can be documented with evidence through each project phase. Because the SEED process advocates for a bottom-up approach to problem solving that truly activates community concerns, this process requires an inclusive and participatory process.

Why Evaluate?

Evaluation involves a detailed assessment of project results based on benchmarks and performance measures embedded in the design process. Evaluation is the translation of project plan or program successes, failures, and challenges. Questions posed during evaluation:

- How were goals defined and accomplished?
- What was done well and what was not?
- Did appropriate project planning create the intended effects?
- What proof of accomplishment demonstrates that goals were met as anticipated? (Gamble et. al 2005, 88)

Designers, communities, stakeholders, funders, and clients all have a need to assess the outcome of design work, just as clients and communities have a need to assess how goals were achieved for purposes of defining community benchmarks and working together toward common goals. The SEED Evaluator provides a road map, a directional pointer that can indicate vital strengths and weaknesses. The SEED Evaluator builds in an assessment component to its process because it is something we need—designers and those we design for need to understand the impact of the work, and we need to be able to learn from and leverage transferable knowledge in any given project for collective learning.

Abendroth and Bell

SEED Certification

SEED Certification is awarded to projects that have demonstrated the effective use of design to overcome social, economic, and environmental issues in a community. One qualifier for SEED Certification comes from meeting the threshold, a value set by project designers with the community based on the SEED mission and principles/ steps. This, along with meeting determined benchmarks and goals is another qualifier. The SEED Evaluator makes meaningful the documentation of project evidence, which is used strategically to assess for certification. Project narratives and visuals submitted to the SEED Evaluator are examined by project reviewers who are trained specialists in their specific design disciplines, who are SEED experts, and who understand the challenges of designing in the public's interest.

Being certified means that a project accomplished what it set out to do in achieving community goals; it also means that its designers can effectively answer four key questions:

1) What are the critical issues being addressed?
2) What is the anticipated design result, and how is it an appropriate response to the design problem?
3) How will results be measured?
4) How has the community participated in the project?

The Value of SEED Certification

Projects and affiliated communities that achieve SEED Certification can leverage their accomplishment not only for their own goals but also to move forward a process of inclusion and informed decision making in design. SEED Certification is the standard that community organizers, leaders, designers, and funders can use to recognize that a project has achieved levels of success in terms of the quantitative and qualitative measures set forth in the SEED Evaluator process.

There are many design projects that claim to benefit a community, but a SEED-certified project is distinct because it has:

- Significant and documented community participation in project decisions;
- An issue-based approach;
- Measured results of the design product.

Applying for SEED Certification Using the SEED Evaluator

A project lead or team can start a SEED Evaluator application online at www.seednetwork.org. With the SEED Evaluator, applicants can decide to pursue

SEED Certification or to simply use the SEED process provided in Part 1 of the application to help guide a project through a public interest design framework. SEED Certification is a three-part commitment to documenting an implemented design project and includes Part 1: Project Application, Part 2: Project Details, and Part 3: Project Results. Applicants who only wish to use the SEED process (and not apply for certification) can access Part 1 and use it to better understand how their work addresses critical social, economic, and environmental justice issues. Reviewer feedback is provided in either option; however, SEED Certification provides comprehensive reviewer guidance and an in-depth analysis of project results at early implementation and post-implementation.

SEED Evaluator Part 1: Project Application

This section of the SEED Evaluator requires a broad range of information: the project type, partners and stakeholders, and descriptive community information detailing geography, demographics, and historical/cultural implications. Here, the applicant also identifies several of the community's most pressing issues evident in the project. Each social, economic, and/or environmental issue is discussed in relation to how design responds to that issue, what research methods and participation methods are being used, and how success is being measured. While Part 1 is intended to offer an introduction to the project, information should be concise yet detailed in describing the qualities most relevant to the nature of the work and those involved. Responses to these questions will help reveal the depth and breadth of the project and its issues, and will document the inclusion of the community's voice in shaping and working toward common goals.

Once Part 1 is completed, there is an opportunity for reviewer feedback to determine the project's prospects for moving toward certification. If lacking necessary application detail or if the SEED mission and principles are not fulfilled or are violated, the project cannot move on to subsequent phases of the application. In the latter situation, applicants will be informed as to why the project failed to meet these principles and will be advised on how the project may be revised and resubmitted.

SEED Evaluator Part 2: Project Details

Submitting Part 2 of the SEED Evaluator confirms the applicant's intent to pursue SEED Certification. Part 2 builds on the content submitted in Part 1 by providing opportunities to elaborate on and/or modify information according to the project timeline and as the project evolves. This section allows reviewers to understand the project in terms of background research, design process, extent of stakeholder participation, as well as progress made toward goals in more concrete terms.

Part 2 contains substantive questions that are interrelated in nature, reinforcing the requirement for definitive, process-based benchmarks that are phased into a timeline and that embrace performance measures. Part 2 presents opportunities to upload support documentation that reinforces benchmarking and the timeline.

SEED Evaluator Part 3: Results

Part 3 requests analysis of outcomes including measured results and met goals. The resolution of social, economic, and environmental issues is requested. This section is broken down into two phases for documentation: early implementation and post-implementation analyses. Early implementation allows for adjustments to the project timeline through the filter of issues addressed, while post-implementation supports the project in its final and intended form and includes reflection on results. Reflecting on knowledge gained during the project and what could have been done differently punctuates the conclusion of the SEED Evaluator process. The submission of Part 3 for SEED Certification marks the completed project documentation, inclusive of timelines, support-documentation uploads, and narratives collected during the life of the project. This vital information conveys the successes and challenges of a project and creates a record of best practices in public interest design upon which transferable lessons can be shared and built.

Reference

Gamble, Dorothy, Marie Weil, and Nicole Kiefer. 2005. *Measuring a Movement: Evaluating Outcomes in Sustainable Community Development*. Chapel Hill, NC: The Resourceful Communities Program of the Conservation Fund.

10

Starting a Project: Public Participation and the Feedback Loop

Lisa M. Abendroth, Bryan Bell

This chapter explores ways to engage thoughtfully articulated participation and garner input from stakeholders from the get-go. The importance of feedback is stressed because communication is a constant requirement in this work: the need to establish mechanisms for transparency that keep all parties abreast of project development.

When initiating public interest design work, we need firsthand understanding of the project's defining social and cultural contexts. These factors create a framework for conducting a practice based in civic engagement and informed by social, economic, and environmental issues—human issues—which cannot be easily known by analyzing the needs of a project or a people from afar. This work is done from the ground up, locally, and involves the community from the very beginning. But how do we carry out this process so that it is meaningful to those involved and provides a structure for feedback? How do we leverage our own technical expertise while honoring the very specific and unique needs of our clients?

Social equity—the notion that people should have access to a full range of life-sustaining opportunities—is a founding SEED concept and a SEED Best Practice Value Proposition (chapter 8, page 97). An important aspect of achieving social equity is informed consent, permission appropriate for human subject research, which is essential to all public interest design endeavors.[1] Projects must involve an open, two-way, and democratic process that engages all parties. The extent of the involvement of a community in the decision making process should include input from a full range of participants—providing preferences that the designer can examine and use to advance the project.

The following indicators can help assess the role of social equity in a project:

- *Participation:* How and to what extent have community members and stakeholders been involved in the design and planning processes? Are processes and participation well documented?
- *Effectiveness:* How and to what extent does the project address the community's critical needs and challenges? Who identified these needs? Is the decision making process well documented?
- *Inclusivity:* Is the community or audience clearly defined? How and to what extent does the project promote social equity as well as reflect a diversity of social identities and values of the community it serves?
- *Impact:* How and to what extent are the social, economic, and environmental impacts of the project being measured? Who will benefit and how? How is success defined, and how will it be evaluated?

Embracing participation and feedback methods at the start of a project ensures long-term project results that accurately reflect needs and desires and reinforce social equity. The power of participatory decision making can motivate communities to engage in a design process that builds consensus, establishes priorities, and defines goals in a way that a design team alone simply cannot. Public interest designers value participatory processes because we trust our clients to know what they need and want. This revelation can be humbling—it says that we empower our community partners to lead us to understanding.

Consider public participation and feedback as part of the early research stage that will extend into later stages of design development and implementation: stakeholders should be part of the longer-term process and an analysis of stakeholder groups should be integrated into project launch. Using an asset-based approach—which identifies the strengths, skills, and talent that are derived from the resources within a community—public interest designers can gauge the many ways in which communities can actively participate in the design process, with the goal of recognizing the largest number of stakeholders. By identifying local skills and abilities, we can create solutions that enable locals to be active agents in the outcome.

Based on best practices in this field, important qualities in an informed, participatory process that verifies feedback include:

- *Communication:* its importance and how we connect directly and openly with stakeholders;
- *Participation:* ways of guiding design process beyond the studio confines;
- *Culture:* cultural sensitivity and honoring individual points of view;
- *Interest:* how to generate awareness with stakeholders and promote long-term attachment to a project;
- *Trust:* strategies for building confidence and overcoming the perception of designer as outsider; and,

- *Value:* how to ensure the public recognition of the importance of design through feedback that acknowledges the desires of the community or audience.

Getting started does not have to be difficult, but it does require a willingness to get involved. Find ways to embed yourself in the community; get to know your audience personally. Join a group or become a member of a club associated with the project or the people. Understand decision makers relevant to your project, and be sure you are working directly with them.

Knowing the best ways to harness participation comes from experimentation and practice, but here are a few proven tactics to get started once you have established a relationship:

- *Interviews:* one-on-one, small peer groups where individual voices can be heard;
- *Workshops, symposia, and conferences:* based around activities that are generative;
- *Discussion groups:* focused on specific project themes or topics;
- *Neighborhood community organization forums:* useful as liaison to broader community;
- *Stakeholder advisory group:* a group that always has the design team's ear;
- *Public forums:* often necessary and needed in larger projects;
- *Community charettes:* used to create or vet design iterations;
- *Group meals:* sharing food in a group setting builds camaraderie;
- *Women- and minority-owned business groups:* engage a wide breadth of voices.

The next two chapters describe the participation and feedback processes of three projects—the Detroit Collaborative Design Center's Impact Detroit Community How-To Guides (case study pages 194–7), Detroit Works Project Long Term Planning, and the Owe'neh Bupingeh Preservation Plan and Rehabilitation Project (case study pages 202–5), located in Ohkay Owingeh, New Mexico. These projects share reinforcing strategies for engaging stakeholders in what can broadly be referred to as community development and include education and empowerment as forms of activated participation. They show the importance of meaningful and productive engagement and how this was achieved in specific community contexts. These projects are exemplars, demonstrating effective strategies for inclusive participation and frameworks for feedback that make contribution a measurable project goal.

Key concepts discussed in the following two chapters:

- Incremental development as a mechanism for starting a project;
- Civic engagement inspires leadership;
- Community-building activities increases capacity toward other goals;

- Two-way, open dialogue;
- Value of community expertise;
- Processes must continually evolve and ensure meaningful, productive participation;
- Community development partners are essential liaisons to the community;
- Work must occur across a broad range of social, cultural, and economic boundaries;
- Reinvestment in place happens through long-term relationships maintained over time;
- Traditional methods and knowledge inform technical design processes;
- Investment in goal setting activates long-term outcomes;
- Build education into the process to empower participants through mutual knowledge sharing.

Notes

1   Read more about the topic of data-collection and informed consent for human subjects research in chapter 13 (pages 121–3).

11

Moving Forward Together: Engagement in Community Design and Development

Ceara O'Leary, Dan Pitera

Civic engagement strategies implemented by the Detroit Collaborative Design Center are focused on ensuring meaningful public participation that is a catalyst for developing equitable urban spaces. Long-term engagement in participatory community design and development provides a variety of lessons learned.

At its core, the Detroit Collaborative Design Center (DCDC) values civic engagement—which mobilizes communities and generates great and meaningful design—as the essence of effective leadership. DCDC defines civic engagement as the open and ongoing two-way dialogue between all stakeholders—essentially, people talking and working together to move forward together. DCDC plays a leadership role in design by facilitating this sharing of knowledge, identifying connections, and developing creative solutions that blend technical knowledge with community expertise. The work of DCDC, a multidisciplinary and nonprofit architecture and urban design firm based in the University of Detroit Mercy School of Architecture, is rooted in Detroit and project partners include residents, neighborhood organizations, community development professionals, government officials, funders, and other local designers. DCDC believes that people in the city are catalysts for urban innovation and is guided by the question, how can people be key operators in creating new ecological and equitable urban spaces? The participatory processes that the office has developed over the last twenty years are constantly evolving in an effort to more effectively address this question.

This chapter highlights two projects that illustrate the range of civic engagement strategies that DCDC embraces, knowing that discrete projects demand unique tactics that both invite people into the design process and ensure that their participation is meaningful. The Impact Detroit Community How-To Guides (case study pages 194–7) outline steps and resources essential to small-scale community development. The guides help build capacity for neighborhood projects as they equip communities to act as key operators in creating equitable urban environments. Detroit Works Project Long Term Planning (DWPLTP) is a citywide planning effort that included a range of civic engagement strategies that respond to Detroit's diverse population and intentionally vary according to distinct demographics and lifestyles. These projects are products of many voices and vary from a small-scale neighborhood tool with a cumulative impact to broad citywide outreach that seeks to represent all Detroiters.

Impact Detroit Community How-To Guides

Released in 2013, the Impact Detroit Community How-To Guides are the result of lessons learned from past projects and represent an effort to support others tackling similar challenges in neighborhoods throughout Detroit. The guides are products of Impact Detroit, a DCDC initiative that acts as a collaborative resource network for community-development projects in Detroit. Impact Detroit facilitates the connection between emerging initiatives and a wide range of partners who provide resources and help build capacity for project implementation. Recent Impact Detroit pilot projects have called on an array of community-development professionals as collaborative consultants—ranging from lawyers and government officials to graphic designers and marketing professionals—responding to project needs and complementing community participation. The guides incorporate this range of insight and represent the knowledge that DCDC has gained through its work with community partners over the last twenty years.

The guides unpack small-scale community-development processes and accelerate future projects by providing step-by-step guidance and highlighting

11.1
The current collection of Community How-To Guides, available in print and online, Impact Detroit Community How-To Guides, Detroit, Michigan, 2013.

O'Leary and Pitera

available resources. Often, seemingly simple challenges can be significant hurdles for neighborhood organizations or small businesses with limited time and resources. The guides diminish these barriers, make relevant information more accessible, and help Detroiters meet common project goals. One guide called "How Do I Create and Maintain a Block Club?" was created in collaboration with a local community leader, who DCDC supported as he formed a block club. Setting goals, identifying resources, and engaging with neighbors resulted in a strong community association dedicated to improving its neighborhood. While some of the Impact Detroit Community How-To Guides are specific to Detroit neighborhoods and city processes, such as "How Do I Organize a Neighborhood Clean Up Day?" and "How Do I Find Resources for my Small Business?," others are more widely applicable, such as "How do I Prepare a Grant Proposal?" and "How do I Outreach to My Community?"

For each of the guides, DCDC engages community collaborators to generate content and ensure the legibility and accessibility of the material. DCDC also calls upon technical experts to review content. These project partners include business owners, community members, block-club leaders, social-media gurus, and economic-development professionals. The participatory process and peer reviews result in resources that maximize usefulness and also put into action DCDC's collaborative model for design driven by civic engagement. The guides are primarily

11.2
The work of Bleeding Heart Design is an example of a collaborative Impact Detroit project that informed the guides. Impact Detroit Community How-To Guides, Detroit, Michigan, 2013.

distributed through neighborhood-based community development corporations as well as citywide support organizations, such as ARISE Detroit. Both the English and Spanish versions are available on the DCDC website. The Impact Detroit Community How-To Guides engage partners and collaborators in an effort to share the basic steps, resources, and other tips necessary to achieve neighborhood goals and build capacity for future community-development projects.

Detroit Works Project Long Term Planning

A successful civic-engagement process lies in the many opportunities to reach a range of communities, to work across silos and boundaries, and to increase the capacity of all people to more effectively participate. It is DCDC's responsibility to facilitate this process. While the guides unpack small-scale processes, DWPLTP engaged a citywide audience in a large-scale planning effort. Accordingly, the two actions call upon distinct participation strategies. DCDC defines two groups of complementary tactics in order to clearly state the purpose of the engagement and the intended audience: methods used to open the process to a wide variety of people and methods used to make their participation meaningful. The development of the Impact Detroit Community How-To Guides prioritizes meaningful participation by stakeholders. The tactics deployed by DWPLTP focus more intentionally on bringing people into the planning process and joining the conversation.

From November 2011 to November 2012, the DCDC co-led the Civic Engagement team for the citywide DWPLTP planning project. In this far-reaching endeavor, the implementation of a mosaic of tactics opened up the process for a variety of people to participate in the planning effort. A broad spectrum of outreach

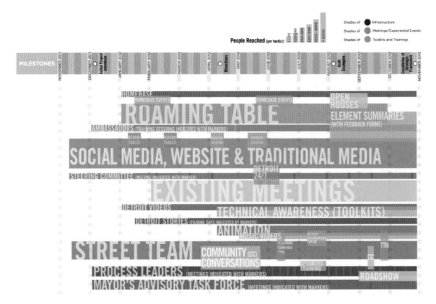

11.3
A diverse array of DWPLTP civic engagement tactics provided a range of ways for Detroiters to participate in the planning process. Detroit Works Project Long Term Planning, Detroit, Michigan, 2011–2013.

O'Leary and Pitera

strategies, such as street team canvassing and a traveling roadshow, connected with people 163,000 times. Additionally, community conversations, open houses, and Detroit stories contributed to 30,700 one-on-one conversations that informed a report titled *Detroit Future City*.

Strategies were developed to connect with a diverse set of stakeholders and residents in a range of different forums. Many people cannot or do not want to attend traditional community-planning meetings or town-hall events. For example, people who work in the evening or have long commutes to or from the suburbs are not able to attend evening meetings. Also, it is rare to find youth or young adults attending community meetings. The civic-engagement efforts of DWPLTP created alternate avenues for residents.

Figure 11.3 illustrates the mosaic of engagement tactics used to reach different audiences. The diagram was reviewed and updated monthly using cumulative participant-demographic data from the previous months. Tactics varied from music videos and an online gaming platform, which successfully engaged a younger audience, to a road show that exhibited the plan at community centers and a team that attended existing neighborhood meetings to share information about DWPLTP. Another engagement strategy was a mobile information station, the Roaming Table,

11.4
The Roaming Table is a mobile engagement station that encounters Detroiters in their everyday lives. Detroit Works Project Long Term Planning, Detroit, Michigan, 2012.

designed to be a hub for DWPLTP knowledge sharing. The Roaming Table was often deployed at neighborhood events, bus stops, grocery stores, and many other sites to create a convenient way for residents to engage with the DWPLTP process.

As the Civic Engagement leaders for DWPLTP, DCDC developed meaningful and productive methods of community participation: Detroiters were invited into the planning process and community expertise effectively blended with professional expertise. People enter design and engagement processes in many different ways. DCDC looks for ways to make everyone's participation meaningful—from the business leader and the nonprofit leader to the pastor and the resident down the street. DWPLTP highlights how communities and designers working together as partners ultimately results in stronger plans and projects.

DCDC works through the exchange of information at various steps in the design process, synthesizing it, finding connections, and developing a series of recommendations. In this way, creative listening and creative thinking leads to creative designing in collaboration with community partners. Throughout this process, the participation of an array of stakeholders leads to well-informed, responsible, and beautiful design. Accordingly, spaces and places designed through effective engagement can reveal hidden histories and instigate future traditions. Designers and planners do not design and plan future traditions; rather, organizations like DCDC work with stakeholders to design community spaces, to design the opportunities for traditions to be made and communities to thrive. For both the Impact Detroit Community How-To Guides and DWPLTP, community participation was an integral part of the design and planning process, which in turn resulted in tools and frameworks that will better guide and support future work in Detroit's neighborhoods.

12

Paths to a Sustainable Future: Native American Community Building

Jamie Blosser

Outreach, participation, and feedback are critical to building relationships and a foundation for deep community investment based on trust. Participatory processes were essential tools in the Owe'neh Bupingeh Preservation Plan and Rehabilitation Project, in which the community used design process to self-determine its future.

Among indigenous communities, successful pathways toward sustainable development are community-based, utilizing a wealth of local knowledge. These pathways can influence design and building principles, and are essential to well-being. Many American Indians view their ancestral lands as a vital aspect of their heritage. Planning and design choices that negatively affect those lands, and lack of participation and leadership by community members in decision-making, can fracture the cultural fabric and deeply affect long term resilience and stability.

The ancestral village of Ohkay Owingeh, a Pueblo community north of Santa Fe, New Mexico—where the Owe'neh Bupingeh Preservation Plan and Rehabilitation Project is located (case study pages 202–5)—suffered deterioration for much of the 20th century.[1] This was primarily the result of federal policies toward Indian communities, which led the U.S. Department of Housing and Urban Development (HUD) to build subdivision-style wood-frame homes rather than constructing and maintaining traditional Pueblo residences. As a result, whereas the plazas were once surrounded by 150 homes, fewer than half of the remaining 60 adobe homes were full primary residences in 2005.

In 2000 the Ohkay Owingeh Housing Authority (OOHA) began a new development called Tsigo bugeh Village to provide much-needed new housing for

12.1
"North Side of Plaza, looking
East, San Juan Pueblo"
c.1912, photograph, The
Carlos Vierra Collection of
New Mexican Architecture,
Volume 3, Center for
Southwest Research,
University Libraries, University
of New Mexico.

tribal members. This was a low-income housing tax credit project that required serious study by the Tribal Council to ensure that outside investment would not adversely impact their sovereignty. A key goal of the project was that it would be designed according to Ohkay Owingeh values and heritage.[2] Community design meetings were held for the first time—potential residents were asked about what they needed in a home and elders told stories about what it had been like to live in the Pueblo. The tradition of the Pueblo's massing, orientation, and scale were incorporated into the contemporary development. OOHA wrote management policies to reflect not only HUD Fair Housing and other grant compliance regulations but also the traditional protocols of the Pueblo.

This project was a great success, largely because it was based upon the Pueblo's architectural heritage, and it became clear upon its completion in 2003 that the most important next project would be the rehabilitation of the historic Pueblo. However, there were significant obstacles, including: finding homeowners, creating deeds for centuries-old homes, determining appropriate preservation and construction approaches, and funding a combined affordable housing and historic preservation project.

In 2005 an informal conversation developed between Tomasita Duran of OOHA, Shawn Evans of Atkin Olshin Schade Architects, and myself. Without significant predevelopment and planning funds, it would be difficult to move

12.2
Exterior of completion of phase two, demonstrating infill rehabilitation, Owe'neh Bupingeh Preservation Plan and Rehabilitation Project, Ohkay Owingeh, New Mexico, 2012.

12.3
High school students learning ArcGIS at the Ohkay Owingeh Community Library, Owe'neh Bupingeh Preservation Plan and Rehabilitation Project, Ohkay Owingeh, New Mexico, 2006.

forward thoughtfully with the construction of the project. Shawn had already been tracking preservation funds in New Mexico, and we decided to apply for—and received—a small grant from the New Mexico State Historic Preservation Office (NM SHPO) to establish a preservation education program for tribal youth.

The youth preservation and education project taught surveying, drafting, ArcGIS software and GPS technology to six high school students for eight weeks. The students presented their work at the end of the summer to the Tribal Council, who were so proud that they sent the students to Sacramento to present at the National Congress of the American Indian (NCAI). Four of the students were awarded Gates Millennium Scholarships to attend college. Another student is currently a journeyman apprenticing as a plumber for the on-going rehabilitation project.[3]

This NM SHPO grant, while small, provided the foundation for the project. While the preservation and education project was underway, we were awarded another grant to establish an oral history program.[4] An anthropologist familiar with Ohkay Owingeh, OOHA and AOS Architects helped prepare survey questions with a tribal member, Josephine Binford, who is bilingual in English and Tewa, the tribe's native language. She then conducted the interviews with elders, many of whom preferred to speak in Tewa. The questions were centered on what it was like growing up in the Pueblo and what traditions they remembered. Tribal youth had the important job of acting as the audiovisual crew; since many of them did not grow up speaking Tewa, the experience underscored the importance of their native tongue.

These community building activities provided a pathway toward successful applications for grants to conduct historic building inventories, archival research, and documentation.[5] Eventually, we were awarded a large HUD grant that provided sufficient predevelopment funding to undertake a full preservation plan, and one of the first activities was the establishment of an advisory committee of Pueblo residents and homeowners.[6] Their role was to identify the owners of various properties so that we could begin to understand the criteria for development.

At this point, we understood the scope of the project as a multi-year, multi-million dollar endeavor. In order to properly phase the project, the design team needed to understand what the priorities would be once construction funding was secured: Would the project begin by rebuilding homes that were in total ruin, or would that exceed the allotted costs per home? Would families with a history of maintaining their property be given priority? Was it more important to stabilize and rehabilitate the central plaza area than the outer rings? Multiple meetings were held to establish ownership and priorities.

This was important work; however, it was clear that the residents could not address more sensitive questions related to larger cultural and sovereignty goals for the project. Questions related to appropriate materials, archaeological protocols, and tribal goals versus federally imposed requirements all required thoughtful dialogue with cultural leaders. In response, the Tribal Council established the Ohkay Owingeh Cultural Advisory Team (OOCAT). We held many meetings with the OOCAT to understand the Pueblo leaders' views on preservation and culture, and their desired solutions. One significant meeting included the discussion of applying traditional mud plaster versus cement stucco on the rehabilitated adobe homes. The conversation began with a materials science seminar by Ed Crocker, a renowned

Hutch Naranjo and Jamie
Blosser building an horno
at Tsigo bugeh Village,
Tsigo bugeh Village, Ohkay
Owingeh, New Mexico, 2002.

adobe professional, a twenty-year cost benefit analysis by the design team, and a site visit to an adobe home that had been well maintained with mud plaster. The OOCAT decided on a hybrid approach, utilizing mud plaster with some modern details, which exemplifies their preservation philosophy of respecting the past while living in the present.

These conversations made clear that the Pueblo leaders had their own strong preservation philosophy, based on their traditions and culture—and that their philosophy sometimes conflicted with federal requirements.[7] It was imperative to bring the tribe together with the NM SHPO and funding sources to determine mutually agreeable ways to move forward.[8] Shawn combined his research and analysis of archival photographs with a mapping of the historic Pueblo. The photographs clearly demonstrated that the Pueblo is dynamic, not a static object fixed in a distant, romanticized past. This research helped open a dialogue between the tribe, NM SHPO and funders, and led to an agreement about the Pueblo's preservation approach. As a result, a Memorandum of Understanding (MOU) was developed: it outlined a streamlined approvals process of the phased implementation of the preservation plan, including allowing only one umbrella environmental clearance for the multi-year project.

The first phase of construction began in 2010 with the rehabilitation of twenty homes for qualified low-income families. The design team incorporated significant preservation, training, and Indian Preference requirements in the bid process for contractors. Local tribal members would be trained in indigenous methods and materials to gain new skills for employment. Avanyu General Contracting, a woman- and Indian-owned firm in northern New Mexico, was awarded the contract and organized a construction crew of over 40 percent tribal members. Pat Taylor, an expert in adobe and traditional earthen building, trained the crew. The crew became so skilled at earthen building and restoration that, when the project tapered off, Pat hired them for other projects around the country, including the Presidio in San Francisco.

Tomasita also realized that without home-maintenance training, this work would not be sustainable in the long term. She committed a portion of OOHA's annual budget to cover the costs of homeownership mud-plastering trainings with Avanyu for the next five years. Participation is now mandatory for a family to receive a rehabilitated home.

The planning, design and construction process of Owe'neh Bupingeh acted as a catalyst for a critical dialogue regarding the heritage and fabric of community members' lives. Each of the phases engaged and respected the history, culture and values of the Ohkay Owingeh community. The project would not have been possible without the effort made by all team members to build relationships that fostered mutual trust and alignment of long-term goals. Through various outreach, participation, and inclusion methodologies, the Owe'neh Bupingeh Preservation Plan and Rehabilitation Project team demonstrated how a thoughtful design process can strongly impact the resilience and sovereignty of an indigenous community.

Notes

1   Pueblo Indians, or Puebloan peoples, are Native American societies in the Southwest made of many different tribes, cultural differences, and languages.
2   HUD established the Native American Housing Assistance and Self Determination Act (NAHASDA) to fundamentally shift the ways in which Native American communities receive housing assistance, to include the opportunity for self-determination.
3   The Gates Millennium Scholars Program selects students each year and funds their tuition through graduation, to attend any university or college they choose.
4   The Chamiza Foundation funded the program.
5   Various other grants were awarded from the McCune Foundation, the National Trust for Historic Preservation, and National Park Service.
6   The HUD Rural Housing and Economic Development grant allowed latitude for planning and pre-development. It was replaced by the HUD Rural Innovation Fund (RIF) grant.
7   Section 106 of the National Historic Preservation Act requires that projects utilizing federal funds in places designated on the National Register of Historic Places follow the Secretary standards.
8   The NM SHPO is contracted to confirm compliance with the Secretary of Interior Standards for the Treatment of Historic Properties.

13

Sustaining Collaboration: Extended Engagement

Lisa M. Abendroth, Bryan Bell

Collaboration is a staple of a public interest design practice. Knowing how to devise, construct, and then deploy scenarios for long-term engagement is part of the designer's required toolkit. This subtopic examines strategies where the community or audience imparts a defining value of what may support collaboration and how. Research and data-collection also have roles in this subtopic.

One of the enduring building blocks of a public interest design practice is extended engagement. This chapter discusses methods for sustaining meaningful alliances during the life of a project. How do designers equip themselves to coordinate collective understanding and achieve consensus while being vigilant to the iterative steps used in design development? How can sustained collaboration benefit the lasting evolution of a project? What skills are necessary for this type of work?

Chapters 10–12 discussed broad strategies for getting started with participation to effectively launch a project; here, partnerships define the on-going character of the work. Collaboration reveals the close partnering that occurs between design teams, participants, and stakeholders. It is something that has typically occurred in the confines of a studio, but public interest designers pursue this endeavor where the audiences or communities reside.

Sustained involvement with stakeholders requires planning and working together toward a common goal. This deepens and diversifies the level of input from that of isolated acts of participation alone and may manifest itself through a variety of constructs. A community that re-creates its narrative of place through storytelling, for example, engages in a shared and replicable activity that could only be the result of a multifaceted collaborative effort.

A Word About Research

Regardless of what specific strategies are used (many of which can be adopted from the participation tactics list on pages 322–5), collaboration as a mechanism for research should be embedded within the public interest designer's process. Research conducted through a framework of extended engagement reasserts the need to understand the impact of the work in various phases of implementation. Performance measurement and documentation gathered through a defined research process, which includes qualitative and quantitative methods, supports this goal.

Qualitative research helps define the nature of a design problem and is open to descriptive variables that may be subjective. Research methods can include observations and flexible or semistructured interviews—the format for recording information can involve audio, visual, and written documentation (e.g., field notes, visual mapping, sound or photographic recordings, to name a few). Quantitative research is not very flexible, as it relies on collected data to establish meaningful connections through numeric-assessment methods provided in predetermined controls. Patterns, categorizations, and statistical outcomes are typical results, which can be used to help answer questions.

The SEED process supports a balanced and informed research and data-collection process in order to reveal community voice through collaboration. The method used and the data gathered, as well as participating individuals or groups, should be clearly documented so that community or audience context is understood by all involved in the project. Research does not need to be logistically difficult, expensive, or time consuming; however, research supports the understanding of the nature or context of the problem and thereby provides a platform on which to build collaboration. Stakeholder observations, discussion groups, and informal community gatherings can qualify as forms of research, so consider the possible scope of relevant methods.[1]

The next two chapters describe the collaborative processes of two distinct projects—Firm Foundation (case study pages 190–3), located in the waterfront city of Banjarmasin, Indonesia, and People Organizing Place—Neighborhood Stories (case study pages 262–5), situated among six Dallas neighborhoods. These projects integrate a variety of tools and strategies to motivate long-term stakeholder engagement, including:

- Design workshops
- Game interactions
- Community action planning
- Physical model building and exploration
- Community meetings
- Sponsored events connected to local organizations
- Narrative collection through interviews, informal conversations, and discussion groups

These two projects share the use of storytelling and design workshops to connect people to the experience of a design problem. These strategies allow stakeholders from two very different contexts to become committed collaborators in their respective projects. Both storytelling and workshops can bring people together to reflect and share in a common activity or goal. Together, these projects demonstrate effective strategies for engagement in which the community are considered the "experts."

In redefining the role of designer as that of a guide, a conduit for understanding, and a mediator in the process of design development, the following concepts are discussed:

- Invest in time as a tangible quality of the project;
- Use the community design center to engage thoughtful decision making;
- Reveal the character and quality of a project through engagement and research;
- Understand that not all strategies are transferable—evaluation of each context is important;
- Realize that some engagement techniques may not reap benefits;
- Build relationships across a range of stakeholder groups;
- Continuously engage stakeholders;
- Coordinate activities that extend the meaning of the project (sponsor events);
- Amplify underrepresented voices;
- Create interactions (games and model building) that tease out design direction, user-group preference, and community-centered goals;
- Use storytelling and reflection as devices to elicit personal perspectives;
- Listen and observe;
- Disturb the status quo, invite participants to "dream," envision their ideal outcome through drawing or model making;
- Celebrate community, literally;
- Use scenarios to identify problems and related causes;
- Make meaningful connections between seemingly unrelated issues.

Notes

1   All forms of research require adherence to ethical codes of conduct. Human subjects included in research are best protected by informed consent and a protection of human rights that can include anonymity and privacy protection, access to research information, insurance of protection from harm, and the ability to conclude participation at any time. To learn more about human subjects research, see the Collaborative Institutional Training Initiative (CITI) at the University of Miami, available at https://www.citiprogram.org.

14

Storytelling for Social and Environmental Impact in Design

Michael Haggerty

An effective participatory design process involves bringing skills to the project and also using local methods of communication. In the Firm Foundation initiative, the designers utilized "community action planning" to facilitate dialogue and an intervention on water-related vulnerability in an Indonesian riverfront community. The team adapted these tools to a context in which residents used storytelling for collective decision making.

In Indonesia, storytelling is a rich tradition, rooted in Javanese Hindu myth performances known as *wayang kulit*, the shadow theater. Between 2009 and 2012, as the Yayasan Kota Kita team of architects, planners, and activists traveled the country on project assignments, we noticed how Indonesians derive equal pleasure from telling stories as they do from listening. In every Indonesian city, narratives are projected into the public realm—through loud speakers in mosques, as symbols on batik clothing, and from buskers at food stalls.

Stories are for Indonesians—living in the world's largest Muslim democracy—a way of communicating and connecting with each other as well as narrating their experiences in a rapidly urbanizing society. Our team of architects and planners worked with community leaders and the municipal government to invite residents from the city of Banjarmasin to Firm Foundation (case study pages 190–3), a participatory design initiative. All thirty residents brought stories. Yet we did not call the initiative a project or a workshop; rather, when the participants arrived for a week of design activities, our team received them with "Welcome to the journey!"

14.1
A new waterfront public space brings social activities to the river. Yayasan Kota Kita, Firm Foundation, Banjarmasin, Indonesia, 2013.

14.2
Residents create concept designs for waterfront improvements with design team member Stephen Kennedy. Yayasan Kota Kita, Firm Foundation, Banjarmasin, Indonesia, 2013.

The idea of a journey immediately lent a narrative quality to the collaboration. At the onset of the initiative, our team spoke about a city on a beautiful deltaic floodplain with rivers that became contaminated. We shared technical information about how river degradation had happened quickly, as the population grew without infrastructure for sanitation and waste management. Then the residents told us stories about the risks to health and livelihood they face due to the fact that they inhabit houses built densely on stilts over the water. Lastly, we used community action planning tools to formulate new stories—ideas for concrete steps residents, in partnership with local government, could take to address these problems.

Our team had seen and heard about community action planning while working in Indonesia, and we utilized this method during Firm Foundation to complement our public interest design sensibility. Community action planning is a method of collaborating with residents to analyze the problems they are facing, prioritize actions they want to take, and integrate the impacts they want to see with their capacities. This method was widely practiced in Indonesia following the 2004 tsunami, when

14.3

Design team-member Ahmad Rifai leads a problem tree exercise, during which residents analyze the root causes of issues in their community. Yayasan Kota Kita, Firm Foundation, Banjarmasin, Indonesia, 2013.

most of the country's architects and engineers worked alongside international development organizations to rebuild the Aceh province.

Community action planning is an effective tool for design because its very structure illustrates—in this case through storytelling—the interrelationships that govern vulnerability. The process usually begins with an exercise called a problem tree: residents create a list of problems, and then evaluate each one to identify its root causes. It is a powerful tool for understanding cause-and-effect relationships in the built environment.

Reaching the root cause of a problem often means perceiving everyday-life relationships that may not be readily apparent. During Firm Foundation, for example, our team learned that waste management is a major issue for residents in the community where we were working. Children often miss school when they get sick from poor air and water quality, which occurs because rubbish is burned or thrown into the river. There is no municipal waste management in the project area, and the road connections are too precarious for waste collection vehicles since houses are located along narrow wooden boardwalks over the water. Children missing school is the result of a factor that at first seemed peripheral to the problem—waste management.

Other community action planning tools are similarly pedagogical and synthetic. The team used a card game to facilitate a discussion about transforming specific neighborhood sites through new programs. The participants also worked extensively with physical models to conceptualize changes to the built environment, and then evaluated the spatial implications of their ideas.

Investing significantly in the engagement process means spending much more time working directly with residents than many designers are accustomed. Yet doing so broadens the potential impact of an intervention, since the relationships and reciprocities between vulnerabilities are more thoroughly understood. Designers can therefore operate systematically, targeting the root causes of problems and integrating the residents' many aims.

The outcome of our project was modest in comparison to the many issues residents faced. We partnered with the local community empowerment program, known as PNPM Mandiri, to build a thousand-square-foot public space over the

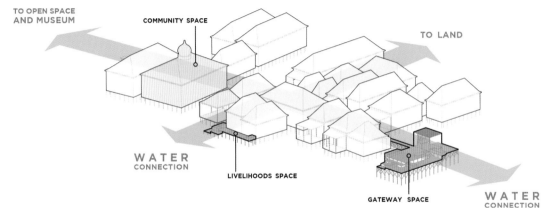

TO OPEN SPACE AND MUSEUM

COMMUNITY SPACE

TO LAND

WATER CONNECTION

LIVELIHOODS SPACE

GATEWAY SPACE

WATER CONNECTION

14.4
The project's place-making concept was to create a gateway to the area linking the riverfront with community assets. Yayasan Kota Kita, Firm Foundation, Banjarmasin, Indonesia, 2013.

water. It was a recreational space for children, a meeting area for the women's group, and a place for vendors to dock their boats. Almost immediately, the vendors lined up with their wares, and the family living next to the public space opened a part of their house to use as a food stall. While the new space did not directly address the issues that result in contaminated water, the design and construction processes initiated a dialogue about long-term, future improvements.

So a new story is beginning in this corner of the city in which water, livelihoods, public space, and mobility are interdependent. A place that had previously been perceived as marginal is now a visible model for riverfront development. With public activities now drawn to the waterfront, residents are talking about taking on other issues, like how to manage the waste that pollutes the river.

Community action planning also requires time investment because it is often difficult for residents to imagine alternatives to the existing environmental conditions that are the status quo. It was not easy for residents to contemplate changing the waterfront, because the river's polluted condition seemed like the natural state of things rather than something to proactively redesign. This is a real challenge in the field, something humanitarian workers know very well.

Disturbing the status quo means designers become a part of the story, not its sole authors. Arriving in the midst of an ongoing story requires architects and planners to be especially observant of what is already happening. When public interest designers look carefully at native practices of communication, storytelling, and collaboration, it can lead to opportunities to enrich their projects and empower the people they work with by combining their design training with what they find in the field.

15

Amplifying Community Voice: Neighborhood Identity Development

Brent A. Brown, Emily Schmidt

Active and resilient neighborhoods are the foundation of a successful city. People Organizing Place (POP)—Neighborhood Stories is an on-going series of public events and activities, organized in partnership with Dallas neighborhoods, focused on capturing and sharing the voices of neighborhood residents and leaders.

During a one-year period, buildingcommunity WORKSHOP (bcWORKSHOP), a nonprofit community design center, partnered with six Dallas neighborhoods to discover their histories and development and collaboratively craft a pop-up event celebrating the neighborhood's identity and unique contribution to the city (case study, pages 262–5).[1]

Neighborhood identity in Dallas has usually been latent and overlooked rather than celebrated. Among the many competing narratives about the city—from the media, local government, the visitors' bureau, advertisements, and others—those

15.1
Each neighborhood story is celebrated through a pop-up event including a gallery, a film screening, creative sharing, and re-created experiences from past and/ or current social activities. People Organizing Place— Neighborhood Stories, Dallas, Texas, 2012.

offered by Neighborhood Stories amplifies the voice of places often underrepresented or overlooked in these dominant narratives, celebrates individual neighborhoods, and builds consciousness about the role of design in our lives. This advocacy and place-making work is an important aspect of bcWORKSHOP's mission to improve the livability and viability of communities through thoughtful design and making.

For this first series of events, bcWORKSHOP chose six neighborhoods in four different regions of Dallas revealing the variety of forces of change that shape the city and impact local communities. All are neighborhoods with a history of neglect, disinvestment, or substantial change: the Dallas Arts District, La Bajada, Dolphin Heights, Wynnewood North, Tenth Street Historic District, and Mount Auburn. These neighborhoods demonstrate impacts of de facto and de jure segregation, the potential of infrastructure to spur growth as well as sever and isolate, the role of industry in providing employment and influencing quality of life, the polarized effects of suburbanization on the inner city and the growing outer ring, and the successes and failures of preservation in the face of redevelopment.

The character and unique qualities of each Neighborhood Stories event was shaped during the immersive engagement and research phase. This involved evaluating context-specific strategies and discarding the expectation that a successful engagement strategy of one community would translate to another. The basis for and direction of each event relies on continuous engagement with neighborhood stakeholders (residents, former residents, business owners, property owners, elected officials, and others) through participation in neighborhood-association and crime-watch meetings, pop-up displays, walking the neighborhood, one-on-one conversations, personal interviews, flyers placed in local businesses, and more. Some engagement and outreach activities yielded no tangible results, and as a neutral, external group, it was at times difficult to build trust.

15.2
In the Mount Auburn neighborhood of Dallas, a paseo (walk/bike procession) was organized around installations making neighborhood landmarks, historic events, and sharing community answers to questions, like "Where do you live, work, and play?" People Organizing Place—Neighborhood Stories, Dallas, Texas, 2013.

Brown and Schmidt

15.3

Each story exhibit presents neighborhood change through the use of mapping and other visual tools to illustrate physical development, social events, and people. People Organizing Place— Neighborhood Stories, Dallas, Texas, 2013.

Relationship development with a core group of neighborhood stakeholders, who invested in sharing their stories, was the key to the project. bcWORKSHOP had previously partnered with community organizations in three of the six communities on other projects. Dedicating significant time to developing and furthering these relationships prior to planning specific activities was the most important step in the process. In the most successful collaborations, residents themselves led event promotions, secured donations, and served as hosts. Although the level of ownership varied by event, interest from attendees and residents indicated that there is a capacity for a high level of ownership in future events.

Common elements of the events are an exhibit of neighborhood history, screening of a short neighborhood documentary featuring interviews with current and former residents and advocates, and continued collection of the communities' stories through film and writing, all within a reunion-type atmosphere connecting friends and neighbors. A converted shipping-container gallery space displayed historical maps, photographs, and artifacts curated into an exhibit that chronicles the social and physical evolution of each neighborhood. This display developed a collective narrative of experience, marking historical turning points and their causes. While certain elements are repeated, the scale, activities, and tone reflected the distinct character of each community. Each event took place in a meaningful neighborhood location and included activities unique to that place: in La Bajada, attendees sledded down the levee of the Trinity River, while in Tenth Street, church choirs performed on one of the neighborhood's many vacant lots.

More than 1,500 Dallasites have participated in Neighborhood Stories events to date, strengthening community cohesion, amplifying the voice of underrepresented and disenfranchised neighborhoods, and stimulating dialogue on how past policy and infrastructure decisions affect communities unevenly within one city. Exhibit

Amplifying Community Voice

15.4
Neighborhood Stories are cataloged and shared in print and digital form, providing an accessible record for current and future citizens. People Organizing Place— Neighborhood Stories, Dallas, Texas, 2013.

material was published in a booklet and distributed to residents and local institutions, creating a permanent and accessible record of the neighborhood's story. Each documentary film, approximately thirty minutes long, was similarly distributed and also available for free online.

Outcomes varied by event: In Tenth Street, the production of the event and the celebration itself catalyzed the emergence and convergence of local leaders, who are now heading up neighborhood-improvement and safety projects. In Mount Auburn, the event led to the reformation of the neighborhood association, which had been dormant for nearly a decade. In Wynnewood North, cards and the Wynnewoodopoly game were used to collect preferences for the upcoming redevelopment of the local shopping center. These preferences were shared with city staff and the property owner.

In continuing to develop the Neighborhood Stories program, there are two key ways that this set of activities can be deployed. The first is partnering with neighborhoods that elect to use storytelling and communal gathering to reflect on the past and future of local development. The second is the use of these events as a launching point for further community-engaged design work by inviting communities first to a period of reflection and dreaming, then to a consideration of how they wish to see the community develop in the future, and finally to a decision about the role that neighborhood advocates have in securing that development. This program is viewed as replicable in a variety of contexts. It is easily scalable from the collection and sharing of stories about place to holding a large-scale community celebration.

Notes

1   This series was funded primarily through a National Endowment for the Arts ArtWorks grant, Trinity Trust, and Citi Community Development.

16

Doing More: Issue-Based Design and the Triple Bottom Line

Lisa M. Abendroth, Bryan Bell

The importance of designing through the lens of issues—social, economic, and environmental—cannot be over emphasized. Leveraging these considerations into a project expands problem-solving opportunities, and we can literally do more with less because we understand the constellation of problem-impact. Design solutions that accommodate for this create systemic outcomes, unlike others that only address a single concern.

All issues are design issues. This belief captures the spirit of the public interest design movement, as it boldly defines a practice based on doing more as a result of the interconnected nature of the triple bottom line (see the Introduction pages 2–3). This chapter introduces the relevance of the triple bottom line concept and how it applies to a public interest design practice. The SEED process provides a framework for analyzing how a singular design problem reveals a multiplicity of embedded issues—it reveals vital connections important to the long-term sustainability of a project.

By tackling some of the world's most critical issues, public interest designers are transforming lives and demonstrating the value of design in a variety of contexts—often involving underserved or marginalized people and where funding and resource allocation can be scarce. The issue-based approach consolidates the actions of public interest designers and overcomes these inherent burdens in resilient ways.

SEED's mission is to ensure that *every person should be able to live in a socially, economically, and environmentally healthy community*. The SEED Network approaches this vision of health in the broader context of the triple bottom line in which social, economic, and environmental factors create a framework through which a community's long-term and sustainable health can be assessed.

This definition of health extends beyond medical connotations—many projects address health in the traditional sense but also through the broader lens of the holistic well-being of a community (e.g., by skills training, an economic issue with social impact). (See MASS Design Group's Umusozi Ukiza Doctors' Housing in part 2 and part 3, pages 167–71 and 246–9.) Issues related to skills training are not isolated challenges, yet every community and every audience has a unique set of priorities, many which are complex and interwoven.

Community Defined Success

Public interest designers are encouraged to adopt a holistic approach when considering the triple bottom line of community needs, looking comprehensively at the social, economic, and environmental fitness of a project and the people connected to it. The triple bottom line can help guide communities in the prioritization of actions stemming from their needs and goals. The interwoven nature of the issue-based approach can also allow communities to seek out or develop a project that meets several needs at once, for example, education and job creation, or hunger and affordable housing.

Critical issues are the challenges that define life struggles. These help clarify the unique priorities of every community. Issues provide a link between the technical knowledge of designers and the local knowledge of communities, and can help delineate more than one goal that defines the project's purpose. When a breadth of issues is addressed, an enhanced stakeholder engagement process can ensue, bringing diverse individuals together for collaboration. (A comprehensive list of critical issues can be referenced in part 3 in the Issues Index, pages 185–305.)

Design has the unrealized potential to assist communities in addressing their most vital needs. Only recently, for example, has the relationship between design and the environment been clarified, with the important result that the public and designers, together, are creating more sustainable design solutions. With this evolutionary step we ask, what next? What other ways can design make significant contributions to address the many challenges we face around the world—not just environmental but social and economic as well?

Today, both the public and design professionals are realizing that design must be more than a luxury service that only a few can afford. Design, instead, should be an essential tool in directing positive change in the environment and beyond. Employment, disease prevention, and access to clean drinking water are examples of issues that are part of a larger network of human productivity, the solutions to which are essential to the preservation of our world. True sustainable design, lasting design solutions that impact lives, is an extremely rich and complex practice that requires an imperative focus. This is a worthy challenge for design to realize its true potential, evident in projects from the next two chapters.

Savda Ghevra in New Delhi, India, is the site of the sanitation infrastructure Potty Project (case study pages 302–5), which considers social challenges related to the safety of women in relation to open defecation, to family health and productivity, and to the environmental issue of public sewage infrastructure. The SAGE Affordable Green Modular Classrooms (case study pages 270–3) in Oregon and Washington examines the environmental issue of sustainable manufactured classrooms, social challenges surrounding student performance, and the economic issue of affordability to the school districts. These two projects serve as models, demonstrating how a singular problem is linked to a tapestry of related issues.

These projects reinforce the following concepts related to issue-based design:

- Connection between systems (physical infrastructure and political, for example);
- Voice of the community reinforces issue prioritization as point of entry into a project;
- Emphasis on the long-term nature of building lasting relationships and on protraction of process;
- Use of local capacity and skills in project development reveals an asset-based approach to project implementation and maintenance;
- Connection between social health and environmental conditions in the built environment;
- Social impacts (education, health) inextricably tied to environmental and economic considerations;
- Expanded definition of architect, designer, or planner to that of community advocate;
- Role of designer as educator;
- Design process supports integrated social, economic, and environmental goals;
- Understanding the relevance of integrated goals and the inherent value of design that solves more than one problem at a time.

17

Unthinking Sanitation for the Urban Poor

Julia King, Dr. Renu Khosla

The Potty Project in Savda Ghevra addresses a combination of social, economic, and environmental issues that are embedded in the development process—in this case, the complexity of delivering sanitation infrastructure. Understanding of stakeholder needs and political constraints helped shape planning and design outcomes.

At noon on a day in 2010 Savari Devi, 35 years old, ventured out of her house in Savda Ghevra (SG), the largest planned resettlement colony in New Delhi, to defecate in the open (CURE 2010). Suddenly, she was grabbed by three men and dragged into some nearby bushes. Fortunately, a young boy saw what was happening and ran for help, and Devi was rescued. Devi's story is an extreme case, but not uncommon—open defecation leaves women, particularly young girls, vulnerable to sexual harassment and abuse. The issue of inadequate sanitation involves not just the dangers, humiliation, and indignity associated with defecating in the open but also significant costs due to poor health and lowered productivity. The lack of sanitation in India is emerging as a pervasive development challenge and is compounded by rapid urbanization and peri-urbanization.

SG is located about forty kilometers west of New Delhi and is home to more than 8,500 families (approximately 46,000 people), who have been evicted from inner-city slums.[1] The resettlement of SG involves relocation on small, semiserviced plots. Centre for Urban and Regional Excellence (CURE), a development nongovernmental organization (NGO), has been helping SG resident resettlement since 2006.

17.1
Examples of self-built housing
in the resettlement colony of
SG, Potty Project, New Delhi,
India, 2013.

This chapter addresses the complexity of social, economic, and/or environmental issues as told through the Potty Project story of delivering sanitation infrastructure to SG. The project is an interplay of three processes:

1) The design, planning, and installation of a sanitation system, with its particular technical and financial attributes and requirements.
2) A consultation process, which moves from an aggregate of individual wants to collaborative action to a political institution, with representation.
3) The movement in and out of the consultation-to-political process, which involved the authors, the NGO, engineers, local government, and contractors.

The Potty Project (case study pages 302–5) is a community-based sanitation system connecting household toilets to a shared septic tank and an up-flow filter that forms a decentralized wastewater treatment system (DEWAT) to treat the black and gray waters. The cluster septic tank and DEWAT are technologies capable of being built, managed, and maintained by the community, and are adaptable to the rapid, unplanned development of the urban fringe, characterized by a lack of conventional sewerage.

Instead of waiting for the state to extend mostly inadequate and certainly expensive services, the project could be a model in the early stages of a resettlement for collaborative building of the primary connective tissue or infrastructure. A *gali* (street) is an aggregate of individual houses, while a sanitation system binds individuals together through collective need. It builds a direct connection between the physical and political collaboration necessary to obtain general health and decency, central to the project.

17.2

A series of cards were made with ten issues, including sanitation, health care, and education, distributed to the attendees, and used to generate discussion on life in SG. Then a series of *chapattis*—round disks, playing on the imagery of the bread accompanied at each meal—were distributed and used to cast votes on the most pressing concern to that individual. The use of chapattis is an original participatory technique used by CURE in many of their projects—the playful nature lightens the gravity of the important, but often-loaded, issues. Potty Project, New Delhi, India, 2013.

17.3

Models and colored straws were used to show how the proposal could adapt to housing type. This form of design-play is iterative and becomes a social event that engenders a sense of ownership. This was crucial to community acceptance. Potty Project, New Delhi, India, 2013.

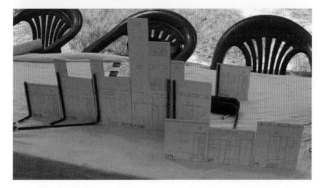

The Potty Project began when, during a community meeting, sanitation emerged as the single biggest issue, particularly with women.[2] The challenge was how to engage and foster optimism without raising false hope.

Long-term engagement occurred through repeated interactions in large design workshops and smaller street meetings. Models showing typical sanitation conditions and retrofitting options captured community attention. Of particular interest was that this approach demonstrated the capacity to customize solutions to individual needs, home spaces, structural quality, resources (affordability), and to capitalize on people's investments.

Once there was sufficient community support, CURE needed to secure funding and government approval, which took more than a year. This—maintaining the community's confidence in CURE, the designers, and the project—was the real test of community engagement and was made possible by the continued presence

17.4
Members of the local community built aspects of the sanitation infrastructure. Potty Project, New Delhi, India, 2014.

of the NGO teams and parallel livelihood projects. Almost two years after the first meeting, construction began.

It was the demand for sanitation and the process of engaging to develop the technology and financing models that brought the community together. Certain involved community members organized themselves into street management teams. The street leaders acted as a bridging body between CURE, technical consultants, and community and helped establish a network of people and systems for the longer (post-construction) management.

For the project to develop, it was important to build on and expand local capacity and skills, as well as institutionalize operation and maintenance strategies. The emergence of community representatives signaled higher political awareness and function, and, of course, trust. The most positive advance rose from the shared management of the project: a formally organized and registered Residents Welfare Association (RWA), the first of its kind in a slum resettlement colony in Delhi. RWAs are typically associated with organized upper- and middle-class neighborhoods. The sanitation project became a tool for people's empowerment and a means by which residents could directly negotiate with the state, without CURE's support.

For any solution to work and be sustainable, retrofitting of such infrastructure requires community buy-in. This is a complex metabolism (particularly when imagined at a master-planning scale) where important nuances are easily lost. Retaining that local, bottom-up capacity on an urban-planning scale is a challenge for the future.

In conclusion, sanitation systems in industrialized countries evolved through successive improvements more than a century ago. Individual practices using bucket latrines were replaced by communal systems of piped water and sewerage. It is simplistic to think that sanitation in developing countries can upgrade in a single step. India will continue to face huge urban growth, and the ensuing sanitation challenge cannot be served by conventional sewerage approaches which neither individuals nor the state can afford.

References

CURE (Centre for Urban and Regional Excellence), ca. 2010. Sanjha Prayas: Bhagidari with the Poor: Socio Economic Study Report—Savda Ghevra Resettlement Colony.

Notes

1   SG is planned to house 20,000 families totalling around 120,000 people as part of a site and service scheme. In addition, currently 10,000 apartments are under construction and due for completion by 2015.
2   The community meeting was held on the March 10, 2011 in a SG park where more than thirty male and female residents attended.

18

A Balanced Approach to the Demand for Classrooms

Margarette Leite, Sergio Palleroni

Social, environmental, and economic integration was inherent to the project process: a solution that addresses the social consideration of healthy learning environments must also meet environmental and material fabrication criteria and economic factors related to tight school budgets.

The SAGE (Smart Academic Green Environment) Affordable Green Modular Classrooms project (case study pages 270–3) is a response to the growing realization that modular classrooms are becoming the primary structures in which children in the United States will be educated for the foreseeable future. Today, modular classrooms, often referred to as "portables," provide more than 50 percent of new classroom spaces. Economic factors that have led to a national crisis in school funding have resulted in increased investment in these inexpensive and poorly made modular classrooms. While these classrooms may provide a cheap, quick solution for schools, a growing body of evidence shows that choosing cost savings over quality may be creating significant health risks and performance-related deficiencies for many students.

The project was initiated by us through academic channels as a way to begin a community-wide discussion about what could be done to address some of the negative aspects of modular classrooms. Following a somewhat typical path for university-based initiatives in its early stages, the project included a symposium and a community design charette, which brought together all of the stakeholders, from parents and teachers to school officials and members of the modular-construction industry. In addition to arriving at nine potential responses to current conditions, the symposium helped bridge one of the main roadblocks to addressing the problems

of modular schools: the distrust among stakeholders. The conference and charette demonstrated a shared commitment to changing the system and helped advance the next steps in the process.

Students of architecture and engineering were encouraged to become involved in the project by investigating the nine potential solution scenarios generated at the charette, with the cooperation of the alliance of stakeholders. The charettes and the follow-up research and coursework created a network of community members that served as grassroots supporters of alternative classrooms for Oregon students. In addition, it laid the groundwork for a collaborative relationship between design faculty, students, and an Oregon-based modular-building manufacturer, Blazer Industries. This collaboration has proven crucial to the success of the project.

Simultaneously, a series of opportune occurrences helped to propel the project forward. The project team was able to take advantage of Oregon Solutions, a unique state-mandated focus on K–12 education. The Green Modular Classrooms project was designated an official Oregon Solution by Governor John Kitzhaber in 2011. This designation, while not financially supported, resulted in project-management assistance from the state and identified the issue as regionally significant, bringing greater awareness of the issue to the citizens. It fostered momentum and a broader support that helped bring together important stakeholders. This consortium was critical to addressing the multifaceted issues that included financial accessibility, building-code interpretation, and energy-efficient engineering.

The Green Modular Classrooms taskforce met regularly during one year, with the mission to create a prototype classroom. At the end of the year-long design process, the Modular Building Institute invited the team to showcase the classroom at the 2012 U.S. Green Building Council's (USGBC) international Greenbuild Conference. Pacific Mobile, a local modular distributor and collaborator in the Oregon Solutions process, stepped in to purchase this first prototype, the SAGE classroom. The classroom was built at Blazer Industries and shipped to San Francisco for the conference, where it received significant attention. Since the conference, several

18.2
Interior rendering of the SAGE
Classroom, SAGE Affordable
Green Modular Classrooms,
2012.

18.3
The new SAGE classroom
at Hazelwood Elementary
School, SAGE Affordable
Green Modular Classrooms,
Lynnwood, Washington, 2014.

modular distributors—chosen by the project team for their reputation and commitment to improving the quality of modular construction—have signed contracts to distribute SAGE classrooms. A legal framework for maintaining quality control over the SAGE classroom ensures that the integrity of the product is not compromised by price cutting. Portland State University faculty and students helped create this framework both as community service and as a means to generate a nominal amount of revenue from royalties to fund future research and development of the SAGE classroom.

The triple bottom line of social, economic, and environmental integration was inherent to the project process. Any solution that seeks to alleviate unhealthy conditions for the greatest number of students would, by necessity, need to address the environmental quality and healthfulness of the materials that go into its fabrication. Furthermore, an emphasis on health requires an assessment of natural light and fresh

18.4
The SAGE prototype at the 2012 Greenbuild Conference, San Francisco, SAGE Affordable Green Modular Classrooms, San Francisco, California, 2012.

air, which have impacts both environmental as well as on a child's ability to learn. Also, to maximize reach, it must address the immediate economic effects of reducing initial costs as well as long-term savings of energy-efficient designs. The SAGE classroom costs only 20 to 25 percent more and provides a 50 percent improvement in energy efficiency over other modular classrooms typically used in Portland's public schools, and is 33 percent or less than the cost of other green modular classrooms. With the use of photovoltaic panels—the number of which are relatively small at SAGE's low electrical demand—the classroom can also be made energy neutral.

The first fifteen SAGE classrooms in Oregon and Washington were set in place for the 2014–15 school year. These pilot classrooms will be monitored for performance and user comfort to inform future research and improvements. In addition, they will serve as teaching tools for schools that want to provide their students with opportunities to learn about the environment in terms of solar orientation, weather, and materials, as well as about understanding the energy impact of choices in lighting, heating, and ventilation.

Other unintended but critical components of the project's success included the expansion of the typical role of the architect: the architect's services included creating and structuring community awareness and participation, developing a business model for the dissemination of this innovative product, and acting as an advocate for schools through presentations and lectures throughout the community. This last role is perhaps one of the most impactful, as it serves to empower parents, teachers, and students to make informed decisions about their own schools and communities through education.

19

Assessing Results: Defining and Measuring Success

Lisa M. Abendroth, Bryan Bell

Design evaluation can be an effective means of assessing project impact. How is success defined in a project, and in what ways are public interest designers responsible for measuring successes as well as lessons learned? As public interest design grows into a profession, it is imperative that designers be accountable and play a more active role in the assessment of project results—whether through post-occupancy or implementation assessments performed internally or in tandem with a certified third-party reviewer.

There are three fundamental questions in any public interest design project: 1) What are the critical issues faced by the community? 2) What does success look like? 3) How will that success be measured? The success of a project can be envisioned and communicated by defining clear goals, and success can be measured through an evaluation of the results. These are important considerations for any project. Two other important features described here include setting benchmarks and performance measures. Defining goals and setting benchmarks can lead to documenting impact measurements through qualitative or quantitative data. By implementing and communicating the steps involved in the process of defining and measuring success, a designer can create a culture of transparency, which builds trust and encourages community participation.

 Achieving a critical mass of projects that support designer accountability through the evaluation of results—projects that serve marginalized people— reaffirms the value of the topic of this chapter. Public interest designers are especially accountable when working in underresourced contexts, as the limited resources need to be effectively directed to address the greatest needs. Failures are particularly damaging when working with marginalized groups.

The evaluation of design outcomes is more crucial today than it has ever been as we try to address increasing challenges that result from the world's decreasing resources. Not all design disciplines—or even well-intended designers—agree on the importance of this action, or even how to accomplish it. But for public interest design to succeed, documenting results of a design intervention should be a foundational step in every project—it is the only way to provide proof of what we set out to do. This goes beyond producing the work; it requires assessing how the design impacted change, both positive and negative, both during early implementation and after.

The following points provide a tangible structure for assessing a project, defined here by how goals were met, benchmarks identified, and performance measurement defined. Integrating these steps into a comprehensive plan will help assure evaluation is timely and that it takes place. It will also help build a shared knowledge base.

The nine steps of the SEED process are described in detail in chapter 8 (pages 93–7). The steps specific to defining and measuring success are summarized below.

Defining Goals (Step 3)

Set goals early in a project and include how goals will be met through timelines and activities. Plan for the inclusion of stakeholders in this step.

Setting Benchmarks (Step 5)

Benchmarks are useful markers that show how goals are being met within the design process. Stakeholder-defined benchmarks further validate the need to understand the relationship between goals and results.

Defining Performance Measurement (Step 6)

Performance measurement results from quantifying benchmarks. A descriptive analysis of how the project is on track toward intended outcomes can be revealed in this step.

Documenting and Reporting Results (Step 8)

Documentation is one way of reporting the results of a project. This step creates an opportunity to authenticate how goals were accomplished and how benchmarks and performance measures were assessed.

Evaluation and Reflection (Step 9)

Accountability is achieved by meeting intended project results. Verification of having met intended goals occurs through a thorough project plan that includes documentation and analysis.

Reflection provides a space for determining what was done well and where improvements are needed in the continuing legacy of public interest design work.

The following two chapters describe how assessment of results impacted two projects—the Durham Performing Arts Center (case study pages 234–7) in North Carolina and the Healthy Laddoo Project (case study pages 186–9) in Pune, India. Both respond to the requirement for project documentation, benchmarking, and evaluation of results in complex circumstances with diverse stakeholders and multiple issues. These projects demonstrate a commitment to long-term development and embody strong connections to place—their partner organizations, funders, and stakeholders are critical actors in the understanding of project results.

These projects explore the following concepts:

- Establish metrics that address multiple issues;
- Verify benchmarks from diverse stakeholders;
- Meet and report on benchmarks;
- Be accountable;
- Use benchmarks in evaluation;
- Use a combination of quantitative and qualitative measures;
- Understand the role of time in project evaluation;
- Define success (what constitutes "good");
- Include measurements early in the project plan;
- Use iteration to support outcome development;
- Know evaluation limitations;
- Reflect on transferable knowledge and lessons learned.

20

Designing Solutions to Childhood Malnutrition

Ramsey Ford, Kate Hanisian

Design Impact's Healthy Laddoo Project demonstrates how measuring project results can be woven into the design process for maximum benefits to all involved. By making evaluation a priority, designers and stakeholders can define and measure the impact of their work, thereby verifying quality and effectiveness of solutions.

Be Sure that "Good" Actually Happens

Design is powerful because it has the ability to both imagine and realize a potential future. And, while this forward-looking practice has contributed incredible change to our world, it has historically done a poor job of measuring its own impact. In public interest design, it is imperative that we remove this blind spot from our process, so that we do not just believe we are doing good, but that good actually happens. Measurement is essential to a responsible public interest design project because rigorous measurement is a requirement for securing support to sustain and scale successful interventions, and understanding the impact of the work is crucial in justifying the expense of a design to community partners.

Designers tend to be good storytellers, and measurement enables them to tell even better stories that are supported by data and thus all the more compelling to funders and community stakeholders. In Design Impact's Healthy Laddoo Project (case study pages 186–9), great effort was put into measuring the change in children's nutrition levels during the six-month pilot test of the intervention. The results of the pilot—42 percent of children moving out of the World Health

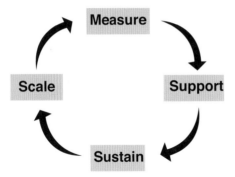

Organization's (WHO) severely malnourished category—were communicated to staff, parents, and funders, and catalyzed continuing support for the distribution of *laddoos*, a traditional Indian cookie. The Healthy Laddoo redesigned this small, round treat as a nutritious food—an example of the virtuous circle that can be created by measurement. Investing in measurement, and incorporating it into your project plan, can help a successful project get support, sustain itself, and even reach more people.

Put Measurement First

The most important aspect of measurement to remember is that it requires time and is not something that is simply done at the end of a project. To fully comprehend the impact of your work, measurement needs to be given priority. Understanding the current state of affairs and identifying the right problems to solve are essential first steps.

Fortunately, a clever designer can learn how to incorporate measurement into the early stages of the process. When approaching any new project, a responsible designer does not start with a solution in mind but looks for a better understanding of the issues at hand. Often, this takes the form of ethnographic research, environmental scanning, and secondary academic research, which often uncover complex and overlapping causes. To act on a complex issue, designers employ sense-making tools, such as a root-cause analysis, to uncover and identify the causal relationships that contribute to an issue. Identifying these relationships helps drive the design process but is also necessary to understand what needs to be measured.

Our process started with an investigation of the local environment and stakeholders, with a secondary research into malnutrition and existing interventions. During the Healthy Laddoo Project, we found that childhood malnutrition was often

Laddoo Nutritional Analysis

COCONUT + WHITE MILLET LADDOO
Ingredients:
Wheat flour (187.5 grams), White millet flour (187.5 grams), Desiccated coconut (125 grams), Flax seed (125 grams), Ghee {50 grams (2 tablespoons)}, Jaggery (350 grams), Cardamom {2.5 grams (7-8 pods)}, Milk (warmed) {250 milliliters (~ 0.75 cup)}

Nutrition Analysis:

Energy Value	404 Kcal/ 100g	Fat	16.1 g/ 100 g
Protein	8.9g/ 100 g	Sugar	10.5 g/ 100g
Carbohydrate	55.9 g/ 100 g	Iron	5.80 Mg/ 100g

PEANUT LADDOO
Ingredients:
Wheat flour (375 grams), Sesame seeds (125 grams), Peanuts (150 grams),Ghee {50 grams (2 tablespoons)}, Jaggery (375 grams), Cardamom {2.5 grams (7-8 pods)}, Milk (warmed) {250 milliliters (~ 0.75 cup)}

Nutrition Analysis:

Energy Value	405 Kcal/ 100g	Fat	16.7 g/ 100 g
Protein	9.4 g/ 100 g	Sugar	5.8 g/ 100g
Carbohydrate	54.2 g/ 100 g	Iron	3.03 Mg/ 100g

caused by a combination of a lack of money, a lack of awareness, and cultural norms. We engaged staff, parents, and children in developing potential solutions and used this research to determine the indicators we needed to measure to understand our impact—the children's height, weight, and hemoglobin counts.

Taking Aim on Impact Measurement

Identifying the right indicators to track is essential to project evaluation. When time for measurement has been included in your project, you can often get an idea of what kind of social, environmental, or economic indicators should be tracked. We also use a simple model called AIM to assess if the proposed indicator is *achievable, impactful, and measurable*. It helps us understand what a good outcome might be for the project.

AIM challenges the designer to consider several questions in selecting indicators and suggesting outcomes for their work. These are captured in Figure 20.4. Asking these questions allows designers to develop outcomes and decide which ones are the most appropriate for their project and measurement capabilities. It is

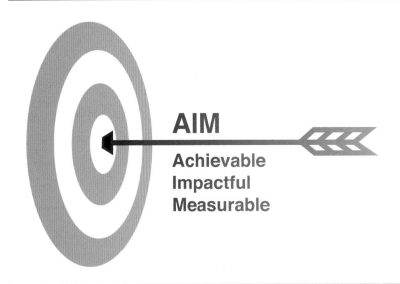

AIM

Achievable
Impactful
Measurable

important to note that this is a qualitative process—there is often more than one correct way to measure the impact of the project.

Iterative Outcome Development

Public interest designers generally focus on developing new solutions, and prototyping plays a major role in this process. Prototyping requires testing and refining, iteratively developing ideas into higher-fidelity models. Measurement and evaluation should follow a similar process of iterative development, moving from simple to complex as a project advances. At the beginning, you may need to only justify the validity of the work to an internal team, which will only require a relatively light amount of measurement. As your solution grows, you will need to refine your evaluation to prove validity, effectiveness, and ability to scale. These more complex evaluations are needed to justify the greater investment of resources for implementation-to-implementation partners and funders.

Recognize Your Limitations

While there is a great deal that a designer can accomplish in evaluating their public interest design projects, it is important to recognize that evaluation can be complex and that you need to know the limits of your ability. Setting up large-scale evaluation programs, like randomized control trials, require the support of professionals with training in evaluation. Do not be afraid to find a partner to support your work.

The AIM Model of Outcome Development

Achievable: How achievable is the outcome?	What are the indicators of success? What level of change would be considered a success? Is this level of change possible in your project?
Impactful: How impactful is the outcome?	Can this impact create the change that is desired? Does the impact have a direct causal relationship to the issue? Is there evidence that connects or correlates the impact to the issue?
Measurable: How measurable is the outcome?	Is the impact possible to measure? How difficult is it to measure the impact? How will you measure the impact?

Before most projects scale to impact millions, they start as smaller local interventions. Much of the public interest design profession is centered on the development of these smaller, emergent solutions, and a major criticism of this movement is its lack of scale. Better measurement is closely tied to increased scale, and the responsible designer will make time to incorporate this into the process. If you are serious about good design, then you need to get serious about measurement. By effectively identifying the most achievable, impactful, and measurable indicators to measure, you set yourself up for the possibility of really making a difference with design.

21

Setting the Stage for Social, Economic, and Environmental Achievement: Benchmarking the Durham Performing Arts Center

Philip Szostak, FAIA

The Durham Performing Arts Center project utilized a comprehensive set of social, economic, and environmental benchmarks to document accomplishment of goals across a range of performance measures. Accountability was quantified by meeting specifically stated standards of achievement in city- and resident-driven development categories.

In serving as architect and developer of the Durham Performing Arts Center (DPAC) (case study pages 234–7), a 2,800-seat Broadway-style theatrical venue, Szostak Design of Chapel Hill, North Carolina, set forth a series of social, economic, and environmental benchmarks deemed most beneficial to a broad spectrum of Durham's citizens. These metrics established targets for workforce development and training, local sourcing of labor and materials, living-wage salaries for the theater's staff, and the use of sustainable technologies.

The goals for each of these benchmarks—developed collaboratively with the City of Durham and community representatives—were written as binding provisions in each contract necessary for the design, construction, and operation of the venue. For example, specific benchmarks were included in the project's contract with its construction manager (CM), coupled with corresponding penalties for failure to reach the goals. Every month during construction, the CM was required to submit documentation of the number of personnel recruited for workforce training, minority participation as a percentage of the overall workforce, the value of local sourcing of construction materials, and labor as a percentage of the total construction

21.1
The Durham Performing Arts
Center, completed in 2008,
has served as a catalyst
for the revitalization of
downtown Durham, North
Carolina. Durham Performing
Arts Center, Durham, North
Carolina, 2008.

contract amount. In addition, the CM presented copies of invoices detailing the use of sustainable construction materials and the percentage of project-construction waste that was either recycled or re-purposed. This documentation was reviewed for contractual conformance, first by the architect's office and then by the city's project manager. Only after confirmation from both parties that the CM achieved the required standard in each category of benchmarking would the CM's application for payment be approved. A contractor has a powerful vested interest in preserving a steady flow of capital into an ongoing project—tying social and environmental performance to the issuance of funding approval proved an extremely compelling tool in ensuring benchmark conformance.

One environmental benchmark was particularly important, given the building site's former use as a municipal bus-maintenance facility. The soils in and around the project were contaminated with a number of potentially hazardous chemical agents, most notably benzene. Prior to the initiation of construction and following a supervised remediation of the contaminated soil, the CM was required to install nineteen monitoring wells both within and outside the new building.

Each month during construction, the contents of these wells were tested to determine whether any hazardous agents were still present in the groundwater. The results of these tests were also submitted and reviewed as part of the application for payment process. This testing continues to this day, though its frequency has been reduced due to the favorable results recorded during construction and early building occupancy.

Similarly, the DPAC co-operators, the Nederlander Organization and Professional Facilities Management (PFM), are contractually obligated to provide periodic accountings of its employment practices, including its adherence to living-wage-

21.2
DPAC impacts, 2008–2013, Durham Performing Arts Center, Durham, North Carolina, 2008.

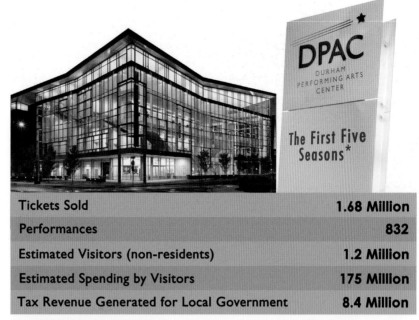

The First Five Seasons*

Tickets Sold	1.68 Million
Performances	832
Estimated Visitors (non-residents)	1.2 Million
Estimated Spending by Visitors	175 Million
Tax Revenue Generated for Local Government	8.4 Million

Source: DCVB, City of Durham; Spending impact calculation using IMPLAN data from IHS Global Insight and DK Shifflet and Associates
*November 2008 - June 2013: four full and one partial season.

salary requirements and equal-opportunity-employment standards. Szostak Design works with Hunter Associates (Salem, Ohio) and the Durham Visitor and Convention Bureau to access conformance with these benchmarks as well as to prepare an annual economic impact assessment of DPAC (since 2009), with particular attention to the realization of the project's original goals. The City of Durham also performs an independent annual audit of the theater's operations, both to determine the city's share of profits in the operation and to ensure conformance with employment and wage targets. In 2013, DPAC returned $1.8 million in shared profit to Durham's coffers by staging 179 performances viewed by more than 383,000 visitors. The value of annual economic activity in Durham's downtown district attributed to DPAC's presence is estimated to be $28 million, which has in turn spurred growth in entrepreneurial development, employment, and wages at all income levels.

In addition to these more broadly focused assessment measures, PFM prepares an event report of each performance held in the venue. The report details attendance numbers and the results of post-performance user surveys (approximately 25 percent response rate). This information includes the distance patrons traveled to attend the event, the use of ancillary dining and hospitality opportunities in the vicinity, and the overall satisfaction with their experience. There are eight areas of assessment: parking, box office, entry experience, staff greetings, assistance from staff, safety and security, restrooms, and elevator wait times. The report also summarizes anecdotal comments from patrons that have led to improvements in the facility's operation and planning. As with the annual reports,

the operator's event report cards are distributed to the architect and city personnel for review.

The annual economic-impact report, audit, and event report cards are available for citizen review on the City of Durham's website, and the performance of DPAC's operator is the subject of an annual City Council presentation. Given the co-operators' excellent record of both financial success and achievement in meeting DPAC's prescribed social, economic, and environmental benchmarks, their contract has been renewed for an additional five years, with options to extend the relationship over the course of the next three decades.

Finally, Szostak Design continues to closely monitor a variety of social media, which offer useful anecdotal evidence of the community's perception of the project and the resulting socio-economic benefits. For example, one recurrent criticism of the facility gleaned from Twitter posts is the dearth of women's restrooms. As a result of the feedback, Szostak Design planned and is presently administering the

21.4
The project's goals for workforce development and training focused on granting community members new skills in the construction industry, designed to enhance their opportunities for long-term, high-wage employment. Durham Performing Arts Center, Durham, North Carolina, 2008.

construction of an addition to DPAC that will increase women's restroom capacity by one-third.

Each of these assessment tools offers the designers, developers, and municipal representatives, as well as the general public, a clearly accountable template of social, economic, and environmental performance. It is a critical method of reflective practice that not only legitimizes the realization of a commonly held set of community goals and ambitions but also serves as a model for all future civic endeavors in the City of Durham.

22

Scaling a Project: Uniting Diverse Stakeholders

Lisa M. Abendroth, Bryan Bell

Public interest design projects can be scaled up to effect broad and long-term change. This chapter considers ways to expand a project through SEED methods of monitoring, evaluation, and communication. Project scaling requires the efforts of many, and diverse stakeholders are central to that effort. Diverse stakeholders can help validate a project's value and realize the most valuable social, economic, and environmental measures. These stakeholders can also contribute rich and varied resources and build capacity even in challenging contexts.

Scaling, a process of expansion in terms of numbers (quantity of people impacted), range (variety of people impacted), or locations (places where people are impacted), suggests a systemic type of project development and implementation across sectors and constituents. Scaling is realized through a guiding vision or plan; through an inclusive process this vision can grow incrementally over time. Stakeholders included in the process can add to the collective vision of the project, and this process can be the very mechanism needed to achieve a project's long- or short-term life. Scaling usually builds off of a series of local endeavors that include a host of partners, such as on-the-ground participants, local, national or international organizations, nonprofits, funders, corporate partners, and nongovernmental organizations (NGOs). These diverse stakeholders comprise the organizational qualities of a project team that impacts broad and universal change within a community or audience group.

Project expansion requires resources—time, funding, human capacity, and the social, economic, and environmental space for progress. Public interest designers can be managers in this development that requires brainstorming, experimentation, and vision for growth over time. Leadership of this type develops capacity in others toward a specific purpose, achieving a successful project vision that is invested in by many. One person is not telling all of the others what to do.

This capacity building can happen in a variety of ways: horizontal (expansion across regions and people), vertical (expansion in strata that includes levels of power), and functional (expansion beyond a single issue) (Hartmann and Linn 2007). Each offers a distinct approach to scaling a project; however, given the organic way in which development can occur over time, most projects incorporate a blend of these. Understanding the opportunities in each method can provide a regulated and/or focused approach to project evolution, especially in terms of anticipated adjustments to program or plan.

Scaling is a goal that can merge with design process. The two can be closely interwoven so as to ensure a thoughtful and innovative approach to identifying opportunity as the project matures. Replication of best practices in the project plan—whether having learned from failures or successes—can help propel the work forward into new developing markets. Know your value chain—not only the players who will make your product or service a reality but also those who may be recipients of built environment outcomes. Map benefits and analyze costs along the value chain so opportunity can be quantified, and consider how producers and consumers benefit.

Pilot programs offer an excellent way to test feasibility in context. The pilot can be a framework for assessing small-scale outcomes of the intended larger-scale project. A variety of requirements can be addressed, including design alternatives, cost variables, material and fabrication options, use monitoring through community or audience groups, distribution, management, and oversight. The broad monitoring and evaluation of these at the pilot stage can support informed decision making later and provide evidence necessary to substantiate funding requests.

Communication of project results can be built into project scaling. The ways in which a project is documented and shared creates a context for organizational-internal and public-external understanding that moves beyond the confines of the project itself. Communication is the very action that verifies understanding and value—how the work is validated beyond its implementation is imperative to the sustained life of a professional practice. By finding innovative and effective ways to educate others about the work we do, we expand understanding and thus grow the viability of the field and create greater demand. All are desired effects of scaling a project.

The two chapters that follow reveal strategies for expanding project relevance in discrete contexts. The Umusozi Ukiza Doctors' Housing project (case study pages 246–9) in the Burera province of Rwanda is a model for how long-term commitment to place-based development—activating vertical, horizontal, and functional scale integration—has affected local, regional, and national healthcare agendas. Likewise, the Easy Latrine Sanitation Marketing program (case study pages 238–41) in Cambodia demonstrates the effectiveness of a steady and determined focus on improving the quality of life at a local and then national level. This project offers lessons on working with diverse stakeholders in the scale up of a market enterprise.

These projects explore the following concepts:

- Identify and develop markets;
- Investigate market or development opportunities;
- Analyze benefits and costs;
- Establish a phased pilot program;
- Build long-term relationships with NGOs and national political entities that are decision makers and funders;
- Build strategy into design goals;
- Replicate processes from one project on-site to another when appropriate;
- Embrace local sourcing;
- Understand existing market failures and successes;
- Define a value chain;
- Consider how producers and consumers benefit from the work;
- Understand results and be prepared to communicate them to constituents;
- Identify a range of stakeholders;
- Monitor, evaluate, and communicate.

References

Hartmann, Arntraud and Johannes F. Linn. 2007. "Scaling Up: A Path to Effective Development." 2020 Focus Brief on the World's Poor and Hungry People. Washington, DC: International Food Policy Research Institute: 2. Accessed on July 23, 2014. http://www.ifpri.org/publication/2020-focus-briefs-worlds-poor-and-hungry-people?print

23

Lessons from Rwanda: Scaling Up Holistic Approaches to Health Facilities

Michael P. Murphy Jr., Alan Ricks, Annie Moulton

Building capacity in a rural Rwandan community demonstrates how dignified health care and supportive doctors' housing address the broader determinants of health— nutrition, income security, education, and safety—while serving as a national model for scaling up health care delivery.

Holistic Health Care in Rural Butaro, Rwanda

In 2008 the Burera province in Rwanda was home to 354,000 people, but almost no doctors (National Institute of Statistics 2011). The Rwandan Ministry of Health, led by Dr. Agnes Binagwaho, and Partners In Health wanted for Burera what they were working tirelessly to achieve throughout the country: dignified health care that addresses the broader determinants of health—nutrition, income security, education, and safety—not just acute and urgent care. The resulting Butaro Hospital, completed in 2011, is a symbol of the possibility of that vision. And, as the architects, we learned a significant lesson: that a building and the building process, if designed right, can help to address well being, especially for communities most in need. Architecture too can heal.

Housing

In 2011 the hospital was open and treating patients. Members of the community came on monthly *umuganda* days (national day of service) to help maintain the hospital but also on other days to help, reflecting a sense of ownership and commitment to the sustainability of the project. And we witnessed something else happening: new doctors arrived from across the country and abroad, willing to live near this new hospital on a hill and test the notion that high-quality care was possible anywhere as long as the local environment was appropriate. At that time, the doctors were housed in a cramped, converted administrative building, formerly used for the war trials after the country's 1994 genocide. Some MASS Design Group staff—including Michael Murphy—had even lived there during the hospital's design, sleeping four to a room. While close quarters offer a certain charm, it was hardly adequate for doctors and their families in the long term. Daniel Ponton, an ardent supporter of the program, asked how surgeons and doctors could possibly perform optimally when living in substandard conditions and remarked that doctors would never stay and that retention rates would be low.

We hatched a new idea—if we offered better housing, could we attract and retain more doctors? Could the housing, by proxy, improve performance and overall quality of health care? From this question emerged the Umusozi Ukiza (healing hill) Doctors' Housing (case study pages 246–9). This prototype was not without criticism. One expatriate doctor questioned the role of architecture when there were so many other needs and so few resources.

As the project neared completion, one of the doctors sent his spouse in Kigali, Rwanda's capital, a photo of the housing. She responded immediately, asking when they would be moving. This response reflected what would become clear: better housing would bring the best doctors. This began to emerge as a potential solution to the "brain drain" that had brought so few doctors into the region.

Equally important was the opportunity to expand the methodologies innovated during the hospital's construction, further developing craft through training programs. The process of design-build in such a rural setting permitted design fellows—recent architecture graduates of the Kigali Institute of Science and Technology—to work closely with the site crew on innovative design and material applications that resulted in a quality design product, with nearly everything custom fabricated. MASS learned about local materials and methods from the site crew; and the site crew acquired considerable experience in material testing. The impact of design thinking in a region where crews are accustomed to building generic units cannot be understated. Members of the site crew even openly discussed wanting to replicate the designs on their own homes.

Scale the Work

Today, Butaro Hospital doctors consider the town their home and provide exceptional care at the facility—in fact, mortality of children under five has dropped by 63 percent, and maternal mortality has been cut in half since the hospital's opening (Farmer et al. 2013, 21). The construction has strengthened the marketable

23.1
Community members work on the roof structure on one of the houses. The project employed some 900 people, 200 of whom learned valuable skills in masonry, carpentry and metalwork. Umusozi Ukiza Doctors' Housing, Butaro, Rwanda, 2012.

23.2

IMPACT BY THE NUMBERS

8 doctors' accommodations were built for a region previously without access to physicians.

30 people were trained in seismic CSEB construction processes, which produced **29,000** earth blocks.

138 people learned masonry skills, **46** of whom became high-skilled, professional masons.

60 people received training in steel bending and carpentry.

50 people learned terracing practices, a skill valued to stabilize Rwanda's agricultural hillsides.

900 jobs created in the construction process.

400,000 US dollars distributed to the local and regional economies.

job skills of the local labor force, and an influx of people, goods, and services have come to Butaro to support the hospital—a Bank of Kigali, shops, and restaurants have opened, and the Rwandan government opened a hydroelectric power plant. Signs of economic growth are omnipresent. Individual lives are affected as well: Anne Marie Nyiranshimiyimana, a master mason and the first female who worked on the Butaro Hospital and the doctors' housing, has inspired a collective of other female masons. Through the building process, Nyiranshimiyimana helped foster equality.

23.3
The volcanic stone outer walls, which have since become a local building tradition, were carefully finished and assembled by newly trained master masons. Umusozi Ukiza Doctors' Housing, Butaro, Rwanda, January, 2011.

Rwanda Innovates

Communicating the value of additional housing is crucial as MASS works to scale this model into new regions. But without global precedence for the quantitative measurement of design interventions, articulating the true impact of the doctors' housing both quantitatively and qualitatively and catalyzing social and economic growth is a challenge for MASS.

Given the immense success of the housing in contributing to the quality of care and retention of physicians, project partners, including Dr. Binagwaho, have acknowledged the need to provide more and diversified housing options for nurses and other medical staff. Expansion to include additional on-site accommodations will contribute to the ministry's broader goal of Butaro being an exemplary teaching hospital and model for holistic and dignified health care. While the current housing provides for single-family homes, the new Butaro Shared Housing will supplement the current housing by providing quality communal-style housing for fifteen medical professionals. These accommodations will foster a sense of community among staff and will also allow for further training, material research, and innovation, building on the successes of the hospital, doctors' housing, and new cancer infusion center.

In the interim, while exhaustive quantitative evaluation is underway in Rwanda, we are reviewing the increasing need for housing for teachers in the Democratic Republic of Congo and for mothers in Malawi. These are two places where the Umusozi Ukiza Doctors' Housing can stand as an example, in the latter case how to rethink maternity waiting homes to reduce maternal mortality rates of expectant mothers in rural villages.

Evidence-based design has shown how architecture can directly better lives: improving performance metrics, reducing recovery times, and increasing health care access. Secondary infrastructure and environments also matter—when we look at indirect metrics like retention, dignity, overall building performance, and economic growth, we see quality infrastructure as integral to long-term development goals. This is our broader ambition—to build systems that support and foster the highest

23.4
Craftsmen put finishing touches on the Umusozi Ukiza Doctors' Housing. Umusozi Ukiza Doctors' Housing, Butaro, Rwanda, 2012.

quality care and inspire those on the front lines to continue their tireless work. To Rwanda we owe a great debt for showing us, as architects, that architecture matters in ways that are beyond the quantifiable. As Partners In Health cofounder, Dr. Paul Farmer, told us, the question we should ask is not what is the cost of having architecture but what is the cost of not having architecture.

References

Farmer, Paul E., Cameron T. Nutt, Claire M. Wagner, Claude Sekabaraga, Tej Nuthulaganti, Jonathan L. Weigel, Didi Bertrand Farmer, Antoinette Habinshuti, Soline Dusabeyesu Mugeni, Jean-Claude Karasi, and Peter C. Drobac. 2013. "Cutting Premature Death in Rwanda." *BMJ*. 346 (7894): 20–22.

National Institute of Statistics, Rwanda. 2011. *EIVC3 District Profile Burera District*, Republic of Rwanda, accessed 04/10/14. http://statistics.gov.rw/system/files/user_uploads/files/books/BURERA.pdf

24

Evolving the Sanitation Marketplace in Cambodia

Yi Wei

An inclusive stakeholder process representing all members of the value chain—both producers and consumers—helps inform the scaling of a sanitation marketing initiative in rural and developing countries. The implementation of the Easy Latrine in a pilot program helps establish a baseline for product and system development in which diverse user groups are active agents in the design and scale-up process.

Forty percent of the world, or 2.5 billion people, do not have access to toilets, resulting in dire consequences. Diarrheal illnesses kill more children than HIV, malaria, and tuberculosis combined. Well-meaning subsidies can depress demand for toilets, stymie private markets, and discourage ownership. Purchasing a latrine is often prohibitively expensive and logistically challenging.

Prior to iDE's intervention, very few private sectors were interested in producing and selling affordable, aspirational, and accessible sanitary latrines to the rural poor. iDE identified the unique needs, desires, and barriers and created a product, the Easy Latrine (case study pages 238–41), that households wanted to buy and businesses wanted to sell, creating a sustainable solution that can be scaled across the country.

Easy Latrine Design Process

The design effort followed a user-centered design methodology that began with in-field contextual observations and interviews with the key stakeholders involved in latrine manufacturing, installation, and use. The observations were distilled and

24.1
Latrine business owner
Mr. Rim uses the "site seller,"
a handy sales tool that helps
him explain to a potential
customer the benefits of
buying an Easy Latrine: you
can dig the hole yourself,
today; you can build it with
whichever shelter you want
and can afford; and, it is
home-delivered. Easy Latrine,
Cambodia, Ongoing.

synthesized into a framework that illustrated the potential opportunities for the design and showed where the design offering fit into the greater sanitation market. Multiple rounds of brainstorming, prototyping, and user testing were undertaken to develop the latrine designs. From the multiple iterations, a design direction emerged that addressed user needs as well as marketing concerns around how to position the benefits and costs of latrine ownership.

User-Research Phase

During the first phase, iDE spent two weeks in the field talking with villagers, concrete-ring manufacturers, retailers, and masons to understand behaviors, needs, and desires regarding latrines. All interviews and observations were performed in context—at the villager's home, at the retailer's store, and at the ring producer's lot. From the user research, eight design principles were established to guide the work:

1) Let everyone go wet: Cambodians have an extremely strong preference for pour-flush latrines over dry pits.
2) Allow self-build at entry level: A simple do-it-yourself package will help lower costs.
3) Work from the bottom up: Focus on designing the underground waste capture and storage components, as those are the elements least familiar to most users.
4) Reflect *in progress*, not *temporary*: Position the latrine as upgradeable over time to avoid users waiting to save for the most expensive model.
5) Divide the pit, slab, and shelter (metaphorically): Doing so makes the task seem easier and more manageable than a seemingly complex black box of parts.

24.2
In addition to innovations in the product, latrine producers have figured out innovative ways to install the heavy concrete product—using rope threaded through holes to lift the rings into the ground. Easy Latrine, Cambodia, Ongoing.

6) Set the stage for the mason: Reduce complexity and eliminate the need for expensive skills, like brick laying, but allow the mason to provide simpler, cheaper services, such as mortaring the pieces together.

7) Show few options but enable many: Offer one simple underground solution to avoid paralysis by analysis, but allow users to customize the shelter according to their financial means and aesthetic preferences.

8) Support procurement: Reduce the complexity of the purchasing process.

Prototype Reviews and Pilot Results

In the course of the design project, iDE took four trips to the field after the initial user research in order to review prototypes—a number of 2-D and 3-D models—with stakeholders—villagers, masons, ring producers, and retailers.

During the sixteen-month implementation phase of the pilot project, which was funded by USAID and technically supported by the Water and Sanitation Program (WSP) of the World Bank, households—without subsidy—purchased 10,621 Easy Latrines. The Easy Latrine served as a catalyst to stimulate general business interest to join the latrine market by providing proof of concept of consistent profit from selling latrines to rural households. For every one Easy Latrine sold by an iDE-trained business, 1.12 other, non-iDE latrines were sold by other businesses. These businesses saw the growth in market opportunity as a result of iDE's performance, resulting in an increase in the baseline rate of latrine adoption by fourfold. A total of twenty-four local businesses were engaged in the manufacture, promotion, and sales of the Easy Latrine. On average, the annual revenue of engaged businesses increased by 259 percent.

Scale-up Results

Given the successful results of the pilot, iDE secured funding from the Bill & Melinda Gates Foundation, the Stone Family Foundation, and WSP to further scale-up the market-based approach, from the original two provinces to a total of seven provinces throughout Cambodia. In just over two and a half years, the scale-up program in Cambodia has facilitated the sale of more than one hundred thousand latrines by more than one hundred local businesses, and creating a ripple effect of 1:1—during the same time, for every latrine sold by an iDE-trained business, another latrine was sold by another business, resulting in the sale of more than two hundred thousand latrines and impacting the lives of more than a million people.

The successful results of the pilot project also helped secure funding for sanitation-market-development efforts in five other countries—Bangladesh, Ethiopia, Nepal, Vietnam, and Zambia. Replicating process, not the product, iDE designs products and business models that are context appropriate.

The consumer includes not only the end user but all stakeholders who influence the experience of the end user, i.e., all members of the value chain who

24.4
The underground portion has been completely installed and is now ready for the family to build a shelter of their choice and their means. The options usually include natural materials (bamboo, leaves, wood), zinc sheets, or concrete. Easy Latrine, Cambodia, Ongoing.

would affect the user's purchasing experience, from before the moment the user even considers the purchase to post-purchase maintenance.

Engagement with users at every step of the design process is key to effective rapid prototyping. You will never know if it will work until you test it out with the user. True innovation does not lie in the product alone. It is essential to get the product right, but the product should act as a catalyst for a thriving business model that serves the needs of both the producers and consumers.

Part 3

Documenting the Value of Public Interest Design: Case Studies and Issues Index

25

The Issues Index: Expanded Opportunity through an Issues Approach

Lisa M. Abendroth, Bryan Bell

The Issues Index presented here is a resource for communities, audiences, and designers to use to understand how design solutions can address a range of discrete yet interwoven critical issues. Cataloged by issues, each case study demonstrates lessons learned and what has worked in specific contexts that may be transferable to new contexts.

Composed of thirty interdisciplinary case studies, the Issues Index documents social, economic, and environmental challenges that are internationally relevant. The result is an aggregate of almost ninety diverse issues that reflect the breadth of global problems affecting many sectors. Organized according to primary and secondary issues, each project case study includes a summary, the goal, the community served, participation methods, results, and the names of collaborators (partners and stakeholders) and design teams. The accompanying narrative and images provide important evidence of civic engagement, participatory design process, and benchmarks toward results that substantiate a relevant public interest design practice.

Projects featured as case studies were originally submitted to the SEED Network. Applicants used the SEED Evaluator tool to document how their project goals, issues, participation, research methods, and results were met. The SEED process establishes a standard for all projects presented in chapter 26 and unifies the actions of public interest designers—it helps us critically assess how the world's most challenging problems are being tackled through the public interest design framework. These case studies exhibit a range of ways of working and varied project results that constructively contribute to the discourse surrounding this field.

While the case studies mark an important moment in the evolution of a young practice, we acknowledge that some are in the early stages of being verified by the SEED process. We express the importance and need for evaluation of results and documentation of outcomes so as to expand the body of knowledge of this field. While these projects continue to develop and move through the SEED Evaluator toward certification, a moment of reflection is captured in part 3 where projects are documented in order to build a foundation from best practices.

The combination of case studies and Issues Index in part 3 functions as a reference guide that can be used to track projects based on similar or related issues. This can be useful in comparing benefits for projects with similar goals. Additionally, the Appendix to the book allows for enhanced cross-referencing of projects based not only on issue but also on discipline, location, or engagement methods used. In combination, these create context and provide a wide view of the healthy diversity emerging in this field.

The issue-based framework was introduced in chapter 16, "Doing More: Issue-Based Design and the Triple Bottom Line" (pages 133–5). The Issues Index shows that designers are expanding the opportunity to impact change by being open to redefining problems and embracing the complexity of embedded issues. By allowing a design problem to be examined through the lenses of macro and micro issues, a single design problem can be broken down into distinct component parts that reflect a tapestry of social, economic, and environmental concerns. This expansion–contraction process is one that should be woven into the planning and design process early on and not simply layered on top of an existing process at the end of a project.

Realizing design problems as human issues effectively moves the discussion away from the designer, as isolated actor, into the realm of the public's interest— the community's interest. It positions designers as mediators who possess specific and often technical skills but who are adept in identifying and translating need so that a broad constituency is activated by a multi-tiered response. When a solution addresses more than one problem and more than one group of stakeholders contributes to determining the outcome and process—the value of design is exponentially increased.

The Potty Project (pages 302–5) case study shows the significance of an issue-based approach. Although the project was defined as a sanitation problem, the design team's participatory process uncovered underlying factors that resulted directly from stakeholders reinforcing that much more than a sanitation system alone was at stake. The issue of women's safety is a growing concern, especially among females in this New Delhi, India, community, who do not have access to safe, sanitary, or private facilities. Elaborated upon in project community meetings, women's safety was identified as a social issue of high priority—one that has its own goals and benchmarks for assessment attached to it.

Secondary issues were identified through a similar process of inclusive and participatory engagement with stakeholders from the community and the local government and was supported by a nongovernmental organization (NGO) development partner, Centre for Urban and Regional Excellence (CURE). A second social concern is family health and productivity, an issue that bridges women's safety and the literal application of a public sewage infrastructure. A family's ability to lead a productive and healthy lifestyle is reinforced by the defining cultural circumstance. A great desire within the community to shift the political balances in favor of those in need puts control in the hands of the people this project serves. The response to a lack of acceptable infrastructure emerges as an incubator for community building and empowerment.

Certainly, sanitation has health outcomes that cannot be ignored. In this project, an analysis of sanitation starts with an assessment of environmental impacts that expand to social well-being (eradication of disease leads to improved health) and reinforce the secondary issue above of family health and productivity. Open defecation and the subsequently polluted natural-water systems are indicators of the environmental implications of the project. Benchmarks specific to the environmental issue of public-sewage infrastructure provide a tangible, time-based measurement of challenges overcome and goals met. Parsing out and framing this infrastructure problem as an environmental issue can help the design team, the NGO, the community, the funders, and the local government meet streamlined and focused objectives while measuring the changing environmental impact of the system.

The importance of unpacking each issue and assessing its capacity to mark social, economic, or environmental change is evident: each discrete issue identified within the larger problem provides an opportunity for validation. When the needs of many are addressed in this manner and through the various phases of a project, designers are able to increase opportunities for meaningful change.

All those involved in the realm of public interest design can work with greater focus when communities and audiences are empowered to identify how their needs can be addressed by design. And while not all projects address each silo of social, economic or environmental concern, the case studies presented in part 3 demonstrate a considerable diversity and breadth of need, and offer important precedents across those three areas. These projects show results and provide evidence of impact and long-term systemic change that can be translated into a recognized value to the communities served.

In order for designers to prove worth through this field, we must engage in radical realignments of process and provide evaluations of outcomes that definitively affirm what was accomplished, and how. Pursuing a community-centered and issue-based approach can help guide that motivated productivity. In a world abundant with challenges, public interest designers are uniquely positioned to respond with an informed and principled practice. That practice must embrace not only the people we serve, and their respective cultures, but also the systems in place that dictate our way of working to a consequential and beneficial end.

26

Case Studies and Issues Index

Lisa M. Abendroth, Bryan Bell

Healthy Laddoo Project
Pune, India

Summary:

Through the development and distribution of Healthy Laddoo, a protein- and iron-rich food supplement, Design Impact and the Deep Griha Society (DGS) are reducing malnutrition in children from low-income communities around Pune. DGS focuses its work with the marginalized and administers a variety of community programs, including a childcare nutrition center. DGS cares for approximately 325 children daily.

Goal: Reduce anemia and malnutrition in Indian children

Laddoo is not only a supplement to daily food intake—it has been identified as a path out of poverty. A well-nourished child can attend school and achieve goals that align with social and economic empowerment well after his or her school years.

26.1
Early laddoo protoypes were tested with Deep Griha staff and parents. Healthy Laddoo Project, Pune, Maharashtra, 2012.

26.2
After the malnutrition issue was identified the staff held
a brainstorm to consider a variety of potential solutions.
Healthy Laddoo Project, Pune, Maharashtra, 2012.

26.3
Extensive research was completed on children's nutritional
needs. Healthy Laddoo Project, Pune, Maharashtra, 2012.

26.4
A plate of healthy peanut
laddoos. Healthy Laddoo
Project, Pune, Maharashtra,
2012.

26.5
The laddoos were made
by hand in small batches.
Healthy Laddoo Project, Pune,
Maharashtra, 2012.

Community:

The seventh largest city in India, Pune has experienced a rampant growth in technology and industry; however, this growth isn't improving the lives of those living in slum communities where education, health, and nutrition are severely compromised. Pune is located in the state of Maharashtra, where a reported forty-five thousand children die yearly of malnourishment.

Participation:

In a call to action from DGS, the snacks were developed in collaboration with a Design Impact fellow, who led the DGS community, parents, and children in the creation and testing of four high-protein, high-iron laddoo variants. Parents were involved in educational outreaches, interviews, and data collection to determine the children's consumption habits. Parents also motivated the program to organize the next step—making the laddoos commercially available.

Results:

The National Agriculture and Food Analysis and Research Institute in Pune conducted the nutrition analysis of the sesame-seed and peanut Laddoo varieties, establishing a health standard for the product. In a study that analyzed the gains of sixty-eight children who consumed one Laddoo every other day for six months, there was a 42 percent increase in the children's heights and weights.

Collaborators:

Deep Griha Society; Hirabai Cowasji Jehangir Medical Research Institute; Elephant Design; Unventured

Design Team:

Design Impact: Anisha Shankar, Jaskeerat Bedi, fellows; Ramsey Ford, design director

2

Environmental: Clean Water Advocacy

Social: Public Space

Economic: Water Economies

Firm Foundation

Banjarmasin, Indonesia

Summary:
Firm Foundation reduces environmental vulnerability and heightens awareness about water issues in Banjarmasin by building a positive relationship between waterfront residents and the city's river systems. The design team, led by the NGO Yayasan Kota Kita in partnership with AECOM and the Indonesian community empowerment program PNPM Mandiri, facilitated a participatory-design process that resulted in a new one-thousand-square-foot public waterfront space.

Goal: Advance understanding of water issues
Three priority issues were communicated to the local government: access to piped water, a restored boat port, and improved sanitation. The design delivered a new port, bringing public activity to the river and supporting the municipal government's recent policies to make the river an asset for city development.

26.6
The project supports water-based economies by facilitating access to boat vendors. Firm Foundation, Banjarmasin, Indonesia, 2013.

0 1 5 M

26.7

The plan makes the river an asset for development by bringing social and economic activities to the waterfront. Firm Foundation, Banjarmasin, Indonesia, 2013.

Community:

The residents of Sungai Jingah in Banjarmasin rely on rivers for fishing, transportation, and informal vending. The river is also utilized for drinking water, sanitation, and solid-waste disposal. Nearly all of the 273 residents in seventy-five households in the project area live in dwellings with toilets that empty into the water below. Community life is negatively impacted by unplanned growth and a lack of waste removal and basic infrastructure.

Participation:

Twenty-seven residents forming three teams that represented different neighborhood areas participated in a three-day planning and design workshop—in the format of a design competition. Using a variety of participatory design tools—including "transect walks," problem tree exercises, model making, and

Firm Foundation

26.8
During a "gallery walk" design team-member Addina Amalia facilitates a discussion about water issues. Firm Foundation, Banjarmasin, Indonesia, 2013.

26.9
The project provides a new space for recreation and gathering in an area where the only public realm is a system of narrow boardwalks over the river. Firm Foundation, Banjarmasin, Indonesia, 2013.

26.10
Located at the intersection of a river and canal at the periphery of Banjarmasin, the neighborhood has become a visible part of the city with the addition of the new public space. Firm Foundation, Banjarmasin, Indonesia, 2013.

card games—each team prioritized issues, identified an improvement site in the neighborhood, and created a concept program and design. Each team presented their solution to a jury of government officials, and the design team developed and constructed the winning concept in collaboration with residents and staff from the community-empowerment program.

Results:
Success was measured by the implementation of improvements to infrastructure. Post-implementation assessments track water hookups and reduction in numbers of toilets that empty into the river, and interviews document changes in residents' attitudes toward water.

Collaborators:
AECOM UrbanSOS Program, Bappeda Kota Banjarmasin, DTRK Banjarmasin, PNPM Mandiri Korkot Banjarmasin, residents of Sungai Jingah

Design Team:
Project lead: Yayasan Kota Kita

Impact Detroit Community How-To Guides
Detroit, Michigan

Summary:
Impact Detroit, an initiative of Detroit Collaborative Design Center (DCDC), developed a series of easy-to-use community-development guides that provide information on often-complex processes. Derived from years of community input, the guides teach people how to realize their own community projects, leveraging the expertise and resources of community stakeholders.

Goal: Foster community development with accessible information
The highly functional guides describe key processes of small-scale community- and business-development projects to make them more achievable for neighborhood groups and individuals. By breaking down the steps with clear graphics and concise text, the guides empower people to tackle goals.

Community:
The guides target audiences in Detroit—individuals, community groups, and business owners—working toward community- and neighborhood-revitalization.

26.11
The guides were translated into Spanish at the request of the Detroit community development organizations in Spanish-speaking neighborhoods. Impact Detroit Community How-To Guides, Detroit, Michigan, 2013.

26.12
Impact Detroit is an initiative of the DCDC that facilitates a network of partners collaborating on the realization of community development projects. Impact Detroit Community How-To Guides, Detroit, Michigan, 2013.

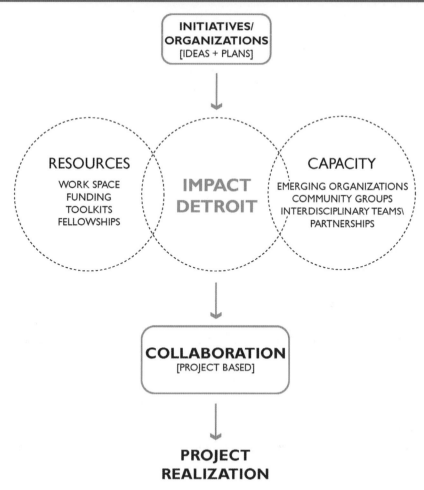

With challenged city services, grassroots and neighborhood-based alliances have been championing social, economic, and environmental renewal efforts.

Participation:
Impact Detroit learned about the need for this tool after years of interviewing, observing, and working in partnership with communities in need of development support. The guides are a direct result of a collaborative process built around feedback and response.

Results:
Results were measured according to the distribution and use of the guides as well as the number of implemented projects. Partner organization ARISE Detroit has distributed as many as four hundred copies at neighborhood forums; other neighborhood organizations have distributed upwards of five hundred copies. Due

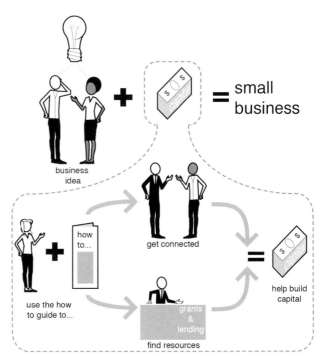

26.13
The content of each guide results from challenges common to community projects and is created in collaboration with DCDC partners. Impact Detroit Community How-To Guides, Detroit, Michigan, 2013.

26.14
Each guide features a simple graphic to grab users' attention and illustrate basic steps. Impact Detroit Community How-To Guides, Detroit, Michigan, 2013.

to demand, the guides are being translated into Spanish and are being supplied to groups outside Detroit. An open source digital version is being explored.

Collaborators:
ARISE Detroit; College Core Block Club; Community Development Advocates of Detroit; Revolve Detroit; Bleeding Heart Design

Design Team:
Impact Detroit, DCDC: Ceara O'Leary, project manager; Virginia Stanard, co-director; Monica Chadha, co-director

26.15

Rebecca Willis, Bleeding Heart Design, talking about the guides that were developed through her neighborhood design work. Impact Detroit Community How-To Guides, Detroit, Michigan, 2013.

Lakota Nation Building at Keya Wakpala Waíçageyapi
Mission, South Dakota

Summary:
Keya Wakpala Waíçageyapi (Turtle Creek Development) is a Lakota resilient community planning project encompassing approximately six hundred acres of tribal lands on the Rosebud Indian Reservation located on the western edge of Mission. A high poverty rate (40 percent unemployment rate) and a lack of infrastructure and economic opportunity are some of the issues this tribe faces.

Goal: Connect people to the heart of the Nation
Reinvigorating traditional culture, familial tribal structure, and the Lakota language while nurturing economic development is the Tribal Nation's goal. The Keya Wakpala Waíçageyapi master plan, which identifies mixed-use development, including renewable and distributed energy, energy-efficient housing, and community-supportive facilities, manifested this commitment.

26.16
Planners, architects, and engineers took community scenarios from the Design Day activities and created one conceptual approach embodying many of the community design and planning inputs. This resulted in the conceptual master plan for the Keya Wakpala resilient community. Lakota Nation Building at Keya Wakpala Waíçageyapi, Mission, South Dakota, Ongoing.

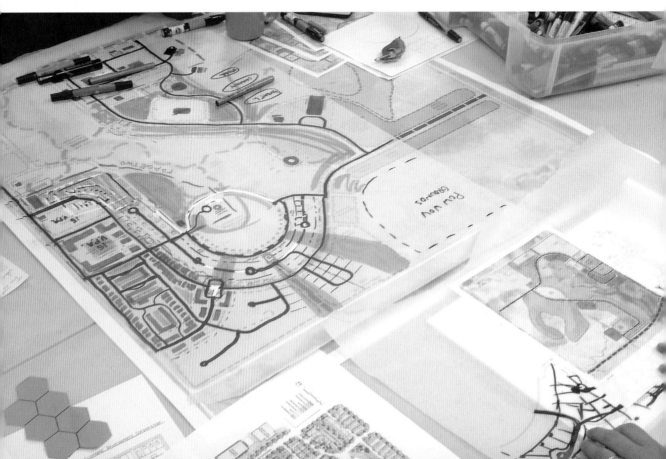

26.17
Conceptual rendering
highlighting housing density
and walkable green spaces
applicable to a tribal setting,
Travis Roubideaux, Lakota
Nation Building at Keya
Wakpala Waíçageyapi,
Mission, South Dakota,
Ongoing.

Community:

The Sicangu Lakota Oyate (burnt thigh nation) of the Rosebud Indian Reservation is one of seven tribes of the Great Sioux Nation. This Tribal Nation is built on the social systems and cultural expressions of *wolakota* (all that is Lakota) and holds paramount its relationship to the land and its people.

Participation:

Participation began with diverse community engagement sessions that included spiritual and cultural leaders who imparted Lakota values and perceptions to the vision statement. Cognitive mapping exercises captured attitudes and desired elements of the new community. Design team participation in cultural activities including comprehension of the language and ceremony is important to developing mutual understanding and respect.

Results:

This development project is in phase two of a much larger twenty-year implementation plan. Anticipated incremental outcomes include addition of jobs, preservation and promotion of language, increased self-sufficiency, sustainable growth, and the strengthening of Lakota values.

26.18
Keya Wakpala conceptual resilient community master plan illustrating overlays of land use, community input, and comprehensive planning based on cultural nuance. Lakota Nation Building at Keya Wakpala Waíçageyapi, Mission, South Dakota, Ongoing.

26.19
Local community members of the Sicangu Lakota Oyate of the Rosebud Sioux Tribe joined in a participatory design process with planners, architects, and engineers to learn more about resilient planning and design principles as well as share an afternoon laying out how the site should be developed. Lakota Nation Building at Keya Wakpala Waíçageyapi, Mission, South Dakota, Ongoing.

26.20

Early cognitive mapping exercises with community members allowed local input at a deeply personal level and often highlighted cultural values and beliefs that would have otherwise been overlooked. The placement and juxtaposition of housing, community spaces, schools, and businesses are then positively rooted in a Lakota world view. Blue Star Studio, Lakota Nation Building at Keya Wakpala Waíçageyapi, Mission, South Dakota, Ongoing.

Collaborators:

Rosebud Economic Development Corporation (REDCO), Rosebud Sioux Tribe (RST), RST Water Resources, RST Water & Sewer, RST Transportation & Roads, RST Land Office, Rosebud Agency Bureau of Indian Affairs, Indian Health Service–Rosebud Service Unit, RST Buffalo Project, Minnesota Housing Partnership, Shakopee Mdewakanton Sioux Community, NW Area Foundation, Enterprise Community Partners, South Dakota USDA Rural Development, Sinte Gleska University, South Dakota State University, South Dakota School of Mines & Technology, Rural Futures Institute at University of Nebraska–Lincoln, Engineers Without Borders–Community Engineering Corps, Enterprise Community Partners, citizens and friends of the Sicangu Lakota Oyate of the Rosebud Indian Reservation

Design Team:

Blue Star Studio, Sustainable Nations, Chad Renfro Design, Development Center for Appropriate Technology, Biohabitats, LeBeau Development, Dream Design International, PAE Consulting Engineers, University of Oklahoma School of Architecture – Division of Regional & City Planning, REDCO

Owe'neh Bupingeh Preservation Plan and Rehabilitation Project

Ohkay Owingeh, New Mexico

Summary:

Located in a Pueblo village believed to be more than seven hundred years old, this preservation and rehabilitation project restores the central historic core and surrounding homes in order to bring families back to the plaza area and positively impact Ohkay Owingeh's cultural heritage. The joint effort of the Tribal Council and the Ohkay Owingeh Housing Authority (OOHA) resulted in a preservation plan, which led to a multi-year rehabilitation project to implement the goals of the preservation plan.

26.21
Justin Aguino making moccasins in front of his newly renovated home. Owe'neh Bupingeh Preservation Plan and Rehabilitation Project, Ohkay Owingeh, New Mexico, Preservation Plan: 2010, Phase I/II: 2012, Phase III: 2013, Phase IV, 2014.

26.22
A family mud plastering, Owe'neh Bupingeh Preservation Plan and Rehabilitation Project, Ohkay Owingeh, New Mexico,
Preservation Plan: 2010, Phase I/II: 2012, Phase III: 2013, Phase IV, 2014.

26.23
Architectural rendering showing completion of all phases, Atkin Olshin Schade Architects. Owe'neh Bupingeh Preservation Plan
and Rehabilitation Project, Ohkay Owingeh, New Mexico, 2010.

Owe'neh Bupingeh Preservation Plan

26.24
National Anthropological Archives, Smithsonian Institution. John K. Hillers. "View of Pueblo and Plaza, Corn Drying on Roof in Foreground," 1877.

Goal: Cultural preservation and revitalization through traditional building

In the latter part of the twentieth century, the indigenous adobe buildings (and construction methodologies) of the Pueblo were displaced by HUD investment in new, subdivision-style wood-frame building. The dwindling numbers and deterioration of the adobe homes pushed most families out of the traditional village. The rehabilitation of the Pueblo core—the spiritual, cultural, and social center of the community—will maintain the people's heritage for future generations. An economic-development aspect was offered in the project: home-ownership guidance and tribal-member training in indigenous construction methods.

Community:

There are 3,357 people in Ohkay Owingeh, as of the 2000 census. It is a community with origins in agriculture. A deep commitment to place is an essential aspect of the Pueblo culture and beliefs.

Participation:

A comprehensive stakeholder advisory process led to a series of participatory meetings, including oral histories with elders; a five-summer education program for six youths; annual community meetings; and at least eight meetings with families. Combining private, government, and nonprofit preservation funds with federal housing funds allowed for a planning phase that ensured significant incorporation of local knowledge.

Results:

Before the project only twenty-five of the remaining sixty-five homes were occupied—many in very poor condition. Today thirty-four have been fully rehabilitated, with the participation of more than seventeen tribal members now trained in construction and the use of preservation methodologies. The project has

26.25
Illustrative plan of proposed infill and rehabilitation in the historic village, excerpted from the Ohkay Owingeh master land use plan. Moule & Polyzoides Architects and Urbanists, Ohkay Owingeh master land use plan, Ohkay Owingeh, New Mexico, 2004.

successfully preserved culturally significant affordable housing. As a result, more than $300,000, annually, has returned to the community. More people are moving back to the Pueblo and participating in community life.

Collaborators:
Project developer, Grant management, Compliance: OOHA; Stakeholders: Ohkay Owingeh Tribal Council and Administration, Ohkay Owingeh Cultural Advisory Team; Advisory Committee; elders and youth, Pueblo residents, New Mexico State Historic Preservation Office, HUD, New Mexico Mortgage Finance Authority, Chamiza Foundation, McCune Foundation, National Park Service

Design Team:
Atkin Olshin Schade Architects; Construction: Avanyu General Contracting

Dimen, Kam Minority Cultural Heritage in China
Guizhou Province, China

Summary:

For centuries Dimen has long resisted modernization and has isolated itself. This project safeguards its unique cultural identity and heritage held within their crafts—papermaking, weaving, indigo dyeing, and embroidery—thwarting cultural extinction.

Goal: Preserve local identity in traditional craft and translate it to contemporary contexts

Maintained by a handful of elderly village matriarchs, traditional artistry is no longer passed on to younger generations. The design team apprenticed with the women

26.26
Wu Mengxi and Marie Lee select Dimen motifs that Wu Mengxi will later screen print. Dimen, Kam Minority Cultural Heritage in China, Guizhou Province, China, Ongoing.

26.27
Dimen villagers working at the Dimen Dong Eco Museum print Dimen motifs on fabric during a screen-printing workshop. Dimen, Kam Minority Cultural Heritage in China, Guizhou Province, China, Ongoing.

26.28
Bags created by Wu Mengxi and Marie Lee as prototypes for artifacts to be later made by local artisans and sold locally and abroad. Dimen, Kam Minority Cultural Heritage in China, Elk Grove, California, Ongoing.

and documented their processes to share their unique culture with others, for posterity, and to foster local identity.

Community:
The Kam people, one of fifty-six ethnic groups in China, make up Dimen. Three hundred years old and once home to 1,300 families, Dimen currently has about 520 households and a population of around 2,200 people.

26.29
Wu Gaitian is re-dyeing and re-pleating a traditional skirt while her husband and a neighbor give each other a hair cut. Dimen, Kam Minority Cultural Heritage in China, Guizhou Province, China, Ongoing.

26.30
Anastasya Uskov learns to make traditional mulberry paper from Wu Meitz, one of the oldest artisans in Dimen. Dimen, Kam Minority Cultural Heritage in China, Guizhou Province, China, Ongoing.

Participation:

Three visits of one-to-six-week periods during three years helped establish the team within the community. During the first two visits, five artisans and their numerous friends participated in demonstrations and interviews about their values, underscored in their relationship to craft. Their processes were recorded through photographs, video, audio recordings, notes, and drawings. During the second visit, local children created stories about village life using photography, and young adults discussed their twenty-first-century village experience. The third trip offered screen-printing workshops that focused on local-identity motifs. Around eighty-five Dimen residents have been directly involved in the project to date.

Results:

Research findings, including collected oral histories, and documentary films showing the craft processes will be made available at the Dimen Dong Cultural Eco Museum. Two craft-making and screen-printing workshops have celebrated local identity. Since the workshops, the Dimen artisans have developed products with local aesthetics that are to be sold domestically and abroad. Five Dimen artisans taught screen-printing of Dimen motifs to several hundred visitors at the Smithsonian Folklife Festival in Washington, DC.

Collaborators:

Dimen Dong Cultural Eco Museum/Western China Cultural Ecology Research Workshop; Dimen village artisans: Wu Meitz, Wu Gaitian, Wu Yingniang, Wu Huazhuan, and Wu Mengxi; University of the Pacific, Jennifer Little

Design Team:

Marie Anna Lee, Anastasya Uskov, Joanne Kwan, Huang Yunyi (Joyce), Zhang Menghui (Ivy), Dong Ran

Kitakami "We Are One" Market and Youth Center
Miyagi Prefecture, Japan

Summary:
The Kitakami "We Are One" Market and Youth Center is an inclusive response to the post-disaster social isolation and economic recovery experienced after the 2011 Great East Japan earthquake and tsunami. The facility offers employment, education, daycare, a gathering place, and a market—all for the long-term recovery of the neighborhood.

Goal: Rebuild community through social and economic development
The social and financial sustainability of the market and center was a focus of the design. The location of the market adjacent to a well-travelled thruway entices the public to visit. The facility's programming ensures continuity in long-term economic recovery: the flexible and open use of its gathering space encourages community participation in events, and its market provides space for locals to sell their freshly grown foods, stimulating the local economy.

Community:
Kitakami is a community of approximately 2,863 people with just under one thousand households. The 2011 disaster resulted in 185 deaths and eighty missing persons with 633 homes destroyed and 463 damaged. Devastation was widespread; many people migrated to larger cities in search of opportunity.

26.31
The completed center is located nearby a temporary housing complex and adjacent to a highway connecting two major cities, making it convenient for local residents and attracting business from travellers with its high visibility. Kitakami "We Are One" Market and Youth Center, Miyagi Prefecture, Japan, 2012.

26.32
The design team led a student design charette where primary school students spent the morning building a vision of their rebuilt village. Kitakami "We Are One" Market and Youth Center, Miyagi Prefecture, Japan, 2012.

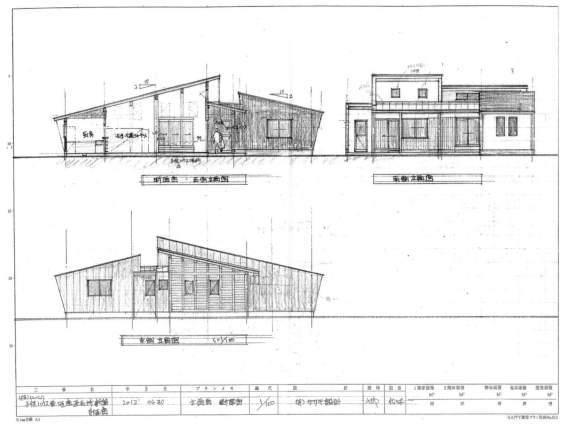

26.33
Fumihiko Sasaki, Kitakami "We Are One" Market and Youth Center, Miyagi Prefecture, Japan, 2012.

Participation:
The project was initiated from within the community. The design team guided a range of residents and city officials through the process and led workshops, during which the interests and needs of the community were carefully reviewed to ensure goals were met. The facility continues to hold outreach workshops—such as a model-making workshop for youth—encouraging the participation of all community members young and old in planning the city's future.

Results:
Project success through long-term recovery will be assessed by the economic growth of the market's businesses. Currently the facility supports three businesses and is staffed by four mothers and an English instructor. Since opening, more than four thousand people have visited.

26.34
Yoshitaka Michihata of "Artwall" from Tokyo kindly donated his labor and material to coat the walls with a diatomaceous earth product that controls humidity in the summer and cleans the air with its fine pores, reducing the risk of sick building syndrome. Kitakami "We Are One" Market and Youth Center, Miyagi Prefecture, Japan, 2012.

26.35
Close collaboration with the client and architect throughout the design process ensured that the client would receive a building, fitting her and the community's needs. Kitakami "We Are One" Market and Youth Center, Miyagi Prefecture, Japan, 2012.

Collaborators:
Funder: Students Rebuild/Paper Cranes for Japan; Community stakeholders: Kitakami "We Are One"; Kitakami Furasato Project; City of Ishinomaki Kitakami Branch

Design Team:
Project lead: Architecture for Humanity; Architect: Sasaki Sekkei; Contractor: Luxs; Community partner: Kitakami "We Are One"

Skill Champ
Chicago, Illinois

Summary:

The founders of Infiniteach, a social enterprise, have spent the past decade working closely with educators and parents of children affected by Autism Spectrum Disorder (ASD). They documented the difficulty in standardizing a curriculum and the time-intensive challenge of creating custom tools for each student's unique needs, interests, and learning objectives. Most importantly, they found that educators and parents often struggle to maintain continuity of learning between school and home.

26.36
Based on best-practice autism strategies, each screen uses a simple and consistent interactive structure (e.g. movement from left to right) so students can focus on the content of each activity. Skill Champ, Chicago, Illinois, 2013 designed.

26.37

Parents and teachers use the Work Session Generator to match skills with motivating themes, quickly and easily creating a series of customized activities. Skill Champ, Chicago, Illinois, 2013 designed.

Goal: Help students with autism learn through an accessible and easily customizable platform

Skill Champ, Infiniteach's first interactive educational product, provides a structured platform that helps early learners with ASD acquire and generalize new skills. Through an intuitive interface, activities teach skills, such as color recognition, object matching, and number identification, and can be customized by motivating themes (e.g., trains, princesses). The platform uses adaptive learning, increasing difficulty based on the child's progress.

Community:

This project serves children with autism and their families, educators, and therapists. ASD is on the rise in the United States, and data from the U.S. Centers for Disease Control and Prevention show that one in sixty-eight children is identified with the disorder.

Participation:

The Chicago autism community actively participated throughout the design process. Taking a human-centered approach, the design team spent entire days in special-

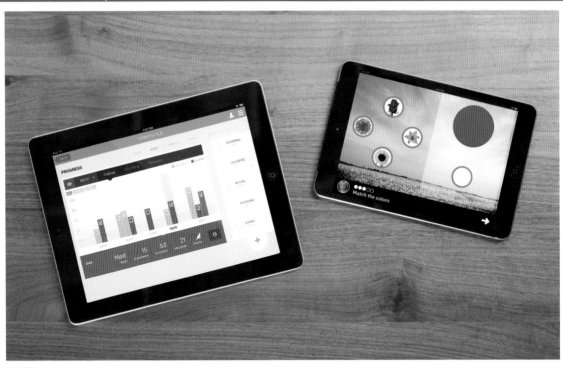

26.38

Skill Champ collects data on each session, so parents and teachers can track student progress, and the app can increase the level of difficulty as each child learns. Skill Champ, Chicago, Illinois, 2013 designed.

26.39

Greater Good Studio visualized initial concepts and facilitated working sessions with parents and teachers to collect feedback and prioritize the app's most desirable features. Skill Champ, Chicago, Illinois, 2013.

26.40
During research in homes and classrooms, Greater Good Studio observed that parents and teachers struggled to customize learning tools for their students' unique abilities and interests. Skill Champ, Chicago, Illinois, 2013.

education classrooms, building empathy for teachers' needs and challenges across the learning cycle. They visited families in their homes, observing how parents support education through tools and technology. Two feedback sessions with parents and teachers followed the initial designs, helping the team improve and prioritize the app's features.

Results:
Infiniteach has a multi-year strategy for Skill Champ: the beta version was released in 2014, and a second-generation version will launch based on customer usage and feedback. The long-term metric is student growth over time; initial success will be measured by the nature, time, and frequency of app use.

Collaborators:
Client: Infiniteach; Stakeholders: children with ASD, their families, and teachers

Design Team:
Greater Good Studio

Piet Patsa Community Arts Centre
Viljoenskroon, South Africa

Summary:

Racial and cultural tensions still exist in post-Apartheid South Africa. Residents of African descent do not have the privileges of those of European descent. Education, economy, and limited upward mobility plague the rural poor. Workshops at the Piet Patsa Community Arts Centre nurture self-worth and confidence building in vulnerable youth through creative expression.

Goal: Use learning to stimulate cultural empowerment

The center offers a physical space that links youth with community leaders from diverse backgrounds. These leaders encourage the youth to develop a personal voice through art and performance-based activities, which help them to cope with extreme life challenges, like victimization and gang violence.

26.41
Mural painting day, Piet Patsa Community Arts Centre, Viljoenskroon, South Africa, 2011.

26.42
Dramatic Need youth painting
east façade of the building,
Piet Patsa Community Arts
Centre, Viljoenskroon, South
Africa, 2011.

Community:

The charity organization Dramatic Need delivers monthly cultural art programming
through the center to approximately 150 underprivileged, at-risk youth, ages five to
twenty years, who live within a thirty-kilometer radius of the peri-urban Rammolutsi
township adjacent to Viljoenskroon.

Participation:

A murals competition engaged users with the project and encouraged community
participation from the start. Jurors from Viljoenskroon and designers from Rammolutsi
were stakeholders. During the center's concept and development phases, Dramatic
Need hosted a series of community-based activities, including interviews and

26.43
Dramatic Need youth designing the mural, Piet Patsa Community Arts Centre, Viljoenskroon, South Africa, 2011.

26.44
Mural competition judging, Piet Patsa Community Arts Centre, Viljoenskroon, South Africa, 2011.

26.45
Construction documents:
floor plan, Chris Harnish, Piet
Patsa Community Arts Centre,
Viljoenskroon, South Africa,
2011.

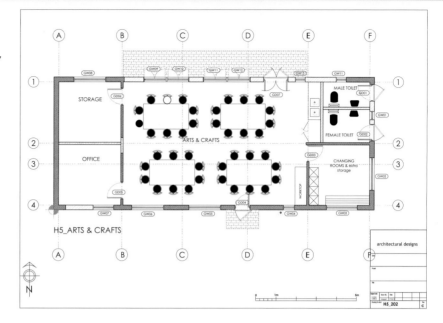

site tours with future students and design charettes with public school officials and community stakeholders. These engagement efforts connected the diverse constituencies and revealed unforeseen neighborhood impacts and vulnerabilities.

Results:
An impact assessment—administered every term—by Dramatic Need quantifies learning outcomes and uses creative assessment models to measure changes in students' behavior and life attitudes through testimonies in a confidential setting. A post-occupancy evaluation revealed students are more self-reflective and in touch with their emotions after having experienced the center programs.

Collaborators:
Dramatic Need: Amber Sainsbury, founder, Shannon Brinkley, program manager, Board of Trustees, future students; Wessel Pansegrouw, contractor; local community and students

Design Team:
Chris Harnish; Mokgadi Mokgobu; PLP Architecture: Andrei Martin

Towns Association for Environmental Quality Green Building Headquarters

Sakhnin, Israel

Summary:

The Towns Association for Environmental Quality (TAEQ), founded in 1993, was the first environmental organization of Israel's Arab minority. TAEQ is a municipal collaborative and offers environmental education to local high school students. The new headquarters expanded the organization's scope to include regional planning, ecotourism, permaculture, and green building.

Goal: Acknowledge culture through green building concepts

The headquarters is a building in which traditional Arab architecture coexists with modern green technology and represents the benefits of environmental and energy conservation, education, and research. Additionally, the headquarters promotes a shared environmental agenda that bridges the cultural and religious differences of the region's Arab and Jewish residents through environmental and social programs.

26.46
The public, including women and youth, participated in open construction days. Towns Association for Environmental Quality Green Building Headquarters, Sakhnin, Israel, 2004.

26.47
Local builders and materials were used to construct the new facility. Towns Association for Environmental Quality Green Building Headquarters, Sakhnin, Israel, 2004.

Community:

Located in Sakhnin, an Arab city in Israel's northern Galilee region, TAEQ serves about eighty-five thousand residents through programs in six member towns, as well as participating schools and organizations in neighboring Jewish communities. Approximately 20 percent of the total Israeli population is Arab, but in Galilee, Jews and Arabs are equally represented. The TAEQ project was designed to preserve Arab cultural heritage and tradition.

Participation:

Local and regional government and community members were engaged in the building design and construction. Approximately forty in-person interviews, which included elders and women, determined the requirement for a strong Arab architectural presence. Asset mapping identified community talent, especially retired building experts, who guided the use of local materials. The design team explored how environmental education impacts the design of classrooms, laboratories, and auditoriums.

Results:

TAEQ's new facility receives sixty thousand visitors a year. Student activities have doubled in participation, with approximately thirty thousand regional high school and

TAEQ Green Building Headquarters

26.48
Community elders advised the design and construction process. Towns Association for Environmental Quality Green Building Headquarters, Sakhnin, Israel, 2004.

26.49
A schematic of the entire TAEQ environmental center, including the forthcoming phase three, which will house a science, space, and technology wing. Towns Association for Environmental Quality Green Building Headquarters, Sakhnin, Israel, 2003.

26.50
The exterior walls of the environmental center are constructed with concrete and covered by locally-gathered stones. Towns Association for Environmental Quality Green Building Headquarters, Sakhnin, Israel, 2004.

university students now completing class projects in both Arab and Jewish schools. By including traditional Arab passive-architectural elements, TAEQ serves as a model of ecofriendly building.

Collaborators:
TAEQ municipality mayors and staff, Sakhnin municipal staff, community members, Israel Ministry of Environment, European Union MED-ENEC Programme, Beracha Foundation

Design Team:
TAEQ executive director: Dr. Hussein Tarabeih; Lead architect: Abed Yasin; Architect: Riyad Dwairy

TAEQ Green Building Headquarters

Economic: Green Microbusiness Growth

Environmental: Solar-Energy Access

Social: Solar-Energy Education

Juabar

Pwani and Morogoro, Tanzania

Summary:

Only 15 percent of Tanzania has access to electricity, with only 2 percent electrification in rural areas, and a mobile phone saturation rate of 55 percent—meaning, twenty million people own phones but lack access to reliable energy to charge them. Developing enterprise opportunities in Tanzania to meet growing energy demands, Juabar offers charging kiosks powered by solar cells that can provide electricity in off-grid areas of Tanzania.

Goal: Develop incremental microbusiness opportunities that support energy access

A Juabar electricity business starts with a phone-charging service, expands to a solar retail outlet, and can grow to a larger solar-energy infrastructure that supports a community. Charging kiosks are the seed to a larger ecosystem of energy services

26.51
The benefits of a Juabar electricity business, Juabar, 2014.

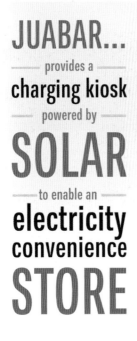

@JuabarDesign

26.52
Issa of Juabar demonstrating how to use the charging system, Juabar, Morogoro Region, Tanzania, 2014.

26.53
Godfrey Mallya of Juabar conducting solar lights sales training, Juabar, Pwani Region, Tanzania, 2013.

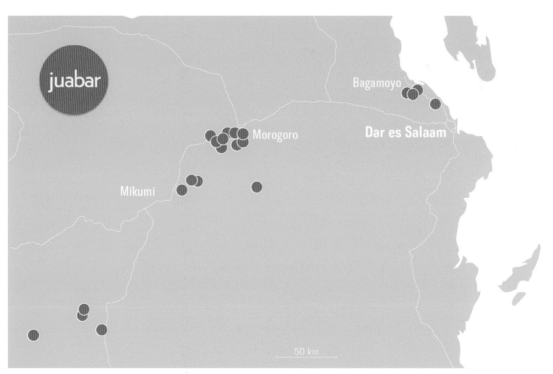

26.54
Juabar locations as of May 2014, Juabar, 2014.

Juabar

that Juabar provides through financing, solar-energy education, sales, and customer-service training.

Community:

Rural Pwani and Morogoro are served by this project. There are two primary stakeholder groups: Juabar kiosk operators (called Juaprenuers) from lower- and middle-class rural populations that operate these electricity convenience stores, and those who use the kiosk for charging. Africa is a "mobile-first continent," and most Africans experience technology through mobile devices. Phones and text-based technologies deliver information to fill a variety of needs, including banking, health, and educational services.

Participation:

The design team engaged with Tanzanians with all levels of energy access, including those with in-home grid electricity and those without. The team conducted research

26.55
Juapreneur gathering: Sales training on personal care products with partner Unilever, Juabar, Morogoro Region, Tanzania, 2014.

that included homestays, in-home interviews, and ethnographic observations. A nine-month pilot with two kiosk prototypes offered local operators an opportunity to work closely with the design team.

Results:

As of 2014, there are thirty-four active kiosk operators (only eight in 2013). Juapreneurs, who lease the kiosks, can earn between 2.5 to 10 times the average Tanzanian through charging services alone. Tanzanian communities require energy infrastructure that builds long-term energy solutions; Juabar supports incremental energy infrastructure, cultivating community energy-service providers.

Collaborators:

ARTI-Energy; Juapreneurs

Design Team:

Juabar Design

12

Environmental: Green Space Access

Social: Well-being

Environmental: Food Production

The Informal Urban Communities Initiative: Comunidad Ecológica Saludable

Lima, Peru

Summary:

When rural people migrate to urban zones, their well-being is often threatened by decreased availability of green spaces. How can access to nature contribute to the social, economic, and environmental health of communities? This project responds by showing how gardening and green spaces enhance well-being and food production.

Goal: Make natural environments an integral part of urban life

The Comunidad Ecológica Saludable (healthy ecological community): Gardens, Green Space, and Health project provides access to nature through the design and

26.56

The processes of garden design, construction, planting, and ongoing cultivation help to build social capital in the community. The Informal Urban Communities Initiative: Comunidad Ecológica Saludable, Lima, Peru, 2013.

26.57
Gardens at individual households have a cumulative positive impact on public space in Eliseo Collazos. The Informal Urban Communities Initiative: Comunidad Ecológica Saludable, Lima, Peru, 2013.

26.58
Many residents are now growing vegetables such as radishes, lettuce, corn, and potatoes. The Informal Urban Communities Initiative: Comunidad Ecológica Saludable, Lima, Peru, 2013.

26.59
Participatory garden modeling workshop using scaled garden kit of parts components. The Informal Urban Communities Initiative: Comunidad Ecológica Saludable, Lima, Peru, 2013.

implementation of twenty-nine household gardens, in which participating households grow food and flowers, recreate, and socialize.

Community:
Eliseo Collazos (EC) is an informal urban settlement in northern Lima, with approximately ninety households and four hundred people. There is very little green space; residents spend much of their time either away at work or indoors. These factors negatively impact quality of life.

Participation:
During participatory workshops, EC community members identified access to nature as one of their highest priorities. The project team worked with residents to

26.60
Residence in Eliseo Collazos before, during, and after the garden project. The Informal Urban Communities Initiative: Comunidad Ecológica Saludable, Lima, Peru, 2013.

develop a garden kit of parts and to design individualized household gardens. During capacity-building and Participatory Impact Assessment workshops, community members learned how to build, plant, and maintain their gardens, and identified benchmarks for project success. EC residents kept journals to document their gardening activities.

Results:
The project team conducted assessments of health and well-being, garden conditions and project impacts at six months and one year. Families and neighbors worked together on garden implementation, sharing skills, and strengthening relationships. Most of the gardens are flourishing, and many families harvest, eat, and sell vegetables and herbs. Others enjoy the green space the gardens provide.

Collaborators:
University of Washington (UW) LARC, SEFS, Nursing, GH, GH and Environment Fellows; Fundación San Marcos; AWB-Seattle; UW GOHealth Fellowship Program; NDSE Graduate Fellowship; LAF Olmsted Scholarship; U.S. EPA P3 Program; UW Royalty Research Fund

Design Team:
EC residents; UW: Ben Spencer, Susan Bolton, Joachim Voss, students; Peruvian Architect: Jorge Alarcon

Durham Performing Arts Center
Durham, North Carolina

Summary:

The Durham Performing Arts Center (DPAC) is a 2,800-seat theater that provides community access to the arts, hosting concerts and more than one hundred performances per year. A key catalyst for downtown revitalization, the project has provided a variety of local jobs through construction and continues to do so with operations that support the local economy and serve the DPAC audience. The project scope also includes clean up of the location, which was an environmental brownfield site.

26.61
A generous public plaza serves as a pre-performance gathering space and frequently features live entertainment and opportunities to meet with members of an event's cast. Durham Performing Arts Center, Durham, North Carolina, 2008.

26.62
At DPAC, patron movement through the building was celebrated to enhance the experience of attending a theatrical performance. Durham Performing Arts Center, Durham, North Carolina, 2008.

Goal: Revitalize an economically challenged zone

The DPAC has attracted capital investment, inspired economic growth, and increased cultural enrichment. Through a participatory process, the project supported the city, local businesses, subcontractors, and the residents by invigorating a central business district with new employment opportunities.

Community:

Located on the southwest edge of Durham, the Hayti District—also referred as the American Tobacco Historic District (once a hub of the tobacco industry)—was a historic settlement known for its locally owned African American businesses that experienced population and job declines in recent years. Today, this area (approximately ten acres) is mixed use, known for its vibrant pedestrian-friendly and cultural environment.

Participation:

Monthly public meetings were held for two years to gather community input. The community suggested hiring local minority- and women-owned businesses, which had an enduring impact. The designer/developer held job fairs and provided assistance to subcontractors who would typically not have been considered for a project of this scale.

Durham Performing Arts Center

26.63
The main house of the theater was designed to optimize the patrons' experience of the performance. Accordingly, the sightlines and acoustics within the venue are excellent, with no seat more than 135 feet from the stage-front. Durham Performing Arts Center, Durham, North Carolina, 2008.

26.64

The venue's lobby spaces were conceived as an illuminated lantern, celebrating the movement of patrons up and through the theater while visually connecting DPAC with its surrounding community. Durham Performing Arts Center, Durham, North Carolina, 2008.

26.65

One key to DPAC's success was the decision to locate the theater in the heart of downtown Durham, within easy walking distance of its central business district. The building is located on the site of a former municipal bus maintenance facility that was deemed a brownfield. Durham Performing Arts Center, Durham, North Carolina, 2008.

Results:

The target of 30 percent of local minority- and women-owned workforce was met during construction. Fifteen full-time-equivalent jobs were supported (generating $612,000 in new wages and salaries); eighty-three construction jobs were supported during development (approximately $3.3 million in wages). Total annual earnings generated by new operations reached approximately $1.3 million, with total indirect earnings equaling $673,200.

Collaborators:

Durham City Government, Durham Chamber of Commerce, Downtown Durham

Design Team:

Architect/developer: Szostak Design; Codeveloper: Garfield Traub; Business plan: Nederlander Productions, Professional Facilities Management; Venue performance metric: Theatre Consultants Collaborative

Easy Latrine Sanitation Marketing
Cambodia

Summary:

Sanitation in Cambodia is dire: an estimated ten million cases of diarrhea and ten thousand deaths each year are due to untreated water and inadequate sanitation disposal. iDE uses a market-facilitation model to support the research and development of user-friendly products, such as the Easy Latrine, a pit latrine composed of a ceramic squat pan, concrete slab, catchment box, PVC pipe, and concrete offset storage rings. Through the Sanitation Marketing (SanMark) program, iDE engages small-scale enterprises to produce and sell the Easy Latrine.

26.66
One of the enterprises that iDE has trained prepares to make a home delivery, a service included in the purchase that significantly reduces barriers for adoption by households. Easy Latrine, Cambodia, Ongoing.

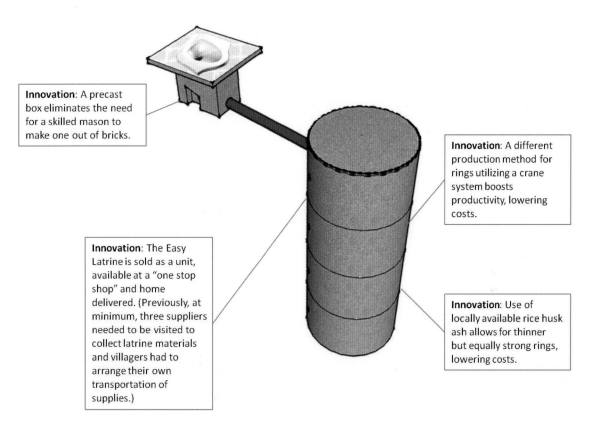

Innovation: A precast box eliminates the need for a skilled mason to make one out of bricks.

Innovation: A different production method for rings utilizing a crane system boosts productivity, lowering costs.

Innovation: The Easy Latrine is sold as a unit, available at a "one stop shop" and home delivered. (Previously, at minimum, three suppliers needed to be visited to collect latrine materials and villagers had to arrange their own transportation of supplies.)

Innovation: Use of locally available rice husk ash allows for thinner but equally strong rings, lowering costs.

26.67
What is innovative about the Easy Latrine is not merely the product, but aspects of the product that remove barriers for enterprises to sell and customers to buy. iDE, Easy Latrine, Cambodia, Ongoing.

Goal: Strengthen sanitation markets

Purchasing a latrine has been prohibitively expensive and logistically challenging in Cambodia. At current rates of latrine installation prior to project intervention, it would have taken more than one hundred years to reach open-defecation-free status. However, when households are treated as customers rather than as charity, this empowerment can encourage adoption, economic growth, and ultimately, well-being.

Community:

This project serves poor rural households without latrines. With the country emerging from a recent civil war, rural Cambodians suffer an almost total lack of social services and infrastructure.

Participation:

iDE designed the Easy Latrine and is supporting small-scale enterprise business by engaging a host of stakeholders to determine the barriers and drivers of latrine ownership. Participants included latrine owners and non-owners, local leaders responsible for community infrastructure, and supply-chain actors.

Results:

iDE launched the two-year pilot SanMark project in two provinces, which has since become a three-year program in seven provinces. During the pilot, twenty-four enterprises entered the latrine market, and since then more than 160 others have joined.

Collaborators:

Product research: Lien Aid, RainWater Cambodia; Advisory team: Ministry of Rural Development of the Royal Cambodian Government; Funders (pilot): United States Agency for International Development, Water and Sanitation Program of the World Bank; Funders (scale-up): Bill & Melinda Gates Foundation, Stone Family Foundation,

26.68
The Easy Latrine is easy to buy, easy to install, and easy to use. Sold as a packaged do-it-yourself product, customers can purchase, install, and use the Easy Latrine in the same day. Easy Latrine, Cambodia, Ongoing.

26.69
Changing the business model from high-margin low-volume, to high-volume low-margin, enterprises are now able to increase net profit while improving the health of their community. Easy Latrine, Cambodia, Ongoing.

26.70
Coupled with aspirational marketing, households associate owning an Easy Latrine with dignity, pride, and convenience. Easy Latrine, Cambodia, Ongoing.

Water and Sanitation Program of the World Bank; Local producers/manufacturers: Enterprises that manufacture, distribute, and market Easy Latrines

Design Team:
iDE WASH staff; iDE Human-Centered Design iLab; Easy Latrine design consultant: Jeff Chapin; Structural engineer: Benjamin Clouet

Manica Football for Hope Centre

Manica, Mozambique

Summary:

Established during the throes of Mozambique's civil war, the Grupo Desportivo de Manica (GDM) recreation club recognizes the possibility of social cohesion through play. GDM reinvigorated its presence in Manica with a campaign for a football club and youth center for boys and girls. It serves nearly five thousand youths and provides needed education and life-skills training in an athletics context.

Goal: Promote change through the use of sports for social good

The Football for Hope Centre is part of GDM's plan for an integrated community club, in which soccer is a tool for positive social change. The facility was designed with the project stakeholders and built using local, natural materials in an innovative way that reinforce the values of the Manica community.

Community:

Manica has an estimated population of three hundred thousand people with approximately 46 percent under the age of fifteen. According to the United Nations Human Development Index, 59 percent of the population lives in poverty. In spite of

26.71
View of the center through the pitch, Manica Football for Hope Centre, Manica, Mozambique, 2013.

26.72
Teaching activity in the main
room of the center, Manica
Football for Hope Centre,
Manica, Mozambique, 2013.

26.73
Hands-on training in
compressed earth blocks,
Manica Football for Hope
Centre, Manica, Mozambique,
2013.

this, the community's spirit and willingness to improve their living conditions remain
high.

Participation:

The design team was fully embedded within the community, from predesign through
construction, with the input of local youth and GDM staff. Research and participation

26.74
The first brick produced,
Manica Football for Hope
Centre, Manica, Mozambique,
2013.

were documented through workshops, charettes, and interviews. The construction
site also became a teaching platform for local sourcing of materials, brick production,
and new construction methods.

26.75
Workers receive their training
certificates, Manica Football
for Hope Centre, Manica,
Mozambique, 2013.

Results:
GDM monitors the return-to-school rates of children and the post-graduation
employment rate: in one year, 219 people went back to school, and 112 people

were employed. A post-occupancy evaluation, typically six to twelve months after building occupancy, will verify that the project has met the needs and requirements of the community.

Collaborators:
Grupo Deportivo Manica, Architecture for Humanity, FIFA, streetfootballworld, Greenfields, Yingli Solar, Yingli Green Energy Europe

Design Team:
Designer, project management: Architecture for Humanity; Architect of record: Jose Forjaz Architects; Structural engineer: Betar Estudos e Projectos; Electrical engineer: GTO Engenheiros Consultores; Contractor: Malacha Construcciones

Umusozi Ukiza Doctors' Housing

Burera, Rwanda

Summary:

MASS Design Group, in collaboration with the Rwandan Ministry of Health and Partners In Health, designed and built the Butaro District Hospital in Burera, a northern, largely rural province that previously had no permanent doctors or health facilities. Upon completion of the hospital, those same partners built the Umusozi Ukiza (healing hill) Doctors' Housing, an eight-unit housing facility built specifically to attract and retain physicians at the hospital—in developing countries like Rwanda, doctors are often lured to higher paying positions in cities and abroad. These projects are a model for the Rwandan Ministry of Health's national initiatives to improve the quality of and to extend universal access to health care.

Goal: Impact the local economy with employment and skills training through collaboration

Focused investment in social capital during the design-build enabled opportunities for collaboration with local artisans, masons, and carpenters. Creative innovations using local materials also ensured that design processes could be repeated

26.76
Housing exterior at night, Umusozi Ukiza Doctors' Housing, Burera District, Rwanda, 2012. Photo: Iwan Baan.

26.77
Umusozi Ukiza Doctors'
Housing interior, Umusozi
Ukiza Doctors' Housing,
Burera District, Rwanda, 2012.
Photo: Iwan Baan.

and commercialized, increasing the local labor market. MASS also leveraged the construction stage to provide paid job training.

Community:
This project addresses the health and employment needs of the Burera community and was designed to attract exceptional doctors to Butaro Hospital as well as leverage the building process to employ and train members of the community.

Participation:
Collaborating with the design team, the local craftsmen tested techniques on-site and fabricated building elements with locally sourced materials. The homes—from the interior design to exterior construction and landscape design—are uniquely Rwandan.

Results:
The project created roughly nine hundred temporary craft- and construction-based jobs that distributed over $400,000 to local and regional economies. An additional

26.78
Housing exterior, Umusozi Ukiza Doctors' Housing, Burera District, Rwanda, 2012.
Photo: Iwan Baan.

26.79
Housing exterior at night, Umusozi Ukiza Doctors' Housing, Burera District, Rwanda, 2012. Photo: Iwan Baan.

26.80
Housing exterior, Umusozi
Ukiza Doctors' Housing,
Burera District, Rwanda, 2012.
Photo: Iwan Baan.

138 people learned marketable masonry skills, thirty were trained in seismic safe building, and sixty received training in steel bending and carpentry. Eight houses accommodate the Butaro physicians.

Collaborators:

Rwandan Ministry of Health; Partners In Health; Daniel E. Ponton Fund at the Brigham and Women's Hospital

Design Team:

MASS Design Group

Social: Nutritious Food Delivery

Economic: Affordable Food

Social: Community Health

Fresh Moves Mobile Market
Chicago, Illinois

Summary:

A study of Chicago's African American communities described the phenomenon of "food deserts," places with inadequate access to healthy, fresh food, in those neighborhoods. Food Desert Action responded to this challenging condition with the Fresh Moves Mobile Market, an urban traveling farmer's market that supports community health.

Goal: Provide accessible nutritious food to people in food deserts

This project provides affordable, fresh produce to people with limited access due to store location, availability of produce, or lack of acceptance of public-assistance cards. Fresh Moves Mobile Market operates year round and visits community anchors, including religious institutions, schools, and community centers, to

26.81
Exterior view of the bus mega graphics on launch day, Fresh Moves Mobile Market, Chicago, Illinois, 2011.

26.82
Exterior view of the bus on launch day with customers entering, Fresh Moves Mobile Market, Chicago, Illinois, 2011.

reconnect people to health- and diet-conscious living. It makes thirty-two weekly stops in seven food desert neighborhoods.

Community:
More than six hundred thousand Chicago residents live in food deserts, primarily on the South and West Sides of the city—overlapping with the highest obesity- and diabetes-rate area. North Lawndale, a neighborhood served by this project, is one of these identified food deserts: a 3.2 square-mile area, it has a population of 41,768 (more than 90 percent African American), with a median income of approximately $18,000.

Participation:
Food Desert Action collaborated with Umoja Student Development Corporation to produce a study on food deserts, which supplied evidence of need. Community design charettes and a bus-deconstruction-day offered opportunities to shape a unique Chicago-market concept.

26.83
Interior view of the bus toward the rear check-out counter, Fresh Moves Mobile Market, Chicago, Illinois, 2011.

26.84
Interior view of the bus with customers and staff navigating the corridor, Fresh Moves Mobile Market, Chicago, Illinois, 2011.

Social: Nutritious Food Delivery
Economic: Affordable Food
Social: Community Health

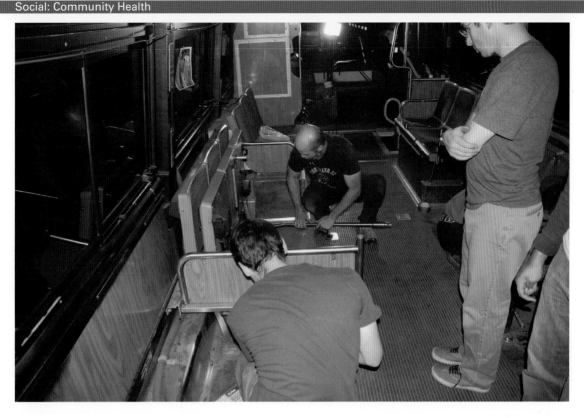

26.85
Interior view of the bus
during the volunteer
bus-deconstruction-day,
Fresh Moves Mobile Market,
Chicago, Illinois, 2011.

Results:

Two renovated Chicago transit buses—one-aisle grocery stores—currently serve the West and South Sides. As a demonstration of market viability, there were almost sixteen thousand customer transactions in 2012, with an average purchase of $5.53. The market has inspired models in Boston, Chattanooga, and Los Angeles.

Collaborators:

Client: Food Desert Action; Stakeholders: Chicago Bus and Truck; Chicago Transit Authority; City of Chicago; Coyote Logistics; Kendall College; U.S. Department of Agriculture

Design Team:

Mobile Market Concepts; Construction and project management: Architecture for Humanity Chicago; Interior fabrication: WM Display Group; Graphic design: EPIC

Rebuild South Sudan Jalle School
Jonglei State, South Sudan

Summary:

During two civil wars and before the enactment of the 2005 Comprehensive Peace Agreement, it is estimated that 2.5 million South Sudanese were killed and 4 million displaced. As part of this peace agreement, South Sudan became an independent nation on July 9, 2011. It is through this lens of recovery that the children of South Sudan became subjects of long-term rebuild and recovery efforts, with an emphasis on educational needs.

Goal: Respond to long-term recovery through education

As the only permanent school within seven miles, the Jalle School represents a new future for the community and a symbolic bond to the homeland, as a place for education and gathering. Climate conditions have traditionally been an obstacle for students, but the new building protects the students from the elements and does not need to be rebuilt after each rain season.

26.86
A rendering of Jalle School design, Marian Nupsund and Jill Kurtz, Rebuild South Sudan Jalle School, Jonglei State, South Sudan, Ongoing.

26.87
Local students pose proudly in front of their future school. Rebuild South Sudan Jalle School, Jonglei State, South Sudan, Ongoing.

26.88
Future students help Jill Kurtz measure the steel structure. Rebuild South Sudan Jalle School, Jonglei State, South Sudan, Ongoing.

Community:

Children of the Dinka tribe, in the Jalle Payam region, are the primary group served.

Participation:

The reunion of South Sudanese Lost Boy Michael Kuany, founder of Rebuild South Sudan, with his community after twenty years resulted in an invitation from the village elders for Rebuild South Sudan to lead the building program. Interviews with local elders, county, state, and national officials all provided necessary input. The project development included local contractors and community members providing on-site project management and material protection (from theft) during recent civil conflicts.

Results:

The project has withstood setbacks since its inception: flooded roads inhibiting the movement of supplies, looted roofing materials, and political conflict have put

26.89
Michael Kuany, Lost Boy of South Sudan and founder of Rebuild South Sudan, Rebuild South Sudan Jalle School, Jonglei State, South Sudan, Ongoing.

26.90
Community elders and leaders
stand in the middle of their
future community-gathering
hall in the school building.
Rebuild South Sudan Jalle
School, Jonglei State, South
Sudan, Ongoing.

the project on temporary pause. Anticipated results include an increase in student enrollment and completion of primary school (state average of 46.7 percent enrolled, 9.8 percent completed), with an increased percentage of students going on to secondary school (state average, 4.2 percent).

Collaborators:
Community of Jalle, South Sudan; John Dau Foundation; Heli-Piles; eMi; Big Ass Fans

Design Team:
Rebuild South Sudan: Michael Kuany, Jill Sornson Kurtz, Blake Clark

Bancroft School Apartments

Kansas City, Missouri

Summary:

The American Recovery and Reinvestment Act designated $200 million for a 150-block area of Kansas City called the Green Impact Zone. The Historic Manheim Park neighborhood (HMP) is at the heart of this effort, with among the highest unemployment and crime rates in the city and the lowest median income. Located in HMP, the Bancroft School Apartments embodies the vision of a dynamic community with a restorative future.

Goal: Restore neighborhood economic and social vitality

The project includes the preservation and rehabilitation of the existing school, including twenty-nine apartments in the building and the on-site construction of twenty-one new units on the property, along with new solar-powered community

26.91
The renovated Bancroft School, Bancroft School Apartments, Kansas City, Missouri, 2013.

26.92
New apartments along the
west side of the site, Bancroft
School Apartments, Kansas
City, Missouri, 2013.

space and protected parking. Community-prioritized goals, such as enhancements
to safety, business, community, education, transportation, and parks, focus on
removing barriers to economic and social vibrancy.

Community:
HMP is located in the northwest section of the Green Impact Zone from Forty-Second
to Forty-Seventh Streets between Troost and Paseo Avenues. The Bancroft School,
built in 1909 and vacant since January 1999, is centrally located in this neighborhood.

Participation:
The community residents were active in setting goals and defining what success
means—through surveys and regular meetings, visioning meetings, conceptual
design meetings, and open forums with facilitated breakout sessions that
characterized this project's iterative and community-driven process. Project
ownership is in the hands of the community, guaranteeing its long-term success.

Results:
Benchmarks for measuring results are set for the second, fifth, and tenth years after
completion and are being accomplished through: school revitalization (complete);
new community programs (underway); removal of vacant properties (underway);
development of park and single-family homes (underway); expansion of commercial

26.93
The new modern apartments are scaled to embrace the neighborhood. Bancroft School Apartments, Kansas City, Missouri, 2013.

26.94
The interior of the school features restored historic elements from the original school. Bancroft School Apartments, Kansas City, Missouri, 2013.

26.95
The photovoltaic array on the roof of the school, Bancroft School Apartments, Kansas City, Missouri, 2013.

properties (future). During the construction phase, crime had decreased by 26.1 percent since the beginning of the project. The project has received LEED Platinum certification.

Collaborators:

Green Impact Zone, Historic Manheim Park Neighborhood Association, Make It Right, Truman Medical Group, Dalmark Group, BNIM, Brush Creek Community Partners, Mid-America Regional Council, Neighborhood Housing Services, Kansas City Police Department

Design Team:

BNIM, BGR Engineers, KH Engineers, Contects, Phronesis, SK Design, Rosin Preservation

People Organizing Place—Neighborhood Stories
Dallas, Texas

Summary:
Neighborhood Stories, a part of bcWORKSHOP's People Organizing Place effort to strengthen Dallas neighborhoods, activates dialogue through film and public activities that reveal local identity and vitality of place. The residents, through their own stories, create a neighborhood chronicle—a collective memory and formalized history.

Goal: Celebrate local identity through community action
By sharing and documenting stories between community members, the neighborhood and city can see Dallas's past and future. The inclusive nature of

26.96
Neighbors remember and mark the memories of places and people in their neighborhood. People Organizing Place—Neighborhood Stories, Dallas, Texas, 2013.

26.97

Gathering and celebrating in the 10th Street neighborhood of Dallas, People Organizing Place—Neighborhood Stories, Dallas, Texas, 2013.

storytelling acknowledges the diversity of each individual while opening up possibilities for a shared vision for the future.

Community:

The design team identified the six participating neighborhoods based on their capacity to represent issues connected to the city's rich history and future: La Bajada, a Mexican American neighborhood threatened by redevelopment; Dolphin Heights, a working-class neighborhood isolated by rail lines and infrastructure; Wynnewood North, a postwar neighborhood with a declining shopping center; Tenth Street Historic District, a persistently vacant African American community; Mount Auburn, a neighborhood built for factory workers with a history of activism; and the Arts District, a downtown arts destination.

Participation:

Engagement is personalized in each neighborhood through an immersive process of research and relationship building, including interviewing, image collection, and documentation of the current built environment. Overarching themes in Dallas's development are explored and analyzed through the lens of each neighborhood.

26.98
Looking inside the Neighborhood Stories Gallery as it is being set up for the La Bajada neighborhood event, People Organizing Place—Neighborhood Stories, Dallas, Texas, 2012.

26.99
Collecting neighborhood preferences for potential redevelopment might occur by playing Wynnewoodopoly. People Organizing Place—Neighborhood Stories, Dallas, Texas, 2013.

26.100
Wynnewood neighbors
watch the film screening as
part of the pop-up event.
People Organizing Place—
Neighborhood Stories, Dallas,
Texas, 2013.

Results:
Success is measured by the level of participation in neighborhood events hosted by the community and design team and in the participants' heightened understanding of the history of that place. Knowing the neighborhood is an integral part of the mission of Neighborhood Stories and is achieved by developing a platform for oral history collection and translation into exhibitions, documentaries, and printed publications.

Collaborators:
National Endowment for the Arts, Art Works grant; neighborhood residents; Trinity Trust; Citi Community Development; stakeholder organizations, businesses, municipal groups, schools, and volunteers

Design Team:
bcWORKSHOP team leaders: Melanie Wood, Lauren Powers, Katharine Dike, Craig Weflen, Jennifer Dowland, Thomas Simpson, Leslie Nepveux

Kensington High School for the Creative and Performing Arts

Philadelphia, Pennsylvania

Summary:

During the last century, South Kensington and Fishtown communities witnessed the death of industry in the region, affecting community stability and growth. The Kensington High School for the Creative and Performing Arts (KCAPA) project fostered student engagement, green-job development, community optimism, and ultimately hope in a previously bleak urban setting. The design of the school provided community cohesion through project planning, programming, and development.

Goal: Provide hope for the future

The community was strengthened through development of the school, site, and adjacent community spaces and properties. An activist group, Youth United for Change (YUC), advanced the concept that smaller schools produce more successful

26.101
Project site after construction, Kensington High School for the Creative and Performing Arts, Philadelphia, Pennsylvania, 2010.

26.102

Project site before construction, Kensington High School for the Creative and Performing Arts, Philadelphia, Pennsylvania, 2008.

26.103

Community gardening day at KCAPA, Kensington High School for the Creative and Performing Arts, Philadelphia, Pennsylvania, 2011.

26.104
KCAPA students learn how to plant vegetables, Kensington High School for the Creative and Performing Arts, Philadelphia, Pennsylvania, 2011.

students. YUC insisted on breaking up the two thousand–student Kensington High School into four smaller schools, of which KCAPA is one.

Community:
The high school students and their families in South Kensington and Fishtown live at or below poverty level. Primarily Latino, this community has a strong connection to family, education, culture, and the arts.

Participation:
Community meetings and design charettes led by the consultant team created a forum to engage students, parents, neighbors, and YUC. A manual that guided design resulted from these meetings.

Results:
The school has seen an increase in retention (ten fold) and in graduation rates (100 percent). Prior to moving into KCAPA, the school lost 247 students in one year; since

26.105

KCAPA students mural painting, Kensington High School for the Creative and Performing Arts, Philadelphia, Pennsylvania, 2011.

occupancy, it has been as low as 22. Student attendance has increased from 80 to 87 percent. Adjacent residential renovations were spurred after construction, and the site has become a central point in a storm-water-management strategy. A 67 percent decrease in school violence since the school's opening has enhanced the feeling of safety (School District of Philadelphia 2012). A LEED Platinum Certified project, this green school combines a healthy learning environment with a pedagogy of sustainability.

Collaborators:
School District of Philadelphia; KCAPA: Principal Debora Carrera, faculty, students, neighbors; AP/BSI; YUC; Concordia; The Philadelphia Education Fund

Design Team:
SMP SRK Architects, Alderson Engineering, Bevan Lawson, Gilmore & Associates, David Nelson Associates

References

School District of Philadelphia. "School Profile: Kensington Capa (Mobility, PSSA, and Serious Incidents)," Accessed on April 24, 2012. https://webapps.philasd.org/school_profile/print/5520

SAGE Affordable Green Modular Classrooms
Oregon and Washington

Summary:
SAGE (Smart Academic Green Environment) classrooms respond to a crisis in school districts today: the need for more teaching spaces and affordable classrooms. This green modular classroom promotes a sustainable solution in up-front savings and long-term operation, as well as in health improvements and enhanced student performance—inclusion of natural light and a healthy environment fosters learning.

Goal: Provide a green modular classroom conducive to learning
Federally funded studies have shown that learning is positively impacted by well-ventilated spaces with natural light and views. SAGE delivers three times the air exchange of a typical modular unit and is constructed with sustainable materials.

Community:
The Edmonds School District in Washington has placed twelve SAGE classrooms on six different campuses, mitigating overcrowding. And in Oregon, the Corvallis

26.106
Rendering of a double SAGE classroom, SAGE Affordable Green Modular Classrooms, 2012.

26.107
The new SAGE classroom at Hazelwood Elementary School, SAGE Affordable Green Modular Classrooms, Lynnwood, Washington, 2014.

26.108
The SAGE concept grew out of three years of research on existing classrooms and their users. SAGE Affordable Green Modular Classrooms, Portland, Oregon, 2009.

SAGE Classrooms

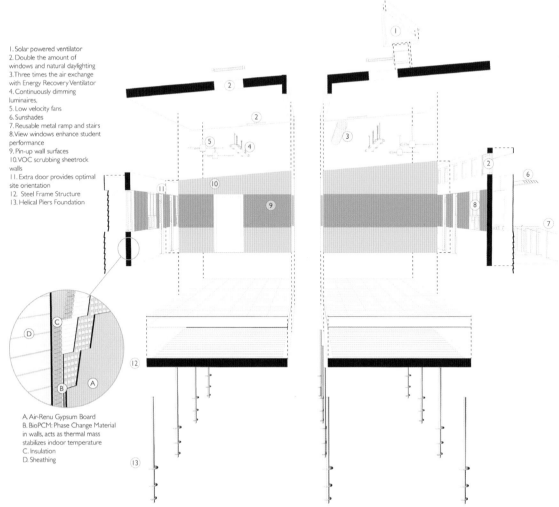

1. Solar powered ventilator
2. Double the amount of windows and natural daylighting
3. Three times the air exchange with Energy Recovery Ventilator
4. Continuously dimming luminaires,
5. Low velocity fans
6. Sunshades
7. Reusable metal ramp and stairs
8. View windows enhance student performance
9. Pin-up wall surfaces
10. VOC scrubbing sheetrock walls
11. Extra door provides optimal site orientation
12. Steel Frame Structure
13. Helical Piers Foundation

A. Air-Renu Gypsum Board
B. BioPCM: Phase Change Material in walls, acts as thermal mass stabilizes indoor temperature
C. Insulation
D. Sheathing

26.109
Diagram of key SAGE features, SAGE Affordable Green Modular Classrooms, 2012.

Waldorf School met their educational mandate for natural, child-centered spaces with a three-classroom SAGE unit.

Participation:
The design team committed to more than four years of community meetings and charettes in response to wasted energy, material contaminants, and air quality measured in typical modular classrooms. The resulting data and designs informed larger community exchanges through the Oregon Solutions Process, a mandate of the State of Oregon governor, in which academic–professional collaboration brought together stakeholders from community health, architecture, engineering, manufacturing, and government.

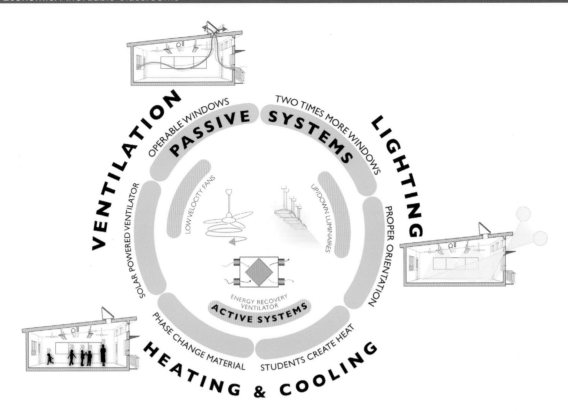

26.110
SAGE systems designed using Whole Building Design principles, SAGE Affordable Green Modular Classrooms, 2012.

Results:

SAGE's environmental performance will be tracked and compared with traditional classrooms and other modular classrooms in the region. Sensors placed in the classrooms will measure impact by monitoring internal environmental conditions, along with energy, water, and waste consumption/production. The design team is assessing student/teacher input on the benefits of SAGE.

Collaborators:

Portland public schools; Portland State University (PSU): Schools of Architecture and Engineering, Green Building Research Lab, Institute for Sustainable Solutions; Blazer Industries; Pacific Mobile Structures; Gerding Edlen, AIA Portland; Oregon Solutions; Oregon State Building Codes; Portland Bureau of Development Services; Northwest Renewable Energy Resources; Energy Trust of Oregon; Oregon BEST; PAE Engineers; McKinstry Engineers; M Space Holdings; EcoReal; Luma Lighting

Design Team:

PSU: Margarette Leite, Sergio Palleroni, Caty Skogland, Seth Moody, Matt Sedor, Taryn Mudge

Lafitte Greenway Revitalization
New Orleans, Louisiana

Summary:
The Lafitte Greenway Revitalization was prioritized after Hurricane Katrina. Because it crosses seven distinct New Orleans neighborhoods, it provided a unique unifying opportunity for the city and the communities. In August 2007, the New Orleans City Council passed a resolution converting the Lafitte Greenway Corridor into a publicly accessible greenway approximately 3.1 miles long.

Goal: Use greenway investment to catalyze sustainable neighborhood development
The project encompassed a master plan and revitalization plan that would not only provide better connectivity and increase the land value of the adjacent neighborhoods but also provide an amenity that would improve the health and welfare of the residents.

26.111
Aerial perspective sketch of the brownfield site known as the Lafitte Greenway after the master plan has been implemented. Design Workshop, Lafitte Greenway Revitalization, New Orleans, Louisiana, In progress.

26.112
Portions of the historic canal are re-envisioned as recreational spaces and provide artistic opportunities to display ecological and historic process. Design Workshop, Lafitte Greenway Revitalization, New Orleans, Louisiana, In progress.

26.113
Transforming the existing city-owned building into an open-air pavilion with community gardens and rainwater collection system offers new solutions for existing structures. Design Workshop, Lafitte Greenway Revitalization, New Orleans, Louisiana, In progress.

NEW ORLEANS, LOUISIANA
AUGUST 2011

AXONOMETRIC VIEWS - VIEW A

DESIGN WORKSHOP

Community:

According to the 2010 census, the corridor population is approximately 13,508 people, with a median age of 33. The seven corridor communities range widely from one end of the greenway to the other. Income differences captured that diversity: the south "river side" of the corridor, primarily renters, averaged a household income of around $18K or less; the northern "lake side," mostly home owners, averaged $35K–$60K.

Participation:

Because the greenway was of interest to the city even before the design team's involvement, community groups were ready advocates. The design team recorded a range of stakeholder needs during workshops and documented community responses using MindMixer and TurningPoint technologies, ensuring measurable public engagement. Comprehensive demographics, traffic-pattern, and land-use maps were created from census data, existing studies, and on-site observations, and more than one hundred pages of text and images verify the site conditions.

26.114
The historic alignment of the Canal is retrofitted as a rain garden with 100 percent native plant material, which helps to achieve environmental sustainability by restoring the native ecology and increasing both wildlife habitat and essential recreation space for the community. Design Workshop, Lafitte Greenway Revitalization, New Orleans, Louisiana, In progress.

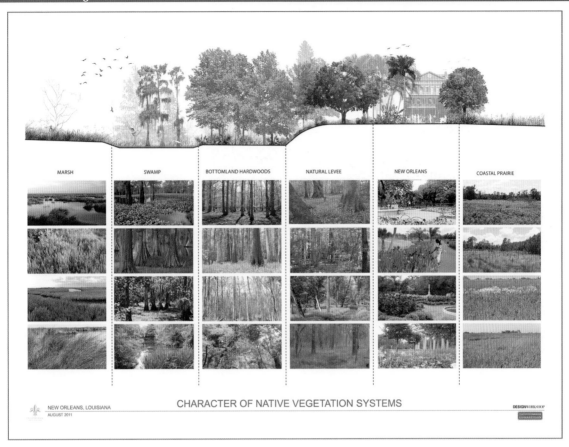

MARSH   SWAMP   BOTTOMLAND HARDWOODS   NATURAL LEVEE   NEW ORLEANS   COASTAL PRAIRIE

NEW ORLEANS, LOUISIANA
AUGUST 2011

CHARACTER OF NATIVE VEGETATION SYSTEMS

26.115

An in-depth analysis of the New Orleans landscape typologies shows the diverse ecotones that bisect the corridor and greenway. Design Workshop, Lafitte Greenway Revitalization, New Orleans, Louisiana, In progress.

Results:

The greenway master plan (as part of the revitalization effort) gave adjacent neighborhoods much-needed open spaces. The greenway further incentivized reinvestment in community through housing development and a renewed sense of community pride and well-being throughout diverse neighborhoods—results vital to long-term recovery.

Collaborators:

City of New Orleans, Friends of Lafitte Greenway, Lake Douglas

Design Team:

Design Workshop, Applied Ecological Services, Bright Moments, Christopher Davala, Eskew+Dumez+Ripple, Elkins, Gandolfo Kuhn, GreenPlay, Julien Engineering, Walter Kulash, Michael Willis Architects, RCLCO, Three Fold Consultants, Moon Design

24

Economic: Transitional Job Training

Social: Community Development

Environmental: Organic Food Production

Growing Home

Chicago, Illinois

Summary:

This project responds to the challenge of building economic self-sufficiency with transitional training and employment opportunities in organic agriculture that targets low-income and homeless people. Growing Home is Chicago's first USDA-certified organic urban farm. Agriculture practices and site building materials were carefully selected to achieve this designation.

Goal: Promote quality of life through economic self-sufficiency

The design team and the Growing Home organization shared the vision that social health is inherently connected to economic and environmental health. Together, they identified three achievable goals: enhance community self-sufficiency

26.116
Initial concept sketch for the Wood Street Site, SHED Studio, Growing Home, Chicago, Illinois, Phase I: 2009, Phase II: 2012.

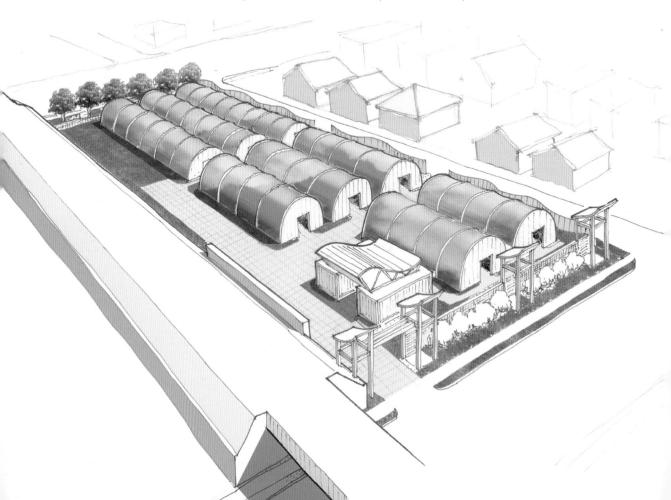

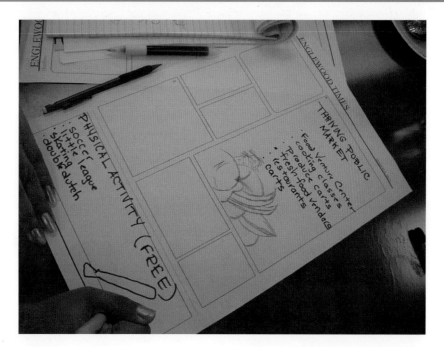

26.117
Community visioning
workshop for the Englewood
Urban Agricultural District,
Growing Home, Chicago,
Illinois, Phase I: 2009, Phase
II: 2012.

26.118
Trainees and staff working inside a hoophouse, Growing Home, Chicago, Illinois, Phase I: 2009,
Phase II: 2012.

26.119
Overall view of site from bridge, Growing Home, Chicago, Illinois, Phase I: 2009, Phase II: 2012.

through entrepreneurship, provide workforce development, and train residents in the production of organic agriculture. Growing Home was a part of the New Communities Program, which was set up to create Quality of Life Plans for targeted neighborhoods in Chicago. The contribution of Englewood (a Chicago neighborhood) to the plan was the creation of an urban agricultural district.

Community:

Since 1960, Englewood has experienced sustained economic and social inequality. Although devastated by disinvestment, this predominantly African American population is reversing their plight by reconnecting to assets that exist within their neighborhood and renewing community ties.

Participation:

The project design and master plan were broken out into two phases: the Growing Home hub site provided the design team with valuable community interaction during phase one, before proceeding to the expansion site during phase two. A full year was spent gathering observations and feedback from stakeholders during community charettes.

26.120
Growing Home farm stand,
Growing Home, Chicago,
Illinois, Phase I: 2009,
Phase II: 2012.

Results:

Currently, Growing Home operates two farms and significantly impacts the community and its economic development: forty to forty-five interns are employed annually; 93 percent of program graduates were placed in employment opportunities in 2013 (total number 300 since program inception); and thirteen thousand tons of produce grown in 2012 (sales of $136,950.00).

Collaborators:

Working group/steering committee: SHED (Sustainable, Humane, and Experimental Design) Studio, Growing Home project manager, farm manager, and job training coordinator; Community: Growing Home program students and staff, Englewood residents, Teamwork Englewood, alderman office representative

Design Team:

Architect: SHED Studio; Interior design: Designs for Dignity

Growing Home   **281**

25

Environmental: Up-cycling

Economic: Local Production

Economic: Street Vending

Can City
São Paulo, Brazil

Summary:
Catadores, Brazil's waste collectors, are responsible for approximately 80 percent of the country's recycling. Unfortunately, many view them as blemishes on the city's image, and there is a movement to prevent the catadores from collecting and selling materials. Can City is a counteraction that supports these workers.

Goal: Create a sustainable system as an income generator
Can City created an inexpensive, sustainable furnace-casting system, which employs cooking oil from food stalls and collected aluminum cans, that catadores can use to make and sell recast products. Increased tourism in Brazil offers a greater opportunity to sell locally produced goods, which will increase livelihood, self-esteem, and potentially even the public's appreciation of these marginalized members of society.

Community:
São Paulo has a diverse and active street culture with food carts, markets, and craftsmen, who make and repair items on city streets. The city lacks infrastructure

26.121
Firing the furnace, Can City, São Paulo, Brazil, 2013.

26.122
Pouring the palm leaf stool, Can City, São Paulo, Brazil, 2013.

26.123
Palm leaf stool, Can City, São
Paulo, Brazil, 2013.

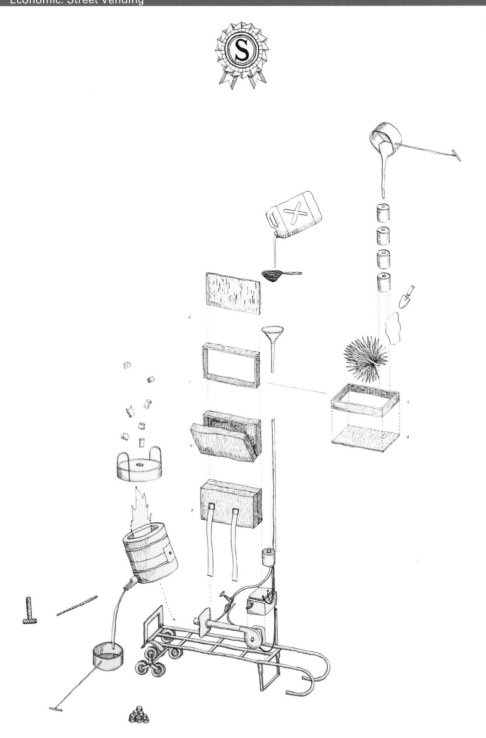

26.124
Exploded diagram of the furnace, Studio Swine, Can City, São Paulo, Brazil, 2013.

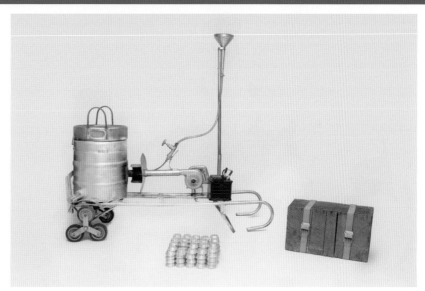

26.125
The mobile foundry, Can City,
São Paulo, Brazil, 2013.

and economic opportunity, spurring entrepreneurs, like the catadores, to take their trade to the streets to earn a living.

Participation:
Can City is the culmination of three years of research and sustainable design development. The design team conducted interviews with local craftsmen, street artists, and vendors to understand their challenges, needs, and desires. Based on gathered data, the team established a network of supporters, who helped launch the Can City project.

Results:
Designed to be an open and adaptable system, Can City is a transportable mobile foundry. Art- and craft-based pieces are cast as unique items on-demand. Benefits include: smaller carbon cost due to local production; burning cooking oil is cleaner than traditional charcoal; and sand for molds is reusable. This manner of up-cycling taps into the strong culture of improvization and the spirit of innovation found in Brazilian vernacular design

Collaborators:
Community organizer: Anya Teixeira, Olivia Faria; Production assistant: Anya Teixeira; Finance: Agatha Faria; Sponsor: Heineken Brasil; Filmmaker: Juriaan Booij; Project production: Studio Swine, Coletivo Amor de Madre; Translators: Paola Croso, Renata Padovan; Catadores from Eco Point: Elcides, Que Que, Wilson, Ricardo, Alan

Design Team:
Project creators: Studio Swine

Klyde Warren Park
Dallas, Texas

Summary:

Constructed over the eight-lane I-35 Woodall Rodgers Freeway, Klyde Warren Park is an urban green space that links Dallas's downtown cultural district with mixed-use neighborhoods to the north. What had previously been an urban blight between downtown and uptown neighborhoods is now a park that celebrates health, innovation, and civic and cultural activity.

Goal: Connect people to the heart of the city

Among the world's largest suspended park infrastructures, the park is socially, economically, and environmentally sustainable. It relies on a system of concrete beams and trenches and hosts more than three hundred trees, several thousand

26.126

Built over an existing freeway, Klyde Warren Park provides a variety of flexible outdoor rooms that support a diverse range of free, programmed activities. Since opening in October 2012, the park has been enthusiastically adopted by the citizens of Dallas. Klyde Warren Park, Dallas, Texas, 2012.

26.127
The groves of trees and arch structures establish a strong architectural rhythm through the park and buffer the interior of the park from the busy adjacent surface streets. Klyde Warren Park, Dallas, Texas, 2012.

26.128
The 5.2-acre park has thirteen programmed spaces including a 3,000-square-foot dog park. Klyde Warren Park, Dallas, Texas, 2012.

shrubs, and thirteen programmed spaces. It serves as both a destination and a link between distinct geographies of the city. Abundant economic growth around the perimeter of the park aids in urban development.

Community:
The pedestrian-friendly park unifies the greater Dallas–Fort Worth community with a world-class amenity—a 5.2-acre public green space that functions as a town square.

Participation:
Stakeholders were engaged throughout the planning process in community meetings, project workshops, charettes, and park-feature surveys. Many donor suggestions for specific features were implemented. The park, now in post-occupancy, continues to promote social interaction and community participation.

Results:
The park's popularity is greater than anticipated: opening weekend attracted approximately forty thousand visitors, with roughly one million visitors during the park's first year. In its first fifteen months, the park hosted about 1,055 programs and forty-six large-scale special events. Luxury residential buildings bordering the park have sprung up as indicators of the demand for accessible, culture-rich urban dwelling.

Collaborators:
Woodall Rodgers Park Foundation; City of Dallas; Texas Department of Transportation; Landscape Architecture Foundation, Case Study Investigation[1]

Klyde Warren Park

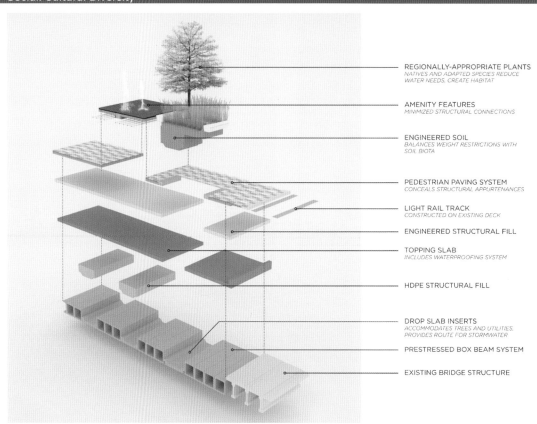

REGIONALLY-APPROPRIATE PLANTS
NATIVES AND ADAPTED SPECIES REDUCE WATER NEEDS, CREATE HABITAT

AMENITY FEATURES
MINIMIZED STRUCTURAL CONNECTIONS

ENGINEERED SOIL
BALANCES WEIGHT RESTRICTIONS WITH SOIL BIOTA

PEDESTRIAN PAVING SYSTEM
CONCEALS STRUCTURAL APPURTENANCES

LIGHT RAIL TRACK
CONSTRUCTED ON EXISTING DECK

ENGINEERED STRUCTURAL FILL

TOPPING SLAB
INCLUDES WATERPROOFING SYSTEM

HDPE STRUCTURAL FILL

DROP SLAB INSERTS
ACCOMMODATES TREES AND UTILITIES, PROVIDES ROUTE FOR STORMWATER

PRESTRESSED BOX BEAM SYSTEM

EXISTING BRIDGE STRUCTURE

26.129
The Office of James Burnett, Klyde Warren Park, Dallas, Texas, 2012.

Design Team:
The Office of James Burnett, Thomas Phifer and Partners, Bjerke Management Solutions, Endres Ware Architects, Focus Lighting Design, Fluidity Design Consultants, Sweeney Associates, Jacobs Engineering, Biederman Redevelopment Ventures, Dal-Tech Engineering, Focus EGD, The Johnson Studio, Archer Western Contractors, McCarthy Building Companies, ValleyCrest Landscape Development

Notes

1   Klyde Warren Park is a Landscape Architecture Foundation, Landscape Performance Series Case Study Brief.

PROJECT WORKSHOP AND STAKEHOLDERS SURVEY RESULTS

PROGRAMS AND FEATURES

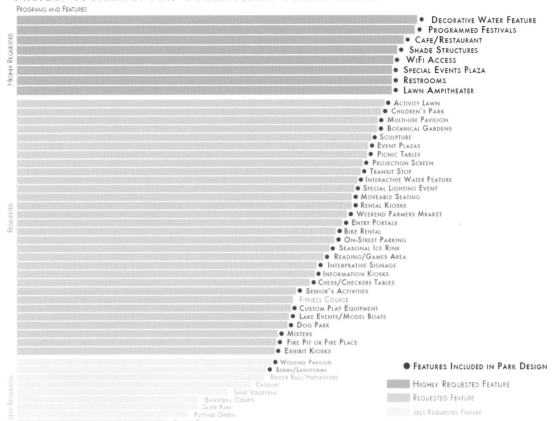

HIGHLY REQUESTED

- DECORATIVE WATER FEATURE
- PROGRAMMED FESTIVALS
- CAFE/RESTAURANT
- SHADE STRUCTURES
- WiFi ACCESS
- SPECIAL EVENTS PLAZA
- RESTROOMS
- LAWN AMPITHEATER

REQUESTED

- ACTIVITY LAWN
- CHILDREN'S PARK
- MULTI-USE PAVILION
- BOTANICAL GARDENS
- SCULPTURE
- EVENT PLAZAS
- PICNIC TABLES
- PROJECTION SCREEN
- TRANSIT STOP
- INTERACTIVE WATER FEATURE
- SPECIAL LIGHTING EVENT
- MOVEABLE SEATING
- RENTAL KIOSKS
- WEEKEND FARMERS MRAKET
- ENTRY PORTALS
- BIKE RENTAL
- ON-STREET PARKING
- SEASONAL ICE RINK
- READING/GAMES AREA
- INTERPRATIVE SIGNAGE
- INFORMATION KIOSKS
- CHESS/CHECKERS TABLES
- SENIOR'S ACTIVITIES
- FITNESS COURSE
- CUSTOM PLAY EQUIPMENT
- LAKE EVENTS/MODEL BOATS
- DOG PARK
- MISTERS
- FIRE PIT OR FIRE PLACE
- EXHIBIT KIOSKS

LESS REQUESTED

- WEDDING PAVILION
- BERMS/LANDFORMS
- BOCCE BALL/HORSESHOES
- CROQUET
- SAND VOLLEYBALL
- BASKETBALL COURTS
- SKATE PARK
- PUTTING GREEN
- SOCCER FIELD

- ● FEATURES INCLUDED IN PARK DESIGN
- HIGHLY REQUESTED FEATURE
- REQUESTED FEATURE
- LESS REQUESTED FEATURE

26.130
The Office of James Burnett, Klyde Warren Park, Dallas, Texas, 2012.

Walk [Your City]
Raleigh, North Carolina

Summary:
Walk [Your City] provides online community-action tools that users can employ to generate signs that promote a more walkable city. Resistance to walking sustains car-dependency and sprawling development patterns that further reduce pedestrian activity. This urban design, signage, and wayfinding project stimulates walking culture and improves public health, pedestrian infrastructure, and the public use of open space.

Goal: Shift the culture toward pedestrian activity
The goal of the project is two-fold: empower citizen activism to implement the Walk [Your City] signage system in compliance with city ordinances and increase the number of individuals who walk to their destination.

26.131
Original WalkRaleigh signs installed on existing signal poles in downtown Raleigh, Walk [Your City], Raleigh, North Carolina, 2012.

26.132
Sign hanging in Raleigh, Walk [Your City], Raleigh, North Carolina, 2012.

26.133
Mayor Trace Cooper installing a campaign to support pedestrian activity while the city raises money for a permanent wayfinding system over the next three years, Walk [Your City], Atlantic Beach, North Carolina, 2013.

Community:

The pilot project was launched in three different Raleigh neighborhoods (downtown Raleigh, the North Carolina State University area, and near the closest grocery store to downtown) and targeted three demographics (business professionals, university students, and shoppers). These ranges were selected for breadth of age, diversity, and site variances.

Participation:

The project designer completed neighborhood surveys to help establish a baseline for people's perception of a walkable distance: fifteen minutes or less. The surveys established a guiding rule: If I can't see it, I can't walk to it! Originally an independent project, Walk [Your City] gained city support after a vote of 1,300 citizens. The project was then reimplemented as a pilot educational program and later incorporated into the City Comprehensive Pedestrian Plan.

Results:

A Kickstarter campaign ignited more than five hundred backers and raised more than $11,000.00. In the first year, there were thirteen thousand downloads of the open-source signage template, with the participation of more than seventy-five communities. A quick response (QR) code embedded in each sign provides walking

26.134
Matt and fellow guerrillas hanging the original WalkRaleigh signs in downtown Raleigh, Walk [Your City], Raleigh, North Carolina, 2012.

26.135
Mayor Michael Martin
and community members
installing the very first
directional signage for Mount
Hope, Walk [Your City], Mount
Hope, West Virginia, 2013.

directions via smartphone and tracks use—thousands of scans are currently being tracked for data patterns. A major health insurance provider recognized the value of this project and has offered substantial financial support.

Collaborators:
Project advisors: Mitchell Silver, former city of Raleigh chief planning and development director; City of Raleigh City Council pilot program

Design Team:
Urban designer/civic instigator: Matt Tomasulo

PackH20 Water Backpack

Haiti, Kenya, Malawi, Guatemala, and Mexico

Summary:

In some of the world's most water-stressed regions, the use of discarded jerry cans for water collection compromises health. Women and children typically carry these cans on their heads for miles, burdening the spine. In addition, the contamination of water sources and toxins from these cans indicate a much needed and culturally acceptable solution for water access and conveyance.

Goal: Change the way the developing world thinks about water access

PackH20 eases the burden of water collection and transport by means of a weight-distributed backpack system. The backpack is durable, puncture resistant, and the lining can be sanitized—solar thermal disinfection keeps internal plastic liners

26.136
A woman in Peru carries water with the PackH20 Water Backpack instead of carrying water in a dirty jerry can. PackH20 Water Backpack, Peru, 2014.

26.137
Illustrations of the final
product, Battelle, PackH20
Water Backpack, 2012.

free from repeated exposure to toxins. The backpack's roll-down closure reduces contamination while the protected spout keeps water safe.

Community:
In developing countries with limited infrastructure, communities are in desperate need of water. PackH20 serves disadvantaged people with a lack of water due to environmental conditions and communities that have experienced a disaster.

Participation:
The design team at Greif, a manufacturer of industrial packaging products and services, worked with Clinton Global Initiative, Partners In Health, and community leaders in Haiti to conduct four field tests to gather input from community leaders on the design. Changes included widening the straps for comfort, altering the spigot location for enhanced water collection and flow, adding reflective tape for night walking, and shaping the bottom of the pack like a bucket.

Results:
PackH20 Water Backpacks have been delivered to communities—more than thirty countries, impacting more than 750,000 people, mostly women and children—through grant funds supported by partner organizations. The twenty-liter version backpack is seven times lighter and smaller than a twenty-liter rigid plastic jerry can, which reduces shipping costs and allows for fast, high-volume emergency-relief shipments.

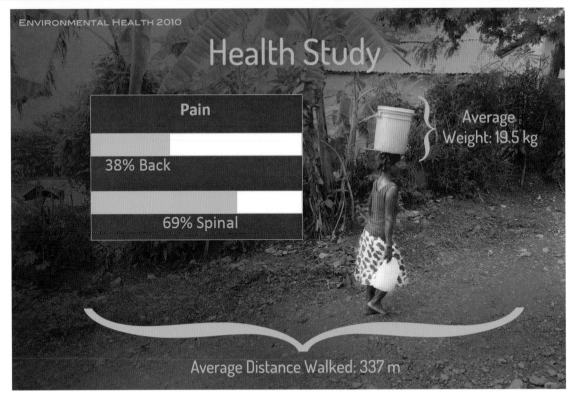

ENVIRONMENTAL HEALTH 2010

Health Study

Pain

38% Back

69% Spinal

Average Weight: 19.5 kg

Average Distance Walked: 337 m

26.138

In 2010, the journal *Environmental Health* published a study on domestic water carrying. The results showed 69 percent of participants reported spinal pain and 38 percent reported back pain. This visual representation depicts the health challenges of traditional water transportation. PackH20 Water Backpack, Kimana, Kenya, 2012.

26.139
A woman in Kenya wearing a water backpack as part of testing, PackH20 Water Backpack, Kimana, Kenya, 2012.

26.140
A woman in Guatemala demonstrates wearing a PackH20 Water Backpack while also carrying a child. PackH20 Water Backpack, Guatemala, 2013.

Collaborators:

Impact Economics, Clinton Global Initiative, Partners In Health, PRODEV, Qorvis MSLGROUP, Partners for Care, Habitat for Humanity International, Operation Blessing International, CxCatalysts, CEMACO

Design Team:

Greif: David B. Fischer, president and CEO, Scott Griffin, chief sustainability officer; Nottingham Spirk team; Battelle

Portable Laboratory on Uncommon Ground

Mahale Mountains National Park, Tanzania

Summary:

Mahale Mountains National Park sustains the local economy through the revenue brought in by tourism. But tourism along with invasive research activities can introduce disease and threaten wildlife health. Past research undertaken in the

26.141
Completed laboratory in situ, Mahale Mountains National Park, PLUG, Mahale Mountains National Park, Tanzania, 2007.

26.142
PLUG arriving by boat on Lake
Tanganyika, PLUG, Mahale
Mountains National Park,
Tanzania, 2007.

26.143
Tool-less assembly process,
PLUG, Mahale Mountains
National Park, Tanzania, 2007.

26.144
A single functionally complex
joint detail resolves all
structural forces within
the system, PLUG, Mahale
Mountains National Park,
Tanzania, 2007.

park negatively impacted the local ecosystem with permanent construction of
research facilities and a lack of waste-disposal infrastructure. Portable Laboratory on
Uncommon Ground (PLUG) is a portable, solar-powered, user-assembled research
station that allows researchers to process samples in the field with minimal impact.

*Goal: Preserve the Mahale chimpanzee population while supporting low-impact
    research*
PLUG leaves no trace, does not require tools for the two-person-team assembly,
and is supported by low-impact compression footings. Photovoltaic panels eliminate
diesel generators, water is sourced from a nearby lake using a photovoltaic helical
water pump and stored in an above-ground polypropylene tank, and second-floor
sleeping quarters reduce the structural footprint.

Community:
The park is a protected environment globally known to tourists and to primate
researchers for its chimpanzee population. Under the purview of the Tanzanian
National Park Authority (TANAPA), the park maintains relationships with the
Tanzania National Wildlife Institute (TAWIRI) and Virginia Maryland Regional College
of Veterinary Medicine (VMRCVM) through the Bush-to-Base Bioinformatics (B2B)
group.

26.145
Lower level of the PLUG lab
in use by researcher from
VMRCVM, PLUG, Mahale
Mountains National Park,
Tanzania, 2007.

Participation:
TANAPA provided design feedback, and B2B researchers validated the solution with outreach to researchers in other camps and local tourist outposts. Performance features were further assessed during a six-month period when VMRCVM–B2B scientists lived and worked on-site.

Results:
Research at the lab is credited with working toward the immediate detection of disease, thus potentially preventing an outbreak that could devastate the park's chimpanzee population. The lab also functions as an education hub, sharing research endeavors related to wildlife preservation and interaction.

Collaborators:
TANAPA, Virginia Tech School of Architecture and Design, Center for Design Research, VMRCVM, B2B, Tanzanian National Wildlife Institute

Design Team:
Virginia Tech School of Architecture and Design students and faculty, led by Matt Lutz and Nathan King; VMRCVM students and faculty, led by Dr. Taranjit Kaur and Dr. Jatinder Singh

Acknowledgment:
This material is based upon work supported by the National Science Foundation (NSF Grant #0238069). Any opinions, findings, and conclusions or recommendations expressed in this material are those of the author(s) and do not necessarily reflect the views of the NSF.

Potty Project
New Delhi, India

Summary:
Located on the western edge of New Delhi, Savda Ghevra (SG) is one of the largest resettlement colonies in the city. It is home to more than twenty thousand families, who live on plots of partially developed land, with homes mostly self-built of brick, concrete, and corrugated-sheet roofs. Infrastructure is marginal: water is brought in by tanker, and there is no sewage disposal. People either use community toilet complexes or defecate in the open.

Goal: Provide household toilets that are safe, dignified, and sanitary
This project addresses the needs of all people in this resettlement but especially women and girls. Females are especially vulnerable to rape and harm: safety in the context of hygiene is a human right.

Community:
The residents of block A of SG are slum dwellers who relocated from the inner city to this fringe "planned" neighborhood. In this community only 3.8 percent of the families have in-home toilets and another 0.5 percent have temporary outdoor facilities. Of the home toilets, only 50 percent connect to a pit or septic tank. The remaining 50 percent discharge into open drains that pose health risks.

26.146
The septic tank services up to 350 households, with an average of six people per household, with a two-year maintenance plan. Julia King, Potty Project, New Delhi, India, 2013.

26.147
Local masons have been used where possible during the construction of the project to increase a sense of ownership. Potty Project, New Delhi, India, 2013.

Participation:

Participation occurred at multiple levels, including small group meetings. Street leaders served as mediators between the design team and residents. Social and community mapping, needs prioritization, focus-groups, in-home surveys, technical assessments, and model generation all aided in the design process. The nonprofit partner Centre for Urban and Regional Excellence (CURE) India had an office in the neighborhood, offering a trusted presence.

Results:

The project provides 322 households (approximately 2,000 people) with the infrastructure to support home toilets, which are connected to a simple transfer and collection method that treats the sewage using a decentralized wastewater treatment system, with the future potential to recycling the black water for reuse. The following metrics will be used to determine success: improved family health and productivity; perception of safety, especially among females; creation of socially cohesive communities; and environmental impact from reduction of open defecation.

26.148

The tanks often overflow into what are incomplete and blocked open drains intended to move greywater, leaving exposed sewage to stagnate and percolate into the ground. Not all houses let their tanks overflow and will get the pits emptied by a local 'Septic Tank Walla'—a man who comes with a truck and mechanically removes the waste. Potty Project, New Delhi, India, 2013.

26.149
Simplified sewers are small diameter pipes laid at fairly flat gradients under the pavement. Here the trenches for these drains can be seen. Potty Project, New Delhi, India, 2013.

26.150
Many meetings were held in local parks and everyone was welcome to attend. Because the issue of sanitation is such a gendered one women were particularly interested in attending these meetings. Potty Project, New Delhi, India, 2013.

Collaborators:

Residents of Savda Ghevra resettlement colony; Academic advisor: Maurice Mitchell

Design Team:

Architectural designer: Julia King; CURE India: Dr. Renu Khosla, Sidharth Shanker Pandey; Chief Engineer: Hussain Zaidi

Glossary

Abduction: Referred to by American philosopher Charles Sanders Peirce as the expectancy of how impending conflicting systems might coalesce (chapter 7, page 83)

Accountability: Demonstrating responsibility in action, especially in evaluation of how goals were met or not met (chapter 8, pages 96–7)

AIM (Achievable, Impactful, Measurable): A model used by Design Impact to understand desirable project outcomes (chapter 20, pages 153–5)

Asset-based Design: An approach to community development design work that identifies the strengths, skills, and abilities of stakeholders and groups involved in a project or process rather than the shortcomings of the problem

Asset Mapping: A resource-driven expression of asset-based design documenting and identifing the wealth of capacity in a community

Benchmark: A point of reference or standard for performance evaluation during the timeline of a project used to inform the expected outcome of a project (chapter 7, page 83; chapter 8, pages 96–7; chapter 21, pages 157–61)

Charette: An individual activity or group collaborative whereby designers and others seek to resolve or understand a problem through comprehensive design process efforts (chapter 18, pages 143–6)

Civic Engagement: Public participation strategies created to help identify community needs or issues and ways to address those (chapter 11, pages 109–14)

Community: A group of people with a shared set of beliefs, interests, or social values

Community Action Planning: A method for community collaboration that assesses problems, prioritizes actions, and identifies impact according to capacities (chapter 14, pages 125–8)

Community-centered Design: A process that assesses individual and/or group needs and wants relative to design and development outcomes

Content analysis: A quantitative or qualitative analysis useful in the systematic comparison of meaning (chapter 7, page 85)

Data: Quantitative or qualitative information used to discover connections, patterns, and meanings that can be helpful in assessing project direction and outcomes

Ethics: A set of guiding principles or standards that guide behavior and conduct (chapter 1, page 13; chapter 7, pages 85–6)

Evidence-based Design: Design decisions created from the analysis of contextual evidence and empirical data; a term with precedents in health care (chapter 7, page 88; chapter 23, pages 170–1)

Goal: The purpose toward which a project is directed (chapter 8, pages 94–5)

Human Subject Research: Any systemic research activity that involves people and the acquisition of information considered private; human subject research often requires Institutional Review Board approval within institutional settings

Institutional Review Board (IRB): An institutional committee that monitors the ethical conduct of researchers in human subject research (chapter 7, pages 85–6)

Issue-based Design: An approach to identifying the strata of community need embedded within and between social, economic, and environmental issues (chapter 16, pages 133–5; chapter 25, pages 181–3)

Measurement: Quantification that shows a sum or aggregate result (chapter 19, pages 147–9; chapter 20, pages 151–5)

Outcomes (see also 'Results'): A consequence stemming from outputs (chapter 6, pages 67–79)

Outputs: The physical results generated by a person, entity, or a project (chapter 6, pages 67–79)

Performance Indicator: A sign or artifact of progress toward goals or results

Performance Measurement: The process of documenting and reporting accomplishment toward goals and/or results (chapter 19, page 148)

Place-making: A framework used in the design and planning of the built environment that acknowledges and activates community assets for promotion of identity, health, and well-being (chapter 14, pages 125–8; chapter 15, pages 129–32)

Problem Tree: A tool for analyzing causal relationships within built environment contexts (chapter 14, pages 125–8)

Public: Diverse social groups with varying values

Public Interest: The management of the well-being, needs, wants, and desires of diverse social groups (chapter 7, pages 81–9)

Public Interest Design: A design practice composed of three tenets—democratic decision making through meaningful community engagement, an issue-based approach, and the requirement for design evaluation (Introduction, pages 1–7)

Public Interest Design Institute (PIDI): The public interest design education and outreach unit of Social Economic Environmental Design (SEED) (Introduction, pages 4–5)

Qualitative Research: Processes that include in-depth analysis of life through contextual observations, interviews, photography, video and written or oral documentation (chapter 13, pages 122–3)

Quantitative Research: Processes based on empirical evidence, facts, numeric references, and analysis of these data to establish broad connections through pattern recognition (chapter 13, pages 122–3)

Results (see also 'Outcomes'): The tangible and measurable consequence of a process that achieves the goal(s) (chapter 19, pages 147–9)

Scaling: A process of impacting people through quantity, variety, or locations (chapter 22, pages 163–5; chapter 23, pages 167–71; chapter 24, pages 173–7)

SEED (Social Economic Environmental Design): A recognized standard for triple bottom line evaluation of design (Introduction, pages 1–7)

SEED Certification: Third-party evaluation and resulting recognition of compliance with SEED standards (mission and principles) at an exemplary level (chapter 9, pages 101–3)

SEED Evaluator: An online communication tool that translates the SEED process allowing communities, audiences, and designers to define goals for design projects and then measure project achievement through a third-party review (chapter 9, pages 99–103)

SEED Network: A principle-based group composed of design professionals and organizations that facilitates action by providing guidelines for pursuing a design process informed by inclusivity and participation as well as creating a community of knowledge for professionals and the public based on a set of shared values (Introduction, pages 2–3)

Stakeholders: Diverse individuals or groups that have a vested interest in a project, and provide needed input toward project process, goals, and results

Sustainability: The ability to endure socially, economically, and/or environmentally over time without negatively impacting other contexts

Triangulation: The use of several methods or sources for data collection helps ensure the soundness of a research investigation (chapter 7, page 84)

Triple Bottom Line: A term coined by author John Elkington, the SEED mission expresses that every person should be able to live in a socially, economically, and environmentally healthy community and provides a framework for an issue-based approach to design that achieves long term sustainable outcomes (Introduction, page 2)

Value Chain: All producer and consumer entities and activities that contribute to the formulation of an emerging or scaled product or service (chapter 24, pages 173–7)

Editor Biographies

Lisa M. Abendroth is a professor at Metropolitan State University of Denver in Colorado, USA. She is a Social Economic Environmental Design (SEED) founding member, a SEED Evaluator coauthor, and a 2013 recipient of the SEED Award for Leadership in Public Interest Design. Abendroth lectures and presents the SEED methodology and case studies in diverse educational contexts including the Public Interest Design Institute. Her research across design disciplines includes writing, curating, and critically assessing solutions that address underserved people, places, and problems.

Bryan Bell founded Design Corps in North Carolina, USA to provide the benefits of design for the 98% without architects. Bell's current work includes public interest design, and the SEED Network, which he cofounded. This work was supported by the FAIA Latrobe Prize and through a Harvard Loeb Fellowship. Bell has published two books in the field, and leads the Public Interest Design Institute and the Structures for Inclusion conference series. He was awarded a National AIA Award and was a National Design Award Finalist. His work has been exhibited at the Venice Biennale and the Cooper Hewitt, Smithsonian Design Museum.

Contributor Biographies

Jamie Blosser is an associate at Atkin Olshin Schade Architects. She founded the Sustainable Native Communities Collaborative (SNCC), an initiative of Enterprise Community Partners, and helped to develop a rural pathway for the Enterprise Green Communities Criteria. SNCC's Case Studies 2013, featuring seventeen exemplary tribal-housing projects, was showcased in Washington, DC, at the National Museum of the American Indian. She was the 2000–3 recipient of the Enterprise Rose Architectural Fellowship. Blosser is a 2014–5 Loeb Fellow at the Harvard Graduate School of Design (GSD), researching resilient planning principles in marginalized communities around the world.

Brent A. Brown, AIA, is a Dallas architect who uses design to enhance livability for all of Dallas's residents. In 2005 Brown founded the buildingcommunity WORKSHOP (bcWORKSHOP), a nonprofit community-design resource that seeks to improve the livability and viability of communities through the practice of thoughtful design and making. He is also the founding director of Dallas's CityDesign Studio, which is stewarding the urban design vision for the city.

Barbara Brown Wilson is an assistant professor of environmental planning at the University of Virginia. Her research and teaching focus is on community-engaged sustainable development and urban, environmental history. Her research often involves collaboration with community partners to identify opportunities for sustainable development that further goals in both research and practice. Wilson has also participated in the founding of several educational and practical public interest design organizations, including the University of Texas Public Interest Design

Program and Design Futures Student Leadership Forum, and the Austin Community Design and Development Center.

Michael Cohen is professor of international affairs at the New School. He worked at the World Bank from 1972 to 1999, during which time he traveled to fifty-five countries and was chief of the Urban Development division and senior adviser to the vice president of Environmentally Sustainable Development. He has written books and articles on development-policy issues, urban development, Africa, and Argentina. Cohen was a member of the US National Academy of Sciences Panels on Infrastructure and Urban Demographic Dynamics.

Roberta M. Feldman, MArch, PhD, is an architectural activist, researcher, and educator committed to democratic design. The cofounder of the University of Illinois at Chicago (UIC) City Design Center, Feldman has collaborated with more than fifty community organizations and development corporations in Chicago's low-income neighborhoods. Feldman is currently Director Emerita of the City Design Center and Professor Emerita at UIC. She continues her research and advocacy with other institutions, including the National Public Housing Museum (as vice chair of Programs and Interpretation on the museum board of directors) and Art Works Projects (chair of the board of directors).

Thomas Fisher is a professor at the School of Architecture and the dean of the College of Design at the University of Minnesota. Educated at Cornell University in architecture and Case Western Reserve University in intellectual history, he has been cited as the fifth most published academic in his field, having authored eight books since 2000, more than fifty book chapters or introductions, and more than 250 major articles. Fisher's recent work has focused on human health and the designed environment and on the ethics related to the creation of sustainable, equitable, and healthy communities.

Heather Fleming is the CEO of Catapult Design, a product- and service-design firm that partners with international organizations to develop sustainable, market-based solutions to poverty. Fleming has more than a decade of experience in product-design consulting and was formerly an adjunct lecturer at Stanford University and senior lecturer at California College of the Arts. In 2010 the World Economic Forum included Fleming in their class of Young Global Leaders, a prestigious community for leaders under the age of forty. She is a prominent advocate for the role of design in international- and economic-development initiatives.

Ramsey Ford is cofounder and design director of Design Impact, a social venture that connects design with low-income communities in India and the United States. With Design Impact, Ford has worked on or directed more than forty-five social-change projects, ranging from local health initiatives to nationwide skill-building platforms.

These projects are all informed by a dedication to community development and empowerment through design.

Michael Haggerty is an urban planner and currently a student in the Master in Architecture program at the Harvard GSD.

Kate Hanisian is the executive director and cofounder of Design Impact. Before founding Design Impact, she earned her master's degree in education, taught for four years in a low-income, underperforming district, and led strategic planning and capacity building for the Ohio Justice & Policy Center, a nonprofit law firm that works for criminal-justice reform. Hanisian has lived and worked internationally, leading youth-development and program-management initiatives in India, Jamaica, and New Zealand. She has spoken and led training sessions in venues ranging from TEDx to the National Endowment for the Arts (NEA).

David Kaisel was most recently a senior designer at Catapult Design, focusing his work on understanding user behavior to harness the influence of design to improve health and welfare, especially in marginalized communities. Kaisel's multidisciplinary background in design, business management, and public health informs his experience, which ranges from the traditional—designing office chairs, client management, and product strategy—to more experimental use of design process, such as coordinating missions for Doctors Without Borders. Kaisel has a BA in Industrial Design from San Jose State University, a Master of Public Health from UC Berkeley, and an MBA from the University of Washington.

Renu Khosla is the director of the Centre for Urban and Regional Excellence (CURE), an Indian nongovernmental organization. She works with slum communities in Indian cities to reimagine slum development and to nudge change in the city narrative—from top down to bottom up—and in people-led development. Through her work she strengthens the capacity of local and state government agencies for participative planning and development, visualizing community information using mobile media and spatial technologies, localizing implementation strategies and de-engineering solutions for greater equity, simplifying institutions, and influencing policy for inclusive development.

Julia King is a British/Venezuelan architect (RIBA II, AA Dip) and PhD candidate in the research department of the Architecture of Rapid Change and Scarce Resources at London Metropolitan University. Her work addresses housing, infrastructure (predominantly sanitation), urban planning, inclusive-development, and participatory-design processes. King runs a design and research practice in Delhi, India, in collaboration with CURE. For her work she was awarded Emerging Woman Architect of the Year in the United Kingdom and won a SEED Award for Excellence in Public Interest Design.

Margarette Leite teaches building tectonics, material sustainability, and community-engaged design at Portland State University's School of Architecture (Oregon), where she is a fellow of the Center for Public Interest Design. She is known for her work with local schools and with disaster-relief communities, which have garnered awards for civic engagement and have been the subjects of numerous publications and documentaries. She has been a featured speaker at various forums on public interest design. Her work on the SAGE green modular classroom received a 2013 SEED Award.

Steven A. Moore is Bartlett Cocke Regents Professor of Architecture and Planning at University of Texas at Austin, where he teaches design and courses related to the philosophy, history, and application of sustainable technology. Moore is a Loeb Fellow of the Harvard GSD, a fellow of the NEA, a recipient of an Individual Scholar Award from the National Science Foundation, and is the author of many articles, book chapters, and six books on the topic of social equity as a dimension of sustainable architecture and urbanism.

Scott Moore y Medina, AIA NCARB, principal architect and community builder at Blue Star Studio, is of mixed heritage from the prairies of Kansas and the mountains of New Mexico. He comes from a long line of teachers, farmers, artists, and preachers. He received his BArch from the University of Kansas, after which he traveled the world. Now a licensed architect, Moore y Medina leads projects at every level and has contributed to works with a solid emphasis on dialogue, respect, and common sense. He is proud to give back to his rural, tribal, and disadvantaged-community roots.

Annie Moulton is chief of staff at MASS Design Group and supports the executive director in development efforts, communications, and advocacy. With a background in international development and public policy, her interest focuses on how the built environment can tangibly impact development challenges. Prior to joining MASS, Moulton worked in Washington, DC, at the Brookings Institution for the Africa Growth Initiative, as well as the Aspen Strategy Group, an initiative of the Aspen Institute. Moulton graduated from the University of Virginia in 2010.

Michael P. Murphy, Jr. is the executive director of MASS Design Group, which he cofounded with Alan Ricks in 2008, and a thought leader in architecture and health care design. Murphy regularly speaks on how architecture can improve people's lives and sits on various boards, including the Clinton Global Initiative Advisory Committee and the Center for Healthcare Design. An architect by training, Murphy was recently listed in *Atlantic Monthly* as one of the "Greatest Innovators of Today." Murphy is a graduate of the University of Chicago and the Harvard GSD.

Ceara O'Leary is a 2012–4 Enterprise Rose Architectural Fellow and a project manager and designer with the Detroit Collaborative Design Center (DCDC).

The DCDC is a multidisciplinary, nonprofit architecture and urban design firm at the University of Detroit Mercy School of Architecture dedicated to creating sustainable spaces and communities through quality design and the collaborative process.

Sergio Palleroni is a professor and senior fellow of the new Institute for Sustainable Solutions at Portland State University. Palleroni's research and fieldwork during the last three decades focused on improving the lives of communities, especially those underserved by architects. In 1988 he founded BaSiC Initiative, an academic outreach program, to serve these communities and has also been involved with nonprofit, governmental, and international agencies, such as UNESCO and the World Bank. Since 2013 he has been the director of the Center for Public Interest Design, a research and community design center. He received a BArch from the University of Oregon and an MSArchS from MIT.

David Perkes is an architect, Mississippi State University professor, and director of the Gulf Coast Community Design Studio. The studio was established following Hurricane Katrina to provide planning, landscape, and architectural design to communities in need. Perkes has a BS in Civil and Environmental Engineering from Utah State University, a Master of Environmental Design from Yale University, and an MArch from the University of Utah. He was a Harvard GSD Loeb Fellow. Perkes was a member of the four-person team that received the 2011 AIA Latrobe Prize to research public interest practices in architecture.

Dan Pitera is the executive director of the DCDC and professor of architecture at the University of Detroit Mercy. The DCDC is a multidisciplinary, nonprofit architecture and urban design firm at the University of Detroit Mercy School of Architecture dedicated to creating sustainable spaces and communities through quality design and the collaborative process.

Jon Red Corn, AIA LEED AP, CEO and director of operations, Blue Star Studio is a member of the Wazhazhi (Osage) Nation. Red Corn has had more than fifteen years of experience in design, fabrication, and construction since graduating with an MArch from the University of Kansas. Red Corn's expertise in advanced integrated systems is geared toward the creation of high-quality, energy-efficient, healthy buildings, which are beautiful, durable, affordable, and easy to maintain. He is passionate about design as a social- and economic-empowerment tool.

Alan Ricks is the COO and cofounder of MASS Design Group, and his work spans design, research, and policy. In spring 2014, Ricks was named a Young Global Leader of the World Economic Forum for the 2014–19 term. Often the only architect at the table, he has worked with the government of Liberia to develop health care policies. Ricks is a graduate of Colorado College and the Harvard GSD.

Emily Schmidt is a planning associate at bcWORKSHOP, where she leads the organization's People Organizing Place, an initiative that strengthens the physical, social, and economic health of neighborhoods. Before joining bcWORKSHOP in 2011, she worked in Chicago and New York City, engaging communities and undertaking research projects for public, private, and nonprofit planning organizations. Schmidt received a BA in American Studies, concentrating in Urban Studies, from Wesleyan University.

Philip Szostak, FAIA, is a Chapel Hill–based architect with more than thirty-five years of experience in architectural design. A graduate of North Carolina State University's School of Design, he first opened Philip Szostak Associates (PSA) in 1980. In 1990 he became the North Carolina principal for NBBJ, the country's second-largest architectural practice. After twelve years of leading the design and management of hundreds of millions of dollars worth of construction, he left NBBJ to reopen PSA, now Szostak Design.

Yi Wei is a social innovator passionately dedicated to making the world a better place by bringing together great ideas and stellar people and aligning incentives to maximize positive impact. Her vision of perfect is a day in which the term *social business* is redundant. A graduate of Harvard University, Wei currently serves as the Innovation Manager at iDE's Global WASH Initiative, fighting the battle against diarrhea through market-based approaches.

Reading List

Aquilino, Marie, ed. 2011. *Beyond Shelter: Architecture and Human Dignity*. New York: Metropolis Books.

Awan, Nishat, Tatjana Schneider, and Jeremy Till. 2011. *Spatial Agency: Other Ways of Doing Architecture*. London: Routledge.

Borasi, Giovanna and Mirko Zardini. 2008. *Actions: What You Can Do with the City*. Amsterdam: Sun Publishers.

Bell, Bryan, ed. 2003. *Good Deeds, Good Design: Community Service through Architecture*. New York: Princeton Architectural Press.

Bell, Bryan and Katie Wakeford, ed. 2008. *Expanding Architecture, Design as Activism*. New York: Metropolis Books.

Carpenter, William J. 1997. *Learning by Building: Design and Construction in Architectural Education*. New York: Wiley.

Cary, John, ed. 2010. *The Power of Pro Bono: 40 Stories about Design for the Public Good by Architects and Their Clients*. New York: Metropolis Books.

Charlesworth, Esther. 2014. *Humanitarian Architecture: 15 Stories of Architects Working After Disaster*. London: Routledge.

Collier, John and Malcom Collier. 1986. *Visual Anthropology: Photography as a Research Method*. Albuquerque: University of New Mexico Press.

Findley, Lisa. 2005. *Building Change: Architecture, Politics and Cultural Agency*. London: Routledge.

Fisher, Thomas. 2010. *Ethics for Architects: 50 Dilemmas of Professional Practice*. New York: Princeton Architectural Press.

Freire, Paulo. 1970. *Pedagogy of the Oppressed*. New York: Seabury Press.

Gaber, John and Sharon Gaber. American Planning Association (APA). 2007. *Qualitative Analysis for Planning and Policy: Beyond the Numbers.* Chicago, IL: APA Planners Press.

Gardner, Howard, Mihaly Csikszentmihalyi, and William Damon. 2002. *Good Work.* New York: Basic Books.

Hammett, Jerilou and Maggie Wrigley, ed. 2013. *The Architecture of Change: Building a Better World.* Albuquerque, NM: University of New Mexico Press.

Hart, Maureen. 1999. *Guide to Sustainable Community Indicators.* Hartford: Hart Environmental Data.

Iveson, Kurt. 2007. *Publics and the City.* Malden: Blackwell Publishing.

Jacobs, Jane. 1961. *Death and Life of Great American Cities.* New York: Random House.

Jones, Tom, William Pettus, and Michael Pyatok. 1995. *Good Neighbors: Affordable Family Housing (Design For Living)* New York: McGraw-Hill.

Kaner, Sam. 2007. *Facilitator's Guide to Participatory Decision-Making.* Hoboken, NJ: John Wiley & Sons.

Ladner, Sam. 2014. *Practical Ethnography: A Guide to Doing Ethnography in the Private Sector.* Walnut Creek, CA: Left Coast Press.

Latour, Bruno. *Reassembling the Social: An Introduction to Actor-Network-Theory.* Oxford: Oxford University, 2007.

Latour, Bruno and Peter Weibel, ed. 2005. *Making Things Public: Atmospheres of Democracy.* Cambridge, MA: The MIT Press.

Lepik, Andres. 2010. *Small Scale, Big Change: New Architectures of Social Engagement.* New York: The Museum of Modern Art.

Mau, Bruce. 2004. *Massive Change.* New York: Phaidon Press, 2004.

Marshall, Catherine and Gretchen B. Rossman. 2010. *Designing Qualitative Research.* Fourth Edition. Thousands Oaks: Sage Publications.

Maxwell, Joseph A. 2012. *Qualitative Research Design: An Interactive Approach* (Applied Social Research Methods, Book 41). Third Edition. Thousand Oaks, CA: Sage Publications.

Morrish, William R. and Catherine R. Brown. 2000. *Planning to Stay: Learning to See the Physical Features of Your Neighborhood.* Minneapolis, MN: Milkweed Editions.

Oppenheimer Dean, Andrea. 1998. *Proceed and Be Bold: Rural Studio After Samuel Mockbee.* New York: Princeton Architectural Press.

Oppenheimer Dean, Andrea. 2002. *Rural Studio: Samuel Mockbee and an Architecture of Decency.* New York: Princeton Architectural Press.

Palleroni, Sergio. 2004. *Studio at Large: Architecture in Service of Global Communities.* Seattle, WA: University of Washington Press.

Papanek, Victor. 1971. *Design for the Real World: Human Ecology and Social Change.* New York: Pantheon.

Pilloton, Emily. 2009. *Design Revolution: 100 Products that Empower People.* New York: Metropolis Books.

Portigal, Steve. 2013. *Interviewing Users: How to Uncover Compelling Insights*. New York: Rosenfeld Media.

Robbins, Bruce, ed. 1993. *The Phantom Public Sphere*. Minneapolis, MN: University of Minnesota.

Sinclair, Cameron and Kate Stohr, ed. 2006. *Design Like You Give a Damn: Architectural Responses to Humanitarian Crises*. New York: Metropolis Books.

Sinclair, Cameron and Kate Stohr, ed. 2012. *Design Like You Give a Damn 2: Building Change from the Ground Up*. New York: Harry N. Abrams.

Smith, Cynthia E. 2007. *Design for the Other 90%*. New York: Editions Assouline.

Smith, Cynthia E. 2011. *Designing with the Other 90%: Cities*. New York: Cooper Hewitt, Smithsonian Design Museum.

Staeheli, Lynn A. and Donald Mitchell. 2008. *The People's Property?: Power, Politics, and the Public*. New York: Routledge.

Turan, Neyran, and Stephen Ramos, ed. 2009. *New Geographies 1: After Zero*. Cambridge, MA: Harvard University Graduate School of Design.

van Lengen, Johan. 2007. *The Barefoot Architect*. New York: Shelter Publications, Inc.

Varnelis, Kazys. 2008. *Networked Publics*. Cambridge, MA: The MIT Press.

Warner, Michael. 2005. *Publics and Counterpublics*. New York: Zone Books.

Internet Resources

AIGA and Cheskin. *Ethnography Primer*. http://www.aiga.org/ethnography-primer/

Association for Community Design. http://www.communitydesign.org

Collaborative Institutional Training Initiative at the University of Miami (CITI Program). https://www.citiprogram.org

"Design and Social Impact: A Cross-Sectoral Agenda for Design, Education, Research and Practice." http://arts.gov/sites/default/files/Design-and-Social-Impact.pdf

Foundation Center. *Research Grant Programs and Fundraising: Foundation Center*. http://foundationcenter.org

Impact Design Hub. http://www.impactdesignhub.org/

McNamara, Carter, MBA, PhD. *Free Management Library*. 1997–2008. Basic Business Research Methods. http://www.managementhelp.org/research/research.htm. (Adapted from the Field Guide to Nonprofit Program Design, Marketing and Evaluation and Field Guide to Consulting and Organizational Development.) Authenticity Consulting, LLC.

Bill & Melinda Gates Foundation. http://www.gatesfoundation.org

Presidio Graduate School. Jonathan Mariano, publisher. *The Dictionary of Sustainable Management*. http://www.sustainabilitydictionary.com

Public Interest Design Institute. http://www.publicinterestdesign.com

Public Policy Lab. *Policy X Design Blog*. http://publicpolicylab.org/pxd-blog

SEED (Social Economic Environmental Design) Network. https://seednetwork.org

Stanford Center on Philanthropy and Civil Society, Stanford University. *Stanford Social Innovation Review*. Blog. http://www.ssireview.org/blog/

The Rockefeller Foundation. http://www.rockefellerfoundation.org

United Nations Department of Economic and Social Affairs, Division for Sustainable Development. *Sustainable Development Knowledge Platform.* http://sustainabledevelopment.un.org

United Nations, Department of Economic and Social Affairs. *The United Nations Division for Sustainable Development in Brief.* http://www.un.org/esa/desa/aboutus/dsd.html

United States Agency for International Development. http://www.usaid.gov

United Nations. *We Can End Poverty: Millennium Development Goals and Beyond 2015.* http://www.un.org/millenniumgoals/

Appendix A:

Methods of Engagement

Methods of Engagement

Engagement and Community Participation

An inclusive and transparent path toward project goals is vital to an informed public interest design practice. Determining appropriate ways to engage stakeholders and community participants can help ensure agency during a project. Through the potential of participatory action, communities are empowered to join in democratic decision making to establish their priorities, define their goals, and build consensus.

The designer or design team can function as a facilitator to engage participation. This role requires neutrality—respect for an unbiased and objective process that honors the social and cultural context of the community or audience. Affording stakeholders ways to contribute to a meaningful process of inclusion that acknowledges the diversity of voices and differences of opinions is essential to a public interest design practice.

Available time and resources will often dictate methods used. Adapting methods to fit the needs of the project through scale or priority can provide opportunities to reinvent processes. Helping communities envision change is at the heart of these efforts. Synthesizing the outcomes of participation is required to discover connections, patterns, and, ultimately, preferences and needs embedded within the multifaceted design problem.

The following methods are grouped according to ways of promoting interaction. Chapters and case studies that utilize methods discussed in this book are cross-referenced and offer a more in-depth and contextually expanded discussion.

Methods

Celebrations
Block parties
Group meals
Local happening (chapter 15, pages 129–32)

Community Assets
Asset-based design/development
Community hiring (case study 13)
Job fairs (case study 13)
Minority-owned businesses (chapter 12, pages 115–20; chapter 21, pages 157–61)
Skills development (chapter 12, pages 115–20; chapter 23, pages 167–71; case study 16)
Workforce training (chapter 21, pages 157–61)

Events
Conferences
Demonstrations (case study 6)
Symposia (chapter 18, pages 143–6)
Workshops (chapter 17, pages 137–41; case study 6, 7, 12, 23, 26)

Games and Play
Board games (chapter 15, pages 129–32)
Card games (chapter 14, pages 125–8)
Online gaming tools (chapter 11, pages 109–14)

Localized Activities
Community action planning (chapter 14, pages 125–8)
Community-embedded design team (case study 15)
Community gatherings (chapter 15, pages 129–32)
Cultural activities (case study 4)
Home visits or home stays (chapter 24, pages 173–7; case study 8, 11)
Neighborhood picnics
Neighborhood walks (chapter 15, pages 129–32)
On-site/field observations (case study 23)
On-site project management (case study 18)
Problem tree exercises (chapter 14, pages 125–8; case study 2)
Street-team canvassing (chapter 11, pages 109–14)
Street-team meetings/advocacy (chapter 17, pages 137–41; case study 30)

Meeting Scenarios
Community-planning meetings (chapter 12, pages 115–20; chapter 17, pages 137–41; case study 4, 21)
Design charettes (chapter 18, pages 143–6; case study 9, 16, 21, 22, 24, 26)
Public forums (case study 13, 19)
Stakeholder advisory groups (case study 5, 14)

Mobility
Mobile information stations (chapter 11, pages 109–14)
Open houses (chapter 11, pages 109–14)
Site tours (case study 9)
Transect walks (case study 2)
Traveling exhibits (chapter 11, pages 109–14)

Oral or Written Communication
Discussion groups (chapter 11, pages 109–14)
Focus groups
Interviews (chapter 12, pages 115–20; chapter 24, pages 173–7; case study 1, 3, 6, 9, 10, 11, 18, 20, 25)
One-on-one conversations (chapter 11, pages 109–14; case study 20)
Oral-history collection (chapter 12, pages 115–20; case study 5)
Phone conversations
Small-group conversations
Sticky-note votes
Storytelling/story collection (chapter 11, pages 109–14; chapter 12, pages 115–20; chapter 14, pages 125–8; chapter 15, pages 129–32; case study 6)
Surveys (digital, in person) (case study 19, 26, 27, 30)

Writing exercises

Outreach and Recruitment
Advertised public hearings
Chalk messages
Classroom visits (case study 8)
Community bulletin boards
Educational outreach (chapter 12, pages 115–20; case study 1)
Facebook groups
Flyers/postcards
Websites

Partnerships
Academic–professional (case study 22)

Community organizations (chapter 14, pages 125–8; chapter 15, pages 129–32; case study 3, 17)
Coordination with local comprehensive plan
Local, regional, state, or national government support
Public–private (chapter 18, pages 143–6; case study 28)

Programs
Phased development (case study 24)
Pilot programs (chapter 20, pages 151–5; chapter 24, pages 173–7; case study 11, 14, 27)

Research
Asset mapping (case study 10)
Behavior mapping (chapter 24, pages 173–7)
Case-study research (case study 26)
Cognitive mapping (case study 4)
Qualitative
Quantitative

Space and Materials
Materials/fabrication testing (case study 16)
Model making (case study 2, 7, 30)
Model/prototype discovery (chapter 14, pages 125–8; chapter 17, pages 137–41; chapter 24, pages 173–7)
Product/prototype field testing (chapter 20, pages 151–5; chapter 24, pages 173–7; case study 1, 8, 11, 28, 29)

Visual Communication
Image collection/exchange (case study 20)
Mural competitions (case study 9)
Photographic or video ethnographies

Appendix B:

Issues Index Cross-Reference Guide

No.	Project Name	Discipline	Participation
1-186	Healthy Laddoo Project	Health and Nutrition Design	Educational outreach, interviews, product testing
2-190	Firm Foundation	Urban Design	Transect walks, problem tree exercises, model making
3-194	Impact Detroit Community How-To Guides	Communication Design	Interviewing, community-organization partnerships
4-198	Lakota Nation Building at Keya Wakpala Waíçageyapi	Tribal Planning	Cognitive mapping, cultural activities, community meetings
5-202	Owe'neh Bupingeh Preservation Plan and Rehabilitation Project	Architecture	Stakeholder advisory group, oral histories
6-206	Dimen, Kam Minority Cultural Heritage in China	Communication Design	Demonstrations, interviews, workshops, storytelling
7-210	Kitakami "We Are One" Market and Youth Center	Architecture	Outreach workshops, model-making workshops
8-214	Skill Champ	Communication Design	Home visits, classroom visits, product testing
9-218	Piet Patsa Community Arts Centre	Architecture	Mural competitions, site tours, interviews, charettes
10-222	Towns Association for Environmental Quality Green Building Headquarters	Architecture	Asset mapping, interviews, community-building activities
11-226	Juabar	Service Design	Homestays, in-home interviews, observations
12-230	The Informal Urban Communities Initiative: Comunidad Ecológica Saludable	Landscape Architecture	Participatory Impact Assessment workshops
13-234	Durham Performing Arts Center	Architecture	Public meetings, job fairs, community hiring input
14-238	Easy Latrine Sanitation Marketing	Business-Model Design	Barrier/driver stakeholder engagement
15-242	Manica Football for Hope Centre	Architecture	Community-embedded design team

Key

No.: (Case study number)-(page number); **Issues:** Social Issue, Economic Issue, Environmental Issue

Primary Issue	Secondary Issue #1	Secondary Issue #2
Children's Nutrition	Children's Health	Nutrition Education
Clean Water Advocacy	Public Space	Water Economies
Community Empowerment	Small-Scale Community Development	Neighborhood Revitalization
Community Renewal	Incremental Economic Development	Healthy Communities
Cultural Heritage	Affordable Housing	Cultural Preservation
Cultural Identity	Craft Preservation	Living Wages
Disaster Recovery	Community Services	Microbusiness Development
Education for Different Abilities	Customized Digital Learning	Social Enterprise
Empowering Rural Youth	Overcoming Racism	Building Self-Worth
Green Energy Education	Promoting Peace	Green Architectural Heritage
Green Microbusiness Growth	Solar-Energy Access	Solar-Energy Education
Green Space Access	Well-being	Food Production
Increasing Employment Opportunities	Downtown Renewal	Brownfield Remediation
Latrine Access	Microbusiness Development	Public Health
Life Skills Education	Job Training	Local Materials Sourcing

No.	Project Name	Discipline	Participation
16-246	Umusozi Ukiza Doctors' Housing	Architecture	Local artisans collaboration, materials/fabrication testing
17-250	Fresh Moves Mobile Market	Urban Design	Charettes, bus retrofit activity, organizational partnerships
18-254	Rebuild South Sudan Jalle School	Architecture	On-site project management, stakeholder interviews
19-258	Bancroft School Apartments	Architecture	Open forums, visioning meetings, surveys
20-262	People Organizing Place—Neighborhood Stories	Neighborhood Planning and Place Making	Relationship building, image collection, interviews
21-266	Kensington High School for the Creative and Performing Arts	Architecture	Community meetings, design charettes
22-270	SAGE Affordable Green Modular Classrooms	Modular Architecture	Academic-professional collaborations, charettes
23-274	Lafitte Greenway Revitalization	Urban Design	Workshops, on-site observations
24-278	Growing Home	Architecture	Phased development, charettes, feedback/response
25-282	Can City	System Design	Diverse stakeholder interviews, support network
26-286	Klyde Warren Park	Landscape Architecture	Park-feature surveys, workshops, charettes
27-290	Walk [Your City]	Urban Design	Neighborhood surveys, pilot educational program
28-294	PackH20 Water Backpack	Industrial Design	Prototype field tests, public-private partnerships
29-298	Portable Laboratory on Uncommon Ground	Architecture and Industrial Design	Researcher and local tourist outreach, on-site testing
30-302	Potty Project	Urban Infrastructure	Street-team advocacy, model making, in-home surveys

Key

No.: (Case study number)-(page number); **Issues:** Social Issue, Economic Issue, Environmental Issue

Primary Issue	Secondary Issue #1	Secondary Issue #2
National Health Care	Local Artisans Collaboration	Local Materials Sourcing
Nutritious Food Delivery	Affordable Food	Community Health
Rebuilding after War	Primary School Education	Flood Resilience
Social Equity	Neighborhood Improvement	Crime Abatement
Strengthening Community	Community History	Community Identity
Student Retention	Community Optimism	Environmental Education
Sustainable Manufactured Classrooms	Student Performance	Affordable Classrooms
Sustainable Neighborhood Development	Community-Based Recreation	Neighborhood Revitalization
Transitional Job Training	Community Development	Organic Food Production
Up-cycling	Local Production	Street Vending
Urban Green Space	Economic Development	Cultural Diversity
Walkability	Sprawl Reduction	Healthful Lifestyle
Water Scarcity	Solar Thermal Disinfection	Toxin and Contamination Reduction
Wildlife Preservation	Tourism	Disease Control
Women's Safety	Family Health and Productivity	Public Sewage Infrastructure

Appendix C:
Case Study Locator Map

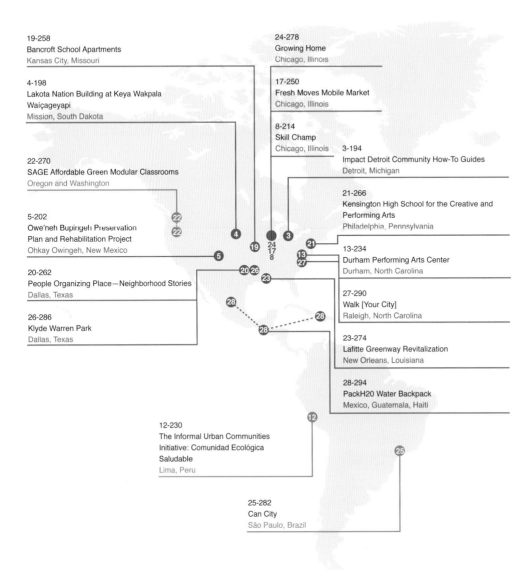

19-258
Bancroft School Apartments
Kansas City, Missouri

4-198
Lakota Nation Building at Keya Wakpala
Waíçageyapi
Mission, South Dakota

22-270
SAGE Affordable Green Modular Classrooms
Oregon and Washington

5-202
Owe'neh Bupingeh Preservation
Plan and Rehabilitation Project
Ohkay Owingeh, New Mexico

20-262
People Organizing Place—Neighborhood Stories
Dallas, Texas

26-286
Klyde Warren Park
Dallas, Texas

12-230
The Informal Urban Communities
Initiative: Comunidad Ecológica
Saludable
Lima, Peru

25-282
Can City
São Paulo, Brazil

24-278
Growing Home
Chicago, Illinois

17-250
Fresh Moves Mobile Market
Chicago, Illinois

8-214
Skill Champ
Chicago, Illinois

3-194
Impact Detroit Community How-To Guides
Detroit, Michigan

21-266
Kensington High School for the Creative and
Performing Arts
Philadelphia, Pennsylvania

13-234
Durham Performing Arts Center
Durham, North Carolina

27-290
Walk [Your City]
Raleigh, North Carolina

23-274
Lafitte Greenway Revitalization
New Orleans, Louisiana

28-294
PackH20 Water Backpack
Mexico, Guatemala, Haiti

Key
No.: (Case study number)-(page number); **Primary Issues Indicated:** Social, Economic, Environmental

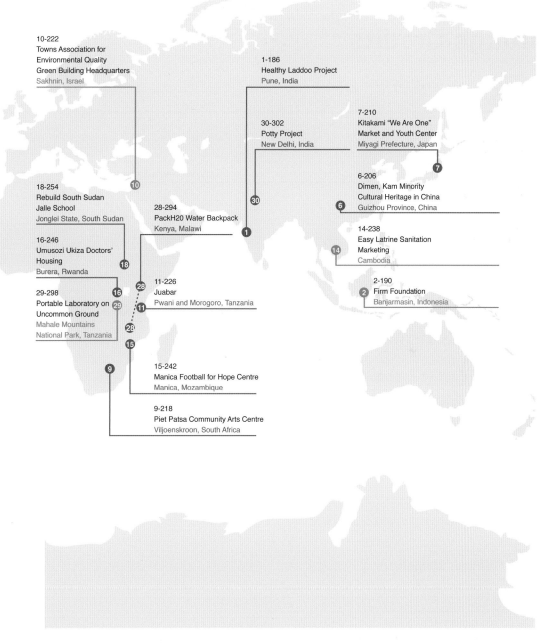

10-222
Towns Association for
Environmental Quality
Green Building Headquarters
Sakhnin, Israel

1-186
Healthy Laddoo Project
Pune, India

7-210
Kitakami "We Are One"
Market and Youth Center
Miyagi Prefecture, Japan

30-302
Potty Project
New Delhi, India

6-206
Dimen, Kam Minority
Cultural Heritage in China
Guizhou Province, China

18-254
Rebuild South Sudan
Jalle School
Jonglei State, South Sudan

28-294
PackH20 Water Backpack
Kenya, Malawi

14-238
Easy Latrine Sanitation
Marketing
Cambodia

16-246
Umusozi Ukiza Doctors'
Housing
Burera, Rwanda

2-190
Firm Foundation
Banjarmasin, Indonesia

11-226
Juabar
Pwani and Morogoro, Tanzania

29-298
Portable Laboratory on
Uncommon Ground
Mahale Mountains
National Park, Tanzania

15-242
Manica Football for Hope Centre
Manica, Mozambique

9-218
Piet Patsa Community Arts Centre
Viljoenskroon, South Africa

Image Credits

Front Cover Images

Row One (left to right)

Dimen, Kam Minority Cultural Heritage in China
SAGE Affordable Green Modular Classrooms
Tsigo bugeh Village, Credit: Peter Aeschbacher
Towns Association for Environmental Quality Green Building Headquarters

Row Two

Durham Performing Arts Center, Credit: © 2014 Tom Arban Photography

Row Three

Umusozi Ukiza Doctors' Housing, Credit: Alan Ricks

Row Four (left to right)

Can City
Growing Home, Credit: Andrew Collings
The Informal Urban Communities Initiative: Comunidad Ecológica Saludable
Skill Champ

Row Five (left to right)

Lakota Nation Building at Keya Wakpala Waíçageyapi, Credit: © 2014 Blue Star Studio
Easy Latrine
Fresh Moves Mobile Market
Juabar, Credit: Juabar

Book Images

Chapters

1 The State of Public Interest Design

1.1 Migrant farmworker housing unit
Design: Bryan Bell, Model: Mathew Heckendorn
1.3 Graphic of AIA survey results
Dasha Orthenberg
1.4 A doctor and patient of the Tuskegee Syphilis Study
The U.S. National Archives and Records Administration

2 What Social Justice Movements Can Teach Us about Public Interest Design

2.1 CORE demonstration
New York World-Telegram and the Sun Newspaper Photograph Collection. Photograph by Phyllis Twachtman, 1964, Library of Congress Prints and Photographs Division, Washington, D.C.
2.2 Poster by the Red Cross Institute for Crippled and Disabled Men
Library of Congress Prints and Photographs Division, Washington, D.C.

7 Post-Occupancy: Implementation and Evaluation

7.1 Raw data matrix
Steven A. Moore

11 Moving Forward Together: Engagement in Community Design and Development

11.2 The work of Bleeding Heart Design
Fares Ksebati, Challenge Detroit

12 Paths to a Sustainable Future: Native American Community Building

12.1 "North side of plaza, looking East, San Juan Pueblo" c.1912,
Photograph: The Carlos Vierra Collection of New Mexican Architecture, Volume 3, Center for Southwest Research, University Libraries, University of New Mexico.

Case Studies

Image Credits

26.114 The historic alignment of the Canal is retrofitted as a rain garden with 100 percent native plant material
John Moon for Design Workshop

26.115 An in-depth analysis of the New Orleans landscape typologies shows the diverse ecotones that bisect the corridor and greenway
John Moon for Design Workshop

24 Growing Home

26.118 Trainees and staff working inside a hoophouse
Andrew Collings

26 Klyde Warren Park

26.126 Built over an existing freeway, Klyde Warren Park provides a variety of flexible outdoor rooms
Aerial Photography, Inc.

26.127 The groves of trees and arch structures establish a strong architectural rhythm and act as a buffer
Mei-Chun Jau

26.128 The 5.2-acre park has thirteen programmed spaces
Dillon Diers Photography

26.129 Credit: The Office of James Burnett

26.130 Credit: The Office of James Burnett

27 Walk [Your City]

26.131 Original WalkRaleigh signs installed on existing signal poles in downtown Raleigh
dtraleigh.com

26.132 Sign hanging in Raleigh
Walk Your City

26.133 Mayor Trace Cooper installing a campaign to support pedestrian activity
Walk Your City

26.134 Matt and fellow guerrillas hanging the original WalkRaleigh signs in downtown Raleigh
Walk Your City

26.135 Mayor Michael Martin and community members installing the very first directional signage for Mount Hope
Walk Your City

28 PackH20 Water Backpack

26.136 A woman in Peru carries water with the PackH20 Water Backpack instead of carrying water in a dirty jerry can
Tony Cece / Operation Blessing International

Index

clients: categorizing business relationships 59–60; sourcing clients and funding 61–3; vetting mechanisms 63–4

collective action, critical activities 20–2, *31*, 31

community action planning *126–8*, 126–8, 139–40, 191, *191–2*, 193

community design: advocacy practices 52–3; affordable and pro-bono services 49–52; community engagement 47–9; nonprofit organization 46–7; professional education 53–4

community design centers (CDCs) 3

Community Development Corporations (CDCs) 23–4

community participation: collaborative storytelling 125–8; discussion techniques *126–7*, 127, 132, *139*, 192; economic recovery 210, *210–13*, 212–13; engagement tactics *112*, *113*, 113–14; long-term engagement strategies 121–3; methods of 94, 106; place-making strategies 129–32, *129–32*; resource accessibility 110–12, 194–6, *194–7*; stakeholder engagement and feedback 105–7

community renewal: brownfield regeneration, New Orleans 274, *274–7*, 276–7; Lakota Nation Building 198–9, *198–201*; neighborhood, Kansas City 258–9, *258–61*, 261; urban agriculture 278, *278–81*, 280–1

Comunidad Ecológica Saludable, Lima 38–9, 230, *230–3*, 232–3

Congress for New Urbanism (CNU) 22, 27

Congress of Racial Equity (CORE) 21, *22*

content analysis 85, 89n

critical issue identification 94, 134

Cruz, Teddy 52–3

cultural identity 206–7, *206–8*, 209

cultural traditions: community renewal 198–9, *198–201*; craft preservation 206–7, *206–8*, 209; respect of 40; storytelling, participatory tool 125–8

Deep Griha Society *186–8*, 186–9

democratic claim makers 20

Design Corps 4, 11

Design Impact 151–3, *153*, 186

Detroit Collaborative Design Center: community engagement 48–9, 109–10; Detroit Works Project Long Term Planning *112*, 112–14, *113*; Impact Detroit Community How-To Guides *110*, 110–12, *111*, 194–6, *194–7*; knowledge broker 21

development assistance: diversity of objectives 69–70; negative public portrayal 68; outcomes and impact evaluation 77–8; output and outcome priorities 70–2, *71*, *72*; Senegal Sites and Services Project 72–7; World Bank's role 67–8

Dimen heritage, China 206–7, *206–8*, 209

disability rights movement 22

disaster recovery 210, *210–13*, 212–13

Dowdell, Kimberly 5

Dramatic Need 219, *219–21*, 221

Durham Performing Arts Center, N. Carolina: documentation and contractual compliance 157–9; social and economic impact *158–61*, 159–60, 234–5, *234–7*, 237

Easy Latrine project, Cambodia: marketing strategies *174*, 175, *176*, *238*, 238–9, *241*; scaling up 176–7; user-centered design 173–5, *174–7*, 238–40, *239–40*

Enterprise Community Partners 28, 29, 53

Enterprise Rose Architectural Fellowship 4

environmental education: green building traditions 222–3, *222–5*, 225; urban high school *267–8*, 269

Erie neighborhood House 51–2

ethical tools: human subject research 123n; monist and relativist thought 35–6; Moral Foundations Theory (MFT) 36–43

evidence based design 82, 88n, 170–1

Firm Foundation, Indonesia 41, 125–8, *126–8*, 190–1, *190–3*, 193

Food Desert Action 250–1, *250–3*, 253

Football for Hope Movement 40

Ford Foundation 53

foundational values: care/harm 38–9; fairness/cheating 37–8

Fresh Moves Mobile Market, Chicago 250–1, *250–3*, 253

Gaspar, Christine 47

goals, definition process 94–5, 148

Green Communities Criteria (GCI) 29–30

Green Design 5, 16

green space: gardening for health 230, *230–3*, 232–3; public recreation 274, *274–7*, 276–7, 286–7, *286–9*

Growing Home, Chicago 278, *278–8*, 280–1

Haidt, Jonathan 36

Healthy Laddoo Project, Pune: children's nutritional improvement 151–3, *153*, *186–8*, 186–9; performance measurement 152–3

homelessness 39

hybrid codes 29